**Doing women's studies**

GABRIELE GRIFFIN | editor

# Doing women's studies

Employment opportunities, personal
impacts and social consequences

## Zed Books

LONDON | NEW YORK

*in association with*

University of Hull

European Union

*Doing women's studies: Employment opportunities, personal impacts and social consequences* was first published by Zed Books Ltd, 7 Cynthia Street, London N1 9JF, UK and Room 400, 175 Fifth Avenue, New York, NY 10010, USA in 2005.

www.zedbooks.co.uk

The publication of this book was made possible by the support of the European Union and the University of Hull.

Cover designed by Lee Robinson/Ad Lib Designs
Set in FF Arnhem and Futura Bold by Ewan Smith, London
Index: ed.emery@britishlibrary.net
Printed and bound in Malta by Gutenberg Press Ltd

Distributed in the USA exclusively by Palgrave Macmillan, a division of St Martin's Press, LLC, 175 Fifth Avenue, New York, NY 10010.

A catalogue record for this book is available from the British Library.
US CIP data are available from the Library of Congress.

ISBN 1 84277 500 6 cased
ISBN 1 84277 501 4 limp

# Contents

# Tables and figure

## Tables

**Figure**

# Acknowledgements

This volume is based on the findings from a research project on 'Employment and Women's Studies: The Impact of Women's Studies Training on Women's Employment in Europe', conducted between 2001 and 2003, and financed by the Directorate General XII (Research) of the European Union. Our thanks therefore go, in the first instance, to the European Union for supporting this project and recognizing the importance of both women and Women's Studies in furthering the aims of the European Union.

Second, we would like to thank all those who provided advice and support to the project at different stages of its development and in a variety of ways. They include Angelos Agalianos, the EU's Scientific Officer for the project; Nicole Dewandre, head of the 'Women and Science' Unit in the European Commission; Chris Zwaenepol, Director of the RosaDocumentation Centre in Brussels; Liz Chennels, Deputy Director of the Women's Unit in the Cabinet Office of the UK government; Helen Wallace, Director of the European Institute in Florence; Chiara Saraceno, Professor of Sociology at the University of Turin, Italy; Ursula Apitzsch, Professor of Sociology at the Johann Wolfgang Goethe University, Frankfurt/Main, Germany; Eva Magnussen, Associate Professor at the Centre for Women's Studies, Umea University, Sweden; and Maria Rita Acciardi, the Regional Equal Opportunities Commission President in Cozensa, Italy. We thank them all for their time and input.

Third, we would like to thank the researchers who contributed to the project through their work: Borbála Juhász (Etvos Lorand University, Hungary); Debbie Wigglesworth (University of Sunderland, UK); Jeannette van der Sanden (Utrecht University, the Netherlands); Laura Viñuela Suárez (University of Oviedo, Spain); Mariagrazia Leone (University of Calabria, Italy); Marianne Schmidbaur (Johann Wolfgang Goethe University, Germany); Muriel Andriocci (University of Toulouse-Le Mirail, France); Salla Tuori (Abo Akademi University, Finland); Simone Mazari (Johann Wolfgang Goethe University, Germany); Sveva Magaraggia (University of Milan-Bicocca, Italy); Zalka Drglin (Ljubljana University, Slovenia).

Last, and most importantly, we would like to thank all the Women's Studies students across Europe who participated in the project on which this book is based, filled in questionnaires and allowed themselves to be interviewed – their contributions are at the core of this project and have fuelled our imagination and thinking.

# Introduction

GABRIELE GRIFFIN

The year 2004 was a key one in the development of the European Union (EU) since ten countries, previously described as accession countries, joined, thus, once more, significantly shifting the contours of that Union, geographically, politically, ideologically, economically and socio-culturally. Nowhere is that more apparent than in the debates this shift raised in relation to intra-European migration, specifically, in this instance, the anticipated migration of people from East European countries to West European ones (White 2004a). But, as Saskia Sassen (1999: xv) argues, 'only five million EU nationals out of a total population of well over 350 million today reside in an EU country which is not their own country of origin'. The EU as an institution, through its extensive mobility programmes such as Erasmus, Marie Curie and so on, actively promotes the mobility of its citizens since that mobility is deemed to be necessary to enhance economic viability, wealth creation and international economic competitiveness. There is thus in some respects something of a tension between national governments' responses to the possibilities of intra-European mobility from east to west, which have been for the most part to restrict access except for those with work permits and in employment sectors where there are active labour requirements, and the EU's position of promoting mobility.

Such tensions are born out of a conflict, much discussed whenever supranational EU-wide changes are proposed as was the case with the introduction of the euro, between the aspirations of Europe as an idea/l, and the realities and specificities of the nation-states that constitute the European Union. As Griffin and Braidotti (2002a: 8–13) discuss elsewhere, one of the key particularities of the European Union is that it seeks to federate neighbouring countries with radically divergent histories, cultures, languages and economies:

> As an ideal, Europe embodies the notions of Enlightenment, democracy, and the free flow of capital. As a reality, it struggles to adjust to the critiques of the Enlightenment that have dominated European thinking since the early twentieth century; to come to terms with its imperialist and fascist histories, its treatment of women and migrants, which are an antidote to the notion of democracy; and to confront uneasily the impact of the so-called

1

free flow of capital, which questions the meaning of the local – if we can call Europe that – in the face of the global. (Griffin and Braidotti 2002a: 10)

One of the measures the European Union has put in place to aid the federation of its constituent countries is the promotion of cross-European research, designed both to 'structure the European Research Area', that is promote greater cohesion, cooperation and interaction among EU member countries' research communities, and to disseminate best practice and policy recommendations, with a view to evening out some of the discrepancies between member countries and different constituencies within these. Such research operates within the context of the EU's concerns to understand better some of the challenges that face it, and to seek ways in which to meet these challenges. One of the key issues for the EU is the question of women's participation in the labour market. In the Amsterdam Treaty of 1997 the EU identified a gap in the employment rates between women and men in Europe with its consequences of the greater economic and social exclusion for women. Thus the *Proposal for Guidelines for Member States' Employment Policies 2000* indicates that 'The current EU [employment] rate of 61% lags far behind the US and Japan' (p. 1). The Commission's communication entitled *Social Action Programme 1998–2000* (Com [98] 259, 29/4/98) points out that 'the employment policy has moved decisively to the top of the European agenda' (p. 1) and that the employment guidelines adopted by the member-states are based 'on the four pillars of employability, entrepreneurship, adaptability and equal opportunities' (p. 4). Within this context member-states agreed to 'actively support employability' (*Council Resolution on the 1999 Employment Guidelines*: 4) and to increase 'possibilities for training, work experience, traineeships or other measures to promote employability' (p. 5). The *Council Resolution on the 1999 Employment Guidelines* recognized that 'women still have particular problems in gaining access to the employment market, in career advancement, in earnings and in reconciling professional and family life' (p. 7) and the *Proposal for Guidelines for Member States' Employment Policies 2000*, finally, indicated the need for 'a continuing commitment over a number of years' to tackle the 'gender gap' (p. 2). This, in political, economic and EU policy terms, constitutes the background to this volume.

The volume is based on data gathered as part of a project funded by the DG (Directorate General) Research of the European Union on 'Employment and Women's Studies: The Impact of Women's Studies Training on Women's Employment in Europe'.[1] That project focused on a particular aspect of the issue of women's employment, namely, What happens to women who undertake Women's Studies training in the labour market?[2]

2

That question was raised for several reasons. One is that the project partners estimated that during the last twenty years or so at least around 100,000 women in Europe (*SIGMA Report*, 1996) have undergone such training and it is known anecdotally that their training has had significant impacts on their employability, adaptability, entrepreneurship, and the promotion of equal opportunities at regional and at European level. However, there are no systematic data on this issue to date. In other words, we know that undertaking Women's Studies training impacts significantly on its students but we do not know how and in what ways.

Second, we know (SIGMA Report, 1996) that Women's Studies training exists in many European countries and in different forms, ranging from widespread, long-term institutionalization in the public higher education sector as is the case in the UK, for example, to its prevalence in NGOs as is the case in Italy and many of the former Eastern European countries. Women's Studies training has also greatly benefited from European training/education mobility schemes such as Erasmus. As countries such as Germany, Slovenia, Hungary and Italy seek to institutionalize Women's Studies, and in order to develop appropriate curricula in the discipline, we need to understand what happens to women with Women's Studies training in the marketplace, how their training impacts upon their employability, how the interdisciplinarity of Women's Studies affects their employment opportunities and choices, and how their training impacts in terms of innovation in the job market and in women's career development as well as on their lifestyles.

The project itself addressed the following issues and questions:

- Women's Studies training differs greatly across countries – how does this relate to individual women's subsequent employment achievements, including changes in the balance between family and work, and changing and managing relationships within the family?
- Women's employment opportunities vary significantly among EU countries – what do women do, once trained, given the structuring of these opportunities?
- What impact does Women's Studies have on the changes women seek to generate in the workplace, and how does it impact on professional and other duties undertaken in the workplace?

This volume presents some of the answers to these questions, thus exploring the interrelationship between women's employment, the institutionalization of equal opportunities, and Women's Studies training in a cross-European perspective. The project, on which it is based and which has already been referred to above, brought together eleven partners from

3

nine European countries[3] and ran between October 2001 and October 2003. It involved, in the main, three phases:

- the collection of background data on women's employment, on the institutionalization of equal opportunities, and on the institutionalization of Women's Studies in the participating countries from 1945 to 2001[4]
- the collection of empirical quantitative and qualitative data[5]
- comparative analyses of these data

The empirical research was carried out during 2002. It combined non-random quantitative survey data elicited through questionnaires from an average of fifty past and fifty current Women's Studies students in each participating country[6] with qualitative data derived from thirty semi-structured interviews (twenty past and ten current Women's Studies students per participating country). The latter were carried out in order to establish the meanings of some of the answers provided in the questionnaires, and to lend depth to the data gleaned from the questionnaires. The project's findings are thus based on over 900 questionnaire returns and 270 interviews. The questionnaire data were non-random, partly because, with the exception of the UK, universities in European countries do not keep exit data about their students – apparently for data protection reasons – and partly because most students access Women's Studies as modules within traditional disciplines, especially at undergraduate level, which renders these students invisible within the system (see Chapter 3 in this volume). This in itself raised interesting questions about the tensions, already hinted at above, between European aspirations for harmonization and the great divergencies that exist among European countries, not least regarding how data are collected and kept.

Within the project we hypothesized that

- the degree of institutionalization of Women's Studies training is significantly related to the impact of the training on women's achievements in the labour market
- the degree of institutionalization of Women's Studies training in individual countries is related to the equal opportunities policies in that country
- both the degree of institutionalization of Women's Studies training and the presence/implementation of equal opportunities policies impact on women's professionalization

These hypotheses were, indeed, borne out by our findings. These findings form the basis of the individual chapters that make up this volume.[7]

In Chapter 1 on 'Employment Opportunities for Women in Europe',

Nicky Le Feuvre and Muriel Andriocci discuss the ways in which the diverse industrial and economic contexts of the various European countries such as Finland's late, compared to the UK's early, industrialization impact on women's employment. They suggest that women's employment needs to be viewed in the light of the public policies, labour market and job opportunities, and the living arrangements or lifestyle options available in any given country. They argue that patterns of Women's Studies students' employment relate to the national, indeed regional, employment patterns of women,[8] but also that Women's Studies students disproportionately enter professional employment and/or continue into postgraduate education, a factor that is important not only in terms of these women's own labour market participation rates but also in terms of subsequent generations, since there is a close correlation between parents' educational attainment levels and that of their children.

Chapter 2 focuses on the institutionalization of equal opportunities in Europe. The chapter highlights the uneven development of that institutionalization, the imbrication of that institutionalization in each country's entry into the EU, the consequent importance of the EU for pushing the equal opportunities agenda, and the still noticeable lack of political will in most European countries to implement effectively the equal opportunities legislation they by now all have. The chapter includes a discussion of the difference in equality discourses which have shaped European thinking on this issue, highlighting, for instance, that the gender neutrality of equality discourses in Finland and France has made it almost impossible to raise gender as an issue in those countries. Isabel Carrera Suárez and Laura Viñuela Suárez show that the lack of effective implementation of equal opportunities means that few women, even in Women's Studies, understand the specificities of that legislation, and that not one woman in our sample had ever used the formal measures of that legislation to seek redress against the discrimination they had all experienced. Additionally, our project showed that despite the growth of equal opportunities as an employment sector and its desirability as such for Women's Studies students, few students found employment in that sector, not least because in countries such as France gender expertise is not part of the standard job requirement of an equal opportunities officer. The chapter suggests that much more needs to be done to publicize citizens' rights under equal opportunities legislation, that its institutionalization should be separated from the party-political good-will that currently governs it in many European countries, and that standardized job specifications need to be created that as a matter of course include gender expertise.

Chapter 3 analyses the conditions and specificities of the institutionalization of Women's Studies in nine European countries, revealing its uneven development across Europe and examining the reasons for this. It shows that Women's Studies has been most readily institutionalized in countries with modular degree structures which allow interdisciplinarity (e.g. the UK), where universities have relative autonomy in relation to the state (e.g. the UK, Germany), where state support for Women's Studies in the form of endowed chairs and studentships prevails (e.g. Germany, the Netherlands, to some extent Finland), and where the women's movement was not opposed to such institutionalization (e.g. Finland, the Netherlands, the UK), while it was hardest to establish in countries with rigid disciplinary structures (e.g. Italy, Hungary), greater control by the state over universities and their curricula (e.g. France, Slovenia), an absence of state support for Women's Studies (e.g. Slovenia, Hungary, Spain), and sustained opposition of the women's movement to any form of institutionalization (e.g. France, Italy, Germany). The chapter analyses degrees of institutionalization across the European countries, and discusses the impact of this differential process on staff and students. Some of the key impacts include on the one hand the invisibility of the discipline in institutions and to the wider public which functions to marginalize both its students and its staff, but, on the other hand, the traits of critical thinking, the ability to argue effectively, the great independent-mindedness, and the tolerance towards divergence that it fosters. The chapter argues that Women's Studies with its transformative agenda regarding gender relations is key to the advancement of women's employment and that its content should be integrated into the curricula of those education levels which most European citizens access, namely the primary and the secondary levels. Since Women's Studies as a discipline has attracted a number of schoolteachers who in the project reported on the positive impact of that training on their classroom practice, it is clear that Women's Studies should also be fully integrated into teacher training.

Such integration of Women's Studies content and methods into teacher training and teacher practice is one of the ways in which Women's Studies professionalizes its students. In Chapter 4 Harriet Silius explores that professionalization. Drawing on data from the EWSI project she distinguishes between professionalism, which she analyses in terms of specific competencies generated through Women's Studies, and professionalization of Women's Studies through the establishment of new professions in the employment sector. Silius shows that Women's Studies students acquire professional competencies of both a generic and a specific kind during their training. The former include enhanced critical thinking, the ability to argue effectively, self-confidence, tolerance towards diversity, and team-working abilities; the latter centre on gender awareness, described by some interviewees as 'feminist lenses', that result in a resistance to sexism and intolerance in the workplace, the willingness to introduce gender issues, fighting against discrimination, standing up for other colleagues, and understanding better the gendered power structures that inform the workplace. The Women's Studies graduates interviewed in the project recognized that Women's Studies competencies were of use in a wide range of professions, and indeed, significant numbers entered a range of occupations not directly related to Women's Studies but where the knowledge and skills acquired through the discipline were useful. Silius points out that the professionalization of Women's Studies has also occurred through the establishment of academic jobs in the subject, through certain kinds of work in women's NGOs and in equal opportunities, and through some women's entrepreneurship. Women with postgraduate qualifications in Women's Studies emerge as predominantly wanting to work in one of three areas: academe/research; equal opportunities; women's NGOs. They are less interested in a career that follows what they perceive to be a male model of making money and progressing up a certain career ladder, and more interested in making a difference and doing work that they consider worthwhile, even if this is to their financial detriment. Our data showed that Women's Studies students disproportionately enter postgraduate education, and also that a very high number (some 68 per cent of our sample) enter professional occupations immediately on finishing their degrees. At the same time, students systematically underestimate the impact Women's Studies has on their employment, and tend to view their professional progress in terms of 'luck' and 'chance' rather than as a function of their own proactivity. This is despite the fact that their proactivity in achieving their professional goals can be demonstrated to them.

Women's Studies impacts not only on women's employment but also on their personal lives and their relationships. Critically, the subject frequently taught its students that they were not the only ones who had had to cope with eating disorders, sexual abuse or domestic violence, for example. Women's Studies thus has as one of its functions putting students' experiences into perspective and giving them a name. Chapter 5 therefore explores some of these impacts. The project data showed considerable variations across the European countries regarding the impact Women's Studies had on women's relationships. These variations depended in part on how women-friendly or misogynistic a culture was (Hungary, for instance, emerged as a particularly macho society; see Juhász 2003), but also on the lifecycle stage interviewees were in. In the UK, for instance, a relatively high proportion of students had children and could therefore report on the impact of their training on their relationship with their children, but this high proportion was associated with the large number of mature students which Women's Studies in the UK has always attracted, and was not matched by similar student profiles in the other European countries. Most respondents, irrespective of age and lifecycle stage, commented on the transformation of their female friendship networks and on the importance that being with like-minded women assumed in their lives both during and after the courses. In some instances the friendships formed during the courses became sources of mentoring and later employment as well as offering the support more generally associated with such friendships. Relationships within families also shifted. Children of students might respect their studying mother more; students attempted to bring up their children in less sexist ways; and they acted as educational role models for their children. Parents of students, on the other hand, could be more wary of the changes in their daughters. Fathers generally were less likely to understand what their daughters were doing but were proud of their educational attainments, while mothers might take a close interest in the subject their daughters were studying and, especially if they themselves had an history of activism, open up new dialogues. Where students were the first generation in their family to go to university – a not uncommon case among Women's Studies graduates – incomprehension could be more pronounced. As Chapter 5 shows, Women's Studies students' greatest degree of change occurred in their relations with their male partners, especially where these had fairly traditional gender role expectations that their female partners began to resist. Interviewees recognized that the changes they were undergoing as a result of their training were not necessarily matched by changes in the partner, and negotiations were often difficult. Students wanted to rewrite the socio-domestic contract in favour of a more egalitarian distribution of domestic labour and greater equity between partners. Where this could not be achieved, partnerships came under strain, but where such renegotiations were successful, partnerships continued. Students also reported an impact of their training on their sexual identity, and in interview various women commented on the fact that Women's Studies enabled them to explore their sexuality or to come out as lesbian. Such comments were particularly prevalent in the more homophobic countries such as Hungary but also in France. In general, the more visible Women's Studies as a discipline is in a given country and the more tolerant that country's dominant culture is towards diversity, the easier it was for Women's Studies students to live the implications and aspirations of their field of study.

Where Women's Studies was largely invisible or not available (as in Italy), or a culture was very intolerant of diversity (as in Hungary), students frequently encountered Women's Studies for the first time while studying abroad. Indeed, educational migration emerged as an important source of learning for many of the Women's Studies students. Chapter 6 focuses on those experiences. It shows that relatively small numbers of female students migrate, and that there are definite patterns of educational emigration and immigration, with, for instance, more students from Italy and Germany emigrating to other countries than from the UK or France. Women's ability to go abroad depended on the financial support they could get and, as our data showed, self-financing was one of the largest sources of funding for migrating students, thus immediately ruling out those who did not have or could not acquire such resources. Female students were mainly prevented from studying abroad through lack of finances, language problems and family commitments. The latter was a particular issue since on the whole only single women without children tended to migrate. Those who did go to other countries most frequently stayed for one semester, and all commented on how they had benefited from that period. Benefits included the encounter with Women's Studies as such, the availability of academic resources in the new place of study, and the divergent teaching methods, as well as language skills acquisition, and a sense of enhanced tolerance towards others. Juhász et al. discuss in particular the significant differences between the continental mass higher education systems with their impersonality and lack of direct contact with teaching staff on the one hand, and the Anglo-American system which they characterize as more participatory, involving smaller groups and more attention from teaching staff. Women's Studies students encountered new paradigms while abroad which they could then introduce into the educational systems in their own countries, and many stated that employers viewed periods spent abroad as positive indexes of flexibility, risk-taking, adventurousness and self-directedness.

While respondents in the project were able to articulate the benefits of educational migration very clearly, we found that the project as a whole brought up many issues regarding cross-cultural differences that emerged indirectly rather than directly. One area in which this was evident was around questions commonly raised on equal opportunities monitoring forms in the UK but not commonly asked in other countries. A key one among these proved to be the question about questionnaire respondents' ethnic background. That question is a standard one on UK forms but is not asked in most other European countries. There are a number of reasons for this, not least the fact that countries with fascist histories which have exploited race and ethnicity as means of articulating xenophobia live with that legacy. Simultaneously it is the case that debates on race and ethnicity within Women's Studies and in the anglophone world more generally have been based on the black–white binary that has dominated Anglo-American feminism and much of postcolonial theory. Chapter 7 draws on the quantitative data of the EWSI project to deliver some startling findings regarding notions of race and ethnicity in Europe. It reveals that women in most European countries conceive of ethnic identity not in terms of skin colour but national and regional identity, thus reinforcing the notion that race and ethnicity obey a different dynamic in many European countries from that posited by Anglo-American feminism. The chapter offers a brief analysis of the implications of this difference for European integration agendas.

European integration agendas such as they manifest themselves in the EU's Framework 6's programme 'Structuring the European Research Area' are also the focus of Chapter 8, which engages with some of the issues involved in conducting comparative research in Europe. Chapter 8 thus offers a meta-discourse on the research process rather than on the findings of the project to which the other chapters are dedicated. As the discussion of Chapter 7 above indicates, cross-cultural differences among the various European nations, arising from their very divergent histories, impact significantly on any European research project as it has to negotiate between its participating members. Not all the issues that arise can be foreseen but all have to be worked on as they arise. Among the ones highlighted in this chapter are the impact of multidisciplinarity on designing and executing a research project, the issue of communication and translation which suggests that even if the same word is used by all participants it is not necessarily interpreted in the same way, the question of comparability of data-bases originating in different countries, and matters of data interpretation. One key aspect of conducting research in Europe is peer education – through collaborating we professionalize ourselves and each other in team-working and in working within European research frameworks. This chapter signals some of the challenges of that process but also suggests that part of the importance of conducting research in a cross-European context is precisely the engagement with those difficulties as a movement towards greater harmony in the European Research Area.

In exploring the interrelationship between women's employment, the institutionalization of equal opportunities and of Women's Studies training, this volume as a whole makes the following key points: since women's labour market participation is significantly determined by their educational attainment, and since Women's Studies attracts women students who in significant numbers want to continue into postgraduate education, it is important that Women's Studies as a discipline is supported on a par with other disciplines in all European countries. The improvement of women's labour market participation in general is in part a function of changes in socio-cultural attitudes towards women and employment, and these changes need to be inaugurated at the educational level to which most European citizens have access, that is primary and secondary education. Here Women's Studies should be mainstreamed into the curricula, and teacher training should include gender awareness training. Much remains to be done to make equal opportunities effective. While all European countries have the necessary legislation in place, few have enforcement measures or sanctions that encourage the effective implementation of equal opportunities. Additionally, gender training is rarely part of the standard job specification for any equal opportunities post. Not only do nation-states need to do much more to publicize the meaning and utility of their equal opportunities legislation; Women's Studies should be used as a locus of information dissemination on the topic.

The uneven development of Women's Studies across the European countries needs to be ameliorated through more state support for the subject, the establishment of endowed chairs and studentships, and the simultaneous establishment of autonomous degree courses as well as mainstreamed modules in the disciplines. Women's Studies as a discipline has significant impacts on its students' employability and personal lives. Students need to be helped to develop discourses about these impacts that they can communicate to employers. Those who take the discipline record long-lasting changes in their knowledge, skills, attitudes and behaviour. They act as change agents in their working and social environments. Their potential should be harnessed more effectively both in the labour market and in their socio-cultural contexts. These are the tasks for the EU under the Bologna process, for national governments and for Women's Studies staff.

## Notes

1 For further information about the project and all reports see the project website <www.hull.ac.uk/ewsi>.

2 The word 'training' was used because Women's Studies education occurs in many different settings and, in countries such as Hungary, Slovenia and Italy, where the discipline is not well established in universities, a significant proportion of that education happens in NGOs and similar bodies, outside the tertiary education sector.

3 They were Harriet Silius, Abo Akademi University, Finland; Nicky Le Feuvre, Université de Toulouse-Le Mirail, France; Ute Gerhard, Johann Wolfgang Goethe Universität, Frankfurt/Main, Germany; Andrea Petö, Eotvos Lorand University, Budapest, Hungary; Donatella Barazzetti, University of Calabria, Italy; Carmen Leccardi, University of Milan-Bicocca, Italy; Rosi Braidotti, University of Utrecht, the Netherlands; Eva Bahovec, University of Ljubljana, Slovenia; Isabel Carrera Suárez, University of Oviedo, Spain; Jalna Hanmer, University of Sunderland, UK; Gabriele Griffin, University of Hull, UK.

11

4 These were published in book form and are available, free of charge, by emailing the project coordinator at g.griffin@hull.ac.uk

5 A volume on the qualitative data entitled *Employment, Equal Opportunities and Women's Studies: Women's Experiences in Seven European Countries*, ed. G. Griffin, will be published by the Ulrike Helmer Verlag, Frankfurt/Main, in the autumn of 2004.

6 The actual numbers of questionnaire respondents per country were as given in the following table:

Actual number of questionnaire respondents by partner country

|  | Past students | Present students |
| --- | --- | --- |
| Finland | 56 | 35 |
| France | 51 | 71 |
| Germany | 56 | 69 |
| Hungary | 51 | 50 |
| Italy | 50 | 50 |
| Netherlands | 80 | 51 |
| Slovenia | 50 | 50 |
| Spain | 43 | 83 |
| UK | 104 | 83 |

7 Chapters 1, 2, 3, 4, 5 and 6 are based on the cross-European comparative reports which project partners produced. Chapters 7 and 8 are based on data derived from the project and on findings which were not included in these reports.

8 There is, for instance, a great difference in women's employment in northern compared to southern Italy, and such regional variations impact on women in those regions (see Barazzetti et al. 2002).

# 1 | Employment opportunities for women in Europe

NICKY LE FEUVRE AND MURIEL ANDRIOCCI

We have prepared this chapter with the aim of providing a basic framework for understanding the employment opportunities for Women's Studies graduates in nine European countries (partners in the EWSI project – see Introduction to this volume). We thus take a systematic look at the national variations in women's labour market participation generally. The project was based on the idea that, due to the particular training they receive, Women's Studies graduates are in a better position to contest the gender stereotypes that shape women's experiences of the work–life interface than are most other women of their generation. In order to verify this hypothesis, we thought it important to provide some knowledge about the dominant 'gender order' (Connell 1987) or 'sexual contract' (Pateman 1988) that characterizes the different European Union (EU) member-states at the beginning of the twenty-first century.

We therefore briefly propose a theoretical framework for understanding the potential influence of Women's Studies on women's employment expectations, aspirations and experiences, before going on to present a general statistical overview of women's employment rates and patterns in the partner countries of the EWSI project. With reference to the recent research on gender and welfare states, we attempt to illustrate the dynamic nature of society-specific gender relations, in relation to women's labour-force participation, to the domestic division of labour and caring, and to public policy decisions. As many authors have stressed, these three dimensions of gender relations have all been contested and transformed in recent years. Since the second wave women's movement has played an important role in redefining the relative positions of men and women in employment and in the family, and in encouraging equal opportunity public policy innovations, and since the knowledge-base for Women's Studies was inspired by the women's movement, it seems logical to conclude that Women's Studies training provides students with the ability to negotiate the terms of existing gender relations. Women's Studies training not only provides students with detailed knowledge of the social processes that produce gender discrimination and inequality, it also enhances their self-confidence and ability to negotiate more egalitarian relationships in their

13

daily lives. In the third part of this chapter, we discuss the potential impact of Women's Studies training on women's employment patterns in the EU and conclude with an analysis of the potential role of Women's Studies for improving the efficiency of European and national equal opportunities measures in the future.

## Theoretical perspectives on women's employment in Europe

In the EWSI project we decided to adopt the 'gendered welfare states' analytical framework developed throughout the 1990s by several European researchers. This approach was particularly relevant for our project, since it places the question of women's employment in a global societal context. It suggests that three dimensions of contemporary European societies, which traditional academic disciplinary boundaries have all too often dissociated, need to be analysed together: first, the process of industrialization and the specific labour market characteristics of industrial and post-industrial societies; second, the family sphere, seen both from the angle of marriage and parenting, and from the angle of the domestic, educational and 'caring' activities carried out there; and, lastly, the state, or rather the public policies which have historically shaped the relationship between the two above-mentioned spheres, and which are also liable to determine the precise forms of this relationship in a given national context, in particular as regards the social positions and roles collectively attributed to men and women (see Figure 1.1).

Figure 1.1 is useful for a comparative analysis of the employment aspirations and opportunities of graduates in Women's Studies, since it relates simultaneously to the social structures that characterize a society at a given time in its history and to the collective representations which constitute the 'mental aspect' of gender relations (Godelier 1984; Guillaumin 1992). We can thus understand not only why job opportunities, for women in general and for Women's Studies graduates in particular, are not identical in all European societies, but also why women's employment aspirations and experiences also vary according to their societal and historic context. Thus: 'State policies can affect, notably, women's demands for employment, the way in which women define themselves as active or inactive within the labour market, the costs and profits generated by the decision to take up paid work, given the costs of child care and other constraints' (European Commission 1996b: 2).

*Women's employment and welfare state regimes* Although academic feminist research has always been interested in the role of the state in maintaining or combating gender inequalities in the labour market, the

14

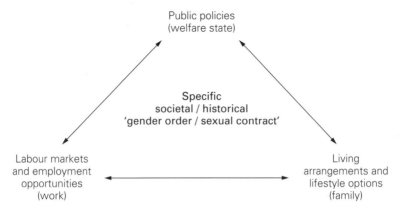

Public policies
(welfare state)

Specific
societal / historical
'gender order / sexual contract'

Labour markets
and employment
opportunities
(work)

Living
arrangements and
lifestyle options
(family)

**Figure 1.1 Societal structures and the gender contract**

debate on European comparisons of women's employment patterns was refuelled in the early 1990s by Gosta Esping-Andersen's (1990) *The Three Worlds of Welfare Capitalism*. Esping-Andersen was not directly interested in the question of gender relations, and was to be severely criticized by a wide range of feminist scholars for his neglect of this question (Daly and Lewis 2000; Jenson 1986; Lewis 1992; Sainsbury 1994, 2001; Ungerson 1990). This book can nevertheless be seen as a major milestone in attempts to analyse the role of the state in shaping women's employment in contemporary western societies. With the explicit aim of analysing the potential for 'convergence' between the different 'welfare regimes' of the EU member-states, Esping-Andersen's work was an extension of the previously available frameworks for analysing the role of the state in contemporary western (capitalist) societies (Titmuss 1963, 1974).

The question of the dynamic nature of these societal models is at the heart of the feminist Birgit Pfau-Effinger's work. According to Pfau-Effinger, the new 'gendered welfare state regime' models need to be refined, notably in order to account for changes over time. Through a comparative analysis of the 'modernization of motherhood', Pfau-Effinger claims that women's employment patterns are not solely determined by state intervention in the labour market and childcare provision. In order better to understand the national and historical variations in women's employment patterns, all the 'gendered' aspects of modern societies need to be analysed. In addition to the 'gender systems' highlighted in previous feminist research on welfare state regimes, Pfau-Effinger introduces the notion of 'gender culture', which refers to the specific set of standards, norms and values that define gender relations and the sexual division of labour in a particular national and historical context. Thus, men and women do not only live in societies

15

Employment opportunities for women

where the objective possibilities for more egalitarian relations between the sexes vary considerably, they also adhere to very different beliefs about the 'ideal' nature of men and women's place in society (Pfau-Effinger 1996). The societal 'gender arrangement' must therefore be analysed in a way that accounts for the 'objective' social structures and for the 'subjective' relationship of individuals to those structures. According to Pfau-Effinger, the nature of the 'gender contract' in each country can be identified by means of the following indicators: (a) the fact that men and women are either assigned to 'specific spheres' or that both sexes are expected to articulate their professional, their parental and their personal commitments to society; (b) the degree to which equal opportunity measures are institutionalized at all levels of society; (c) the fact that childcare and other forms of care are either primarily assigned to individuals and families, to public sector institutions or to the market; (d) the degree to which heterosexual marriage dominates lifestyle choices, in comparison to alternative living arrangements (single-parent families, staying single with or without children, community-based living arrangements, etc.) (Pfau-Effinger 1993: 390). Pfau-Effinger is particularly interested in the ability of different social groups to impose changes on the dominant social structures and norms in a given social context. Although she does not deny that there may be structural inequalities between the different groups involved in the negotiation of new social norms, she insists on the fact that women's ability to initiate changes should not be denied, not only in relation to institutions but also with respect to other social groups (men). Her aim is thus to restore women's potential for action and to take account of the contribution of feminist movements to the negotiation of new social norms (Pfau-Effinger 1999: 67). Pfau-Effinger thus refines the 'male breadwinner' model. She is particularly interested in understanding the factors that explain that a given national welfare state regime has integrated a specific vision of gender relations at a certain time in its history, but she is also concerned with the factors that influence the evolution of this societal model over time. Although she does not pay explicit attention to the question of intra-country variations, her conceptual framework also enables us to consider the 'infra-national variants' identified by Claude Martin (1997).

Hence the comparative analysis of women's employment is no longer envisaged solely from the angle of the state and public policy. A more appropriate typology for the analysis of women's employment should integrate both the structural (social) and subjective (cultural) elements that combine to form the societal framework within which women's labour market participation patterns are determined. As we have seen, this enables us to analyse the evolution of models within a given society over time, and to consider the role of feminist movements (and perhaps even academic Women's Studies) in inducing change. In her own research, Pfau-Effinger defines a typology comprising five different 'gender cultural models'.

1. The family economic gender model. This is the model that corresponds to the pre-industrial situation in most European countries. It is characterized by cooperation between all the individuals who constitute an autonomous economic entity (farming, commerce, craft unit, etc.), which is built around a domestic entity (family, often extended to several cohabiting generations). There may be a strong sexual division of tasks, but men and women are dependent on one another for the survival of the economic entity and for each other's 'welfare'. In a way, it is the pre-industrial model of the sexual division of labour in European societies.

2. The male breadwinner/female home-carer model. This model is based on a differentiation between the public and private spheres to which individuals are assigned according to their sex. Men are considered as the main breadwinners, whereas taking care of the activities connected with the home is primarily assigned to women. The latter are therefore responsible for caring for dependent persons and for performing all the domestic tasks. In this model, men and women are envisaged as complementary, in an organization of 'separate spheres' which are in fact articulated through the marriage contract.

3. The male breadwinner/female part-time worker model. Pfau-Effinger characterizes this model as a 'modernized' version of the 'male breadwinner/female home-carer model' (Pfau-Effinger 1999: 63). Adult men and women are all expected to work at the end of their school years, but the arrival of one or more children in the household serves to redefine the pattern of women's labour market participation. The delicate task of 'reconciling work and the family' falls solely on female shoulders (Junter-Loiseau 1999). In most cases, 'reconciliation' usually takes the form of a reduction in women's paid working time (with a move from full-time to part-time jobs, for example) and an intensification of men's professional investment.

4. The dual-breadwinner/state carer model. Men and women are first and foremost considered as individuals and they are not assigned primarily to either of the two spheres. Each individual is expected to work. A diverse range of 'family patterns' is tolerated, since there is no functional need for men and women to exchange breadwinning and caring services in a stable family unit. When people choose to live together, they operate as

17

'dual-breadwinners', for themselves and for their children. In this model, the 'reconciliation of work and the family' is facilitated by the collective organization of household services, in particular as regards childcare. In countries that adopt this gender cultural model, 'The State is regarded as more competent for fulfilling this task than private households are' (Pfau-Effinger 1999: 63). Despite public policies aimed at increasing men's investment in the family sphere (generously funded parental leave measures, for example), it nevertheless remains the case that women tend to use the policy measures directed at 'reconciliation' to a greater extent than their male counterparts.

5. The dual-breadwinner/dual-carer model. Here, men and women are not only considered equal, they are also 'interchangeable', both in the labour market and as regards unpaid caring activities. Contrary to the previous model, the burden of caring activities does not revert directly to the state (through the provision of a wide range of 'social services' to households), but rather to individual men and women. However, in order to make it structurally (and culturally) possible for individuals of both sexes to combine their professional and caring responsibilities, state intervention is required in order to ensure that 'the labour market is organized in such a manner that structurally allows for parents to fulfil a "dual responsibility"' (ibid.).

From previous comparative research findings, it is possible to add a sixth model to Pfau-Effinger's typology:

6. The dual-breadwinner/market carer model. Here, the 'externalization' of domestic care activities is left to market forces and new inequalities emerge between those households whose 'dual earnings' are high enough to allow the purchase of a wide range of domestic and care services on the labour market and those households that, through lack of economic resources, are excluded from the household services market, except as (low-)paid providers of such services (Crompton 1999; Le Feuvre et al. 1999a).

*Historical comparisons of the east–west divide in Europe* The typology of the 'gendered welfare states' was initially founded on capitalist market economies. The countries of the former Eastern bloc were not explicitly included in the first feminist-inspired analyses summarized in the previous section. According to Pfau-Effinger: 'An extension of the analysis to Central and Eastern European societies and societies outside Europe would, of course, extend the range of gender cultural models' (Pfau-Effinger 1999: 64). In order to include the EWSI partners who previously formed part of the Soviet regime (the former GDR, Hungary and Slovenia), in our analysis,

Le Feuvre and Andriocci | 1

18

we have attempted to identify the principal elements of the 'Soviet social policy regime' which influenced women's employment patterns in these countries. After the Second World War, the countries which were later to form the Eastern bloc switched rapidly from being agrarian societies to socialist-type industrial regimes, based on the Soviet model, collectivization with control and planning of production and consumption. The two pillars of the socialist ideology at the time were: 'That all people, regardless of sex or race, were equal politically, economically and socially [and] that all those capable of working in the paid labour market should do so and rewards in the new society were to be based on this form of worker participation' (Makkai 1997: 189).

This type of regime did not promote an ideology based on a citizen-individual with a series of 'rights', but on an individual defined above all as a worker. Female labour proved necessary in order to achieve the changeover from an agrarian society to a highly productivist, collectivist and centralized socialist economy: 'Following Engels's influential arguments, paid employment was seen as the major avenue through which women's equality should be achieved' (Crompton and Harris 1999: 111). The rights granted to women in the socialist-type countries aimed above all at maintaining their participation in the labour force. It was therefore with that same aim that a relatively widespread network of childcare structures were set up (Makkai 1997). It was thus as mothers and workers that women benefited from certain services. However: 'in Eastern Europe, the necessity for "self-welfare" served to emphasize women's domestic role, despite an official ideology that privileged paid, rather than domestic or caring, work. Support for mothers was linked to the biological maternal role' (Crompton and Harris 1998: 112). It seems difficult to speak of 'social welfare' as such since the socialist-type states extolled the fact that: 'only market economics required social welfare provisions in order to bolster support for a capitalist system that was inherently crisis ridden' (Makkai 1997: 189).

All the measures taken by the socialist states aimed at integrating women in the labour market did not question the gender inequalities which continued to be manifest in other spheres: 'the domestic division of labour has remained highly conventional, despite women's long-term labour-force participation' (Crompton and Harris 1999: 115). The obvious and multiple inequalities between men and women were never taken into account by the socialist states. This was reflected, for example, in the low presence of women in the 'Nomenclatura' and in political decision-making during the state socialist period: 'State socialism gave women equal rights to education, to enter the professions, and so on. The demands of women's market work have been recognized in the State's provision of childcare for working mothers, but domestic work, and the division of labour in the household, was, ideologically, not seen as particularly important – although from the 1960s the "double burden" of state-socialist women was increasingly recognized' (Buckley 1989, cited in Crompton and Harris 1999: 111).

During the 1990s, the transition of socialist regimes to a market economy completely transformed the socio-economic landscape of the countries concerned. This transition had significant impacts on women's employment. First, unemployment, unknown or rendered unknowable during the socialist administration, severely affected women, who also suffered a major drop in their earnings. Furthermore: 'Under post-state-socialism there has been a concerted attack on reproductive rights, with abortion being outlawed in Poland, a two-year reprieve in East Germany, and abortion as one of the first issues discussed for reform in Hungary' (Heinen and Portet 2002; Makkai 1997: 197). Restrictions on the rights concerning abortion, the closure of many childcare facilities, high unemployment rates, the congruence of all these factors underpins a patriarchal ideology based on the 'male breadwinner/female home carer' model which, despite sixty years of women's participation in the job market, remains ideologically strong in most Eastern European countries to date (Pollart 2003). The imposition of full-time work combined with other injunctions – for example, that of becoming involved in the political activities of the state – appears to have contributed to the feeling, for women in particular, that it was not a question of rights, but of obligations coming from a patriarchal and paternalistic state (Gazsi et al. 2002; Makkai 1997). Thus, 'In the public sphere or at the society level a variety of changes were implemented, albeit imperfectly; but in the private sphere little changed. Hence there was no discussion of personal lived experiences – sexuality, domestic division of labour, violence, alcohol and incest remained silent, un-addressed issues' (Makkai 1997: 198). Of course, this was also often the case in many Western European countries.

Furthermore, according to Makkai, the many changes, some of whose characteristics we have identified above, which led to the fall of the socialist regimes, caused a kind of withdrawal to a traditional vision of the family corresponding to the 'male breadwinner/female home carer' model. This model could be imposed even more easily in the absence of women's movements able to propose or negotiate other forms of the 'gender cultural contract' in post-communist societies (Bahovec et al. 2002; Gazsi et al. 2002). In the absence of a vociferous 'feminist lobby' aimed at influencing public policies, the welfare states continue to set up legislative measures inspired by a 'male breadwinner/female home carer' model which is strongly anchored socially, institutionally and culturally (Pfau-Effinger 1999).

Recent research on 'gendered welfare state regimes' (Daly 2000; Pfau-

Effinger 1998, 1999; Sainsbury 1997) enables us to analyse the normative models at work in each national context. By seeing women as 'competent social actors' and underlining the real or potential role of the women's movements, of academic Women's Studies and of EU or national-level policy, in shaping the evolution of the nationally specific 'gender arrangements', this research also allows the impact of feminist knowledge to be incorporated into our analytical framework. This is particularly important as Women's Studies teaching and research not only increase women's awareness of gender inequalities and their ability to act against them, but also provide them with the concepts and arguments that are required to induce change around them (Griffin 2003b).

Based on Eurostat statistics, the national *Background Data Reports* (Griffin, ed. 2002), and the *Qualitative Data Reports* of the EWSI project, the following part of this chapter will provide the basic data necessary for understanding the different 'gender cultural models' that characterize the EWSI partner countries, with the aim of providing a general framework for analysing the influence of Women's Studies training on women's employment patterns in the EU.

## Main features of women's employment in Europe

Despite the importance of the 'male breadwinner/female home carer' in the history of most EU member-states, the data provided in this section illustrate the considerable diversity in women's employment patterns and opportunities that characterizes the various European countries. However, this relative diversity should not mask the labour market realities that are common to women across the EU: the constantly rising level of women's employment rates, the vertical and horizontal segregations of the labour force, the relatively high levels of unemployment and job insecurity among women and the particular difficulties women face in 'reconciling work and family life'.

*Employment rates* In order to compare the countries involved in the EWSI project, it is useful to put women's employment rates into historical perspective. If we consider that women's economic activity patterns started to change (at least in the Western European democracies of the time) in the mid-1960s, it is perhaps useful to see how the countries were classified at that time. At the beginning of the 1960s, European countries were generally grouped under three categories: the so-called 'Scandinavian model' was already characterized by women's continuous economic activity patterns. Indeed, women's employment rates and the modes of women's participation in the labour market were close to those of their male counterparts.

Since the beginning of the 1980s, this model has strengthened even further, but there has been a decrease in employment rates among the under-twenty-fives, linked to an increase in the length of time young women spend in education (Rubery et al. 1996: 287).

At the beginning of the 1960s, the 'Southern European' model was used to describe those countries characterized by very low rates of female employment, where less than 20 per cent of women between the ages of twenty-five and forty-nine were in the labour market, and economic activity curves peaked around the age of twenty-five. Throughout the 1960s, this model did not apply only to Italy, Portugal, Spain and Greece, it also described the position in Austria, Belgium and the Netherlands, although in the latter three countries women tended to give up work after the birth of their first child, rather than on marriage. During the past forty years, these countries have evolved very differently, with a particularly spectacular change in women's employment patterns in Portugal (Ruivo et al. 1998).

Lastly, at the beginning of the 1960s, Germany, Denmark, France and the United Kingdom showed similar patterns of women's employment: 40 per cent of women aged twenty-five to forty-nine were in the labour market and there was a tendency for women to leave paid work after the birth of their first child and to return to work (often on a part-time basis) once their children were older. This pattern is generally known as the 'camel's back' model, since female employment rates fall spectacularly during the child-rearing years. Some forty years on, these countries no longer show such high levels of similarity.

The European landscape of women's employment patterns has evolved in different directions in each country. The categories that made sense at the beginning of the 1960s no longer accurately account for the changes that have taken place since that time. There is, however, one tendency that had begun to take shape in all EU countries early in the 1970s and which has been confirmed ever since:

> The employment rates of 25 to 49 year old women have not ceased to increase in a significant, regular and systematic manner. Within these age groups, which formerly made up the 'slack groups' of women's employment, there are now very high employment levels, sometimes over and above those of other age cohorts. No country has escaped this transformation, which can be characterised on several levels: a) by the fact that women's employment rates have moved closer to those of men; b) by the decreasing influence of motherhood on women's employment rates, leading to more continuous female activity patterns throughout adult life. Between the ages of 25 and 49 years, male and female employment rates have become much

22

closer, sometimes to the point of merging and c) by the fact that women's employment rates in all EU countries have become more similar over time. Despite having followed different paths, the progression of the proportion of women in the labour market has been a common characteristic of all EU member states since the beginning of the 1980s. Although the outcomes are still quite different, the direction of change is the always the same. This increase is largely due to women with dependent children. This group has made the largest contribution to the growth of the working population of Europe. Although the employment rates of all women between the ages of 25 and 49 have literally rocketed, it is the employment rate of mothers that has increased most. (Maruani 1995: 111–12)

TABLE 1.1  Female employment rates (15–64 years), 1993–2000

| Countries | 1993 | 1997 | 2000 |
|---|---|---|---|
| Finland | 59.6 | 60.4 | 65.2 |
| France | 51.5 | 52.5 | 54.8 |
| Germany | 55.1 | 55.3 | 57.8 |
| Hungary | – | 45.4 | 49.4 |
| Italy | 35.8 | 36.4 | 39.3 |
| Netherlands | 52.0 | 57.4 | 63.4 |
| Slovenia | – | 58.0 | 58.5 |
| Spain | 30.8 | 34.4 | 40.3 |
| UK | 61.2 | 63.2 | 64.5 |

*Source*: Eurostat 2001c

Although the progression of women's employment rates has not ceased to rise in Europe there are substantial differences between the EWSI partner countries (see Table 1.1). It is important to note that women's employment rates in the EU are still, on average, lower than those registered in other industrialized countries such as the USA. This is one reason why the Lisbon Treaty (March 2000) set the objective of attaining a 60 per cent female employment rate by 2010 (in comparison to the 51 per cent European average reached in 2000).

It should be noted that men's employment rates also vary quite considerably across the EU: from 82.1 per cent in the Netherlands to 67.6 per cent in Italy. The range for women is between 39.3 per cent in Italy and 65.2 per cent in Finland. However, the historical development of these rates is clearly differentiated. Men have experienced a decrease in employment rates at both ends of the lifecycle (in the under twenty-five and in the over fifty age groups) – due to the increase in the length of studies and general lowering of the retirement age – and a high level of stability between the ages of twenty-five and forty-nine. For women, it is in the 'middle' age groups that the increase has been most spectacular (Maruani 1996). As a result of these different changes, some age groups in some countries show very stark gender differences: 54.8 per cent of men in the fifty-five to sixty-four age group are in the labour market in Spain, compared with just 19.9 per cent of their female counterparts.

Table 1.2 provides some more detailed information on the historical differences in employment patterns in different parts of Europe of women in the forty- to forty-four-year-old age bracket.

TABLE 1.2  Female employment rates (40–44 years) in the Eastern bloc countries, 1950–85

| Countries | 1950 | 1960 | 1970 | 1980 | 1985 |
| --- | --- | --- | --- | --- | --- |
| Eastern bloc countries | | | | | |
| Soviet Union | 66.8 | 77.9 | 93.2 | 96.9 | 96.8 |
| Bulgaria | 78.6 | 83.4 | 88.5 | 92.5 | 93.3 |
| Czechoslovakia | 52.3 | 67.3 | 79.9 | 91.3 | 92.4 |
| East Germany | 61.9 | 72.7 | 79.1 | 83.6 | 86.1 |
| Romania | 75.8 | 76.4 | 79.5 | 83.1 | 85.1 |
| Poland | 66.4 | 69.1 | 79.5 | 83.2 | 84.7 |
| Hungary | 29.0 | 51.8 | 69.4 | 83.2 | 84.7 |
| Northern Europe | 30.9 | 39.9 | 53.8 | 69.9 | 71.1 |
| Western Europe | 34.5 | 39.5 | 46.4 | 55.1 | 55.6 |
| Southern Europe | 22.4 | 25.3 | 29.7 | 35.7 | 37.1 |

*Source*: Gazsi et al. 2002: 370

The data indicate that, at the beginning of the 1960s, with some variation between countries, women in the Soviet bloc countries were more than twice as likely as their female counterparts in Northern, Western or Southern Europe to be in employment. By the 1980s, over 80 per cent of women in this age group in the East were in employment, whereas this was the case for just under three-quarters of women in the Scandinavian and northern countries, just over half in western continental Europe and only one-third in the Mediterranean countries. These differences reflect different patterns of combining motherhood with employment across Europe. However, identifying the specific type of 'gender culture model' in operation in a given country on the sole basis of women's employment rates is not as straightforward as one might imagine. First, average national female employment rates depend on the specific situation of the younger

TABLE 1.3 Male and female employment rates, by age, 2000 (%)

| Countries | Age cohort | Women | Men | Total |
|---|---|---|---|---|
| Finland | 15–64 | 65.2 | 71.1 | 68.1 |
| | 15–24 | 43.8 | 47.0 | 45.4 |
| | 25–54 | 77.6 | 84.6 | 81.1 |
| | 55–64 | 40.7 | 41.8 | 41.2 |
| France | 15–64 | 54.8 | 68.8 | 61.7 |
| | 15–24 | 25.2 | 31.4 | 28.3 |
| | 25–54 | 69.6 | 87.3 | 78.4 |
| | 55–64 | 26.0 | 32.8 | 29.3 |
| Germany | 15–64 | 57.8 | 72.7 | 65.3 |
| | 15–24 | 43.6 | 48.6 | 46.1 |
| | 25–54 | 71.1 | 87.4 | 79.3 |
| | 55–64 | 28.7 | 46.2 | 37.4 |
| Hungary | 15–64 | 49.4 | 62.7 | 55.9 |
| | 15–24 | 29.2 | 37.0 | 33.1 |
| | 25–54 | 66.7 | 79.0 | 72.8 |
| | 55–64 | 13.0 | 33.0 | 21.9 |
| Italy | 15–64 | 39.3 | 67.6 | 53.4 |
| | 15–24 | 22.0 | 30.2 | 26.1 |
| | 25–54 | 50.7 | 84.6 | 67.7 |
| | 55–64 | 15.2 | 40.3 | 27.3 |
| Netherlands | 15–64 | 63.4 | 82.1 | 72.9 |
| | 15–24 | 66.7 | 69.9 | 68.4 |
| | 25–54 | 70.9 | 92.2 | 81.7 |
| | 55–64 | 25.8 | 49.9 | 37.9 |
| Slovenia | 15–64 | 58.5 | 66.7 | 62.7 |
| | 15–24 | 27.4 | 34.7 | 31.2 |
| | 25–54 | 79.6 | 85.5 | 82.6 |
| | 55–64 | 14.3 | 31.0 | 22.3 |
| Spain | 15–64 | 40.3 | 69.6 | 54.7 |
| | 15–24 | 26.4 | 37.0 | 31.8 |
| | 25–54 | 50.6 | 85.4 | 67.7 |
| | 55–64 | 19.9 | 54.8 | 36.6 |
| UK | 15–64 | 64.5 | 77.9 | 71.2 |
| | 15–24 | 53.5 | 58.2 | 55.9 |
| | 25–54 | 73.1 | 87.5 | 80.4 |
| | 55–64 | 41.4 | 59.8 | 50.5 |

*Source*: Eurostat 2001b

and older age cohorts. The longer young women stay in full-time education, the lower the activity rates for the fifteen- to twenty-four-year-old age cohort will be. Likewise, a system of social protection that enables women to receive generous old-age pensions is likely to lead to lower female activity rates among the fifty-five to sixty-four age group than a system where women have difficulty meeting the legal requirements for old-age pensions (Ginn and Arber 1992).

Because of these differences, which are inherent in the national model of the welfare state and in the 'gender culture model', it may be more useful to consider the employment rates of women (and men) in the twenty-five to fifty-four years age group. Thus the data in Table 1.3 show that there are significant differences in women's access to the labour market before the age of twenty-five across all the EWSI partner countries. In five countries (France, Hungary, Italy, Slovenia and Spain), less than a third of under twenty-five-year-old women are in the labour market, whereas over 40 per cent of women from this age group are already working in Finland, Germany, the Netherlands and the UK. This would seem to suggest that women are more likely to be in full-time education up until their mid-twenties in the first group of countries, and that this investment in education is more important for women than for their male counterparts.

There are also important differences in the employment rates of women aged above fifty-four years. Less than 20 per cent of this age group are in the labour market in Hungary, Italy, Slovenia and Spain, whereas over 40 per cent of Finnish and British women aged between fifty-five and sixty-four years are working. France, the Netherlands and Germany occupy an intermediate position in this respect. Once again, these figures may be explained by a variety of factors: in some countries, the legal retirement age for women is sixty years, in others it is sixty-five years. In some countries, we find a clear generation effect in these figures. The vast majority of women who are now reaching retirement age in the Southern European countries probably left the labour market when they married or had children and may never have had a job since that time. Older women in Eastern Europe may have worked throughout their adult lives, but may have left the labour market as soon as their children left home, once the need for a 'second income' became less crucial. In both these cases, it is likely that the activity rates in this age group will change as the younger generations of women, with a more continuous history of labour market participation, reach the age of fifty-five.

Finally, when we look more closely at the twenty-five to fifty-four years age group, the activity patterns are still very different across all the EWSI project countries. Employment rates for this group vary from 79.6 per cent in Slovenia to 50.6 per cent in Spain, with the majority of countries on or above the 70 per cent mark. Thus, although women's employment rates in this age group are systematically lower than those of their male counterparts, they are nevertheless well above the 60 per cent objective of the Lisbon Treaty in all but two countries (Italy and Spain). However, as we shall see below, these fairly similar employment rates mask some very significant differences as far as the patterns of women's labour market participation are concerned.

*Employment patterns (continuous/discontinuous careers)* Even more than women's employment rates, the different patterns of women's employment over their lifecycle give the most accurate information regarding the kind of 'gender culture model' that exists in each national context. Traditionally, research is based on the distinction between three different female employment patterns:

1. The 'female home carer' employment pattern. Here, only women aged twenty to twenty-five, single and/or without children, are predominantly in the labour market. After marriage or a first child, women stop working once and for all and the employment rates for those between the ages of twenty-six and sixty are relatively low. Of course, this pattern of women's work corresponds to the typical ideal of the 'male breadwinner/female home carer' model described by Pfau-Effinger (Pfau-Effinger 1999).

2. The 'camel's back' employment pattern. In this case, a majority of women go into employment after school but many withdraw from the labour market between the ages of twenty-five and forty, when their children are still young. The second peak in this curve, usually from the age of forty, matches a return to the labour market when the children are older. Depending on the country, this return to the labour market can be full-time or part-time. This is a modified version of the 'male breadwinner/female home carer' model. Here, even if women spend a greater part of their adult lives in the labour market they nevertheless remain financially dependent on a (male) 'breadwinner' for several years. Furthermore, in societies that encourage the total or partial withdrawal of mothers from the labour market, we often find tax policy measures that offer substantial advantages to married couples (especially those with children) and to couples that do not achieve 'dual breadwinner' status (the 'one and a half breadwinners' model developed in the Netherlands in recent years is a good example of this kind of policy) (van der Sanden and Waaldijk 2002).

3. The 'continuous' employment pattern. This is the standard male pattern of employment. It corresponds to a situation in which women do not leave work when they have children, even very young children – they combine their jobs with family responsibilities. This pattern therefore reflects the

homogenization of male and female employment experiences (Maruani 1995: 109). In this 'dual breadwinner' model different social policy configurations can be found: either measures that encourage the externalization of part of the education and domestic tasks (according to the logic of the 'dual breadwinner/state carer' or the 'dual breadwinner/market carer' models) or, more exceptionally, policies that aim to encourage a more egalitarian share of domestic and educational responsibilities by men. In all cases, when the state intervenes to encourage women's continuous employment patterns, social policies often translate into a form of political neutrality towards diverse family formations (married couples, unmarried cohabitation, single parenthood, homosexual couples, etc.) and children's birth rank. It is therefore important to note that the policies that influence women's rate and pattern of labour market participation also have an effect on the kind of living arrangements that are promoted within a given 'gender culture model'. As Pfau-Effinger (1993) stressed, the ability of women to adopt alternative lifestyles to heterosexual marriage depends to a large extent on the conditions of access to social benefits and on the possibility for continuous, full-time labour market participation in occupations that offer relatively comfortable levels of income and job security.

*Salaried employment rates* Although European women have always worked on farms and in small-scale trade and cottage industry, women's salaried employment outside the home has indisputably been the major change for the second half of the twentieth century (Schweitzer 2002). Indeed, women who work outside the home are more often in salaried employment than their male counterparts – the rate of salaried employment in 2001 was 88.4 per cent for women as against 81.8 per cent for men: 'the growth in the female working population was very largely the result of salaried employment [and] women's activity has carried the general increase in the proportion of salaried workers in the working population over the last 10 years' (Maruani 1995: 109). Substantial differences exist, however, in terms of salaried employment according to country. These differences reflect both the distribution of national employment among the various sectors of activity – the primary sector (agriculture, fishing), the secondary sector (industrial and manufacturing production) and the tertiary (services) – and the differentiated distribution of men and women within the labour market. In all European countries, women who work outside the home are concentrated in the service sector, in other words, in areas where salaried employment is most highly represented (see Table 1.4).

In addition, the proportion of women in salaried employment varies according to the importance of public services provision in a given national

TABLE 1.4 Male and female salaried employment rates, 1983-2001

| Countries | Women (%) | | | Men (%) | | |
|---|---|---|---|---|---|---|
| | 1983 | 1991 | 2001 | 1983 | 1991 | 2001 |
| Finland | 73.0* | 72.0 | 91.1 | 79.0* | 78.0 | 83.3* |
| France | 84.3 | 87.5 | 92.1 | 81.9 | 82.7 | 86.6 |
| Germany | 86.9 | 90.5 | 91.5 | 87.7 | 88.0 | 86.8 |
| Hungary | – | – | 89.7 | – | – | 81.2 |
| Italy | 73.7 | 75.8 | 78.5 | 69.8 | 69.4 | 68.3 |
| Netherlands | 88.3 | 88.4 | 90.2 | 87.7 | 88.6 | 87.1 |
| Slovenia | – | – | 86.1 | – | – | 80.3 |
| Spain | 66.9** | 74.5 | 83.4 | 70.7* | 74.3 | 77.9 |
| UK | 93.8 | 92.0 | 92.9 | 86.5 | 81.3 | 84.5 |

Notes: * = 1985 data; ** = 1987 data
Sources: data for 1983 and 1991: Maruani 1995: 108; for Finland: Statistics
Finland 1995; data for 2001: Eurostat 2002b

context. Indeed, the public sector offers a greater proportion of jobs to
women than to men in nearly all EU member-states (Eurostat 2002c). The
development of public services has a dual effect on women's employment.
On the one hand, women's access to the labour market is made easier by
the availability of publicly funded facilities such as childcare and care for
the elderly, the sick and the disabled. On the other hand, the setting up of
such services generally increases the demand for women's labour.

*Employment rates according to education level* When analysing the differences between women's activity levels within the various member countries
of the European Union, the fact that variations also occur in women's employment rates within the same country is too often overlooked. Recent
research, however, quite clearly indicates that several factors differentiate
the relation to work of women sharing a common nationality – we will deal
here with the most significant variables, that is to say the levels of education and family situation. As shown in Table 1.5, the overall differences
in women's employment rates between countries vary quite considerably
according to the level of education. In all countries, women who have received some form of higher education are more likely to be in the labour
market than their less well-qualified compatriots.

Indeed, one could almost argue that the societal specificities in women's
labour market participation rates are reduced once one compares women
with a university degree. The cross-national differences in employment
rates are only 7.8 per cent for women with a higher education qualification,

TABLE 1.5  Male and female employment rates (25–59 years), by education levels, 2000

| Education levels | Finland | France | Germany | Italy | NL | Spain | UK | EU-15 |
|---|---|---|---|---|---|---|---|---|
| **Primary** | | | | | | | | |
| Men | 72.2 | 75.3 | 73.0 | 76.9 | 82.7 | 80.4 | 74.8 | 77.7 |
| Women | 64.9 | 53.7 | 51.7 | 32.8 | 49.5 | 35.1 | 60.0 | 47.1 |
| **Secondary** | | | | | | | | |
| Men | 82.0 | 87.3 | 84.1 | 84.4 | 92.4 | 86.7 | 88.6 | 86.2 |
| Women | 74.3 | 71.0 | 69.7 | 61.7 | 74.2 | 57.8 | 77.3 | 69.4 |
| **Higher** | | | | | | | | |
| Men | 87.3 | 85.9 | 87.9 | 83.5 | 90.0 | 81.1 | 89.2 | 86.9 |
| Women | 84.3 | 81.8 | 82.0 | 77.0 | 84.9 | 73.6 | 84.8 | 81.8 |

*Source*: Eurostat 2002c: 181

TABLE 1.6 Male and female education levels, 2002

| | Pre-primary, primary and lower secondary education | | Higher secondary and post-secondary education | | Higher education | |
|---|---|---|---|---|---|---|
| | Women | Men | Women | Men | Women | Men |
| Finland | 24 | 27 | 41 | 44 | 36 | 29 |
| France | 38 | 33 | 37 | 44 | 24 | 23 |
| Germany | 22 | 13 | 60 | 58 | 18 | 29 |
| Hungary* | 40 | 28 | 48 | 61 | 12 | 11 |
| Italy | 56 | 55 | 33 | 35 | 10 | 10 |
| NL | 36 | 29 | 42 | 44 | 22 | 27 |
| Slovenia* | 42 | 29 | 50 | 60 | 12 | 11 |
| Spain | 59 | 58 | 17 | 18 | 24 | 25 |
| UK | 21 | 16 | 51 | 54 | 29 | 30 |
| EU-15** | 38 | 33 | 41 | 44 | 21 | 23 |

Notes: All data concern men and women between the ages of fifteen and sixty-four
* 2000 data; ** Comparison of all 15 EU member-states
Sources: Eurostat 2001a, 2003a

whereas the differences are over 30 per cent when one considers women with only primary school education levels. However, the influence of higher education on women's employment rates also depends on the national 'gender culture' context of the society. Thus, the differences in employment rates between the least and the best qualified Finnish women is only 20 per cent, whereas a 44 per cent difference exists between the least and the best qualified women in Italy (Table 1.6). It is therefore very important that women should have access to the highest levels of the education system, since their levels of qualification impact directly on their employment patterns.

On average, women are still less likely to obtain a higher education qualification than their male counterparts. The qualification levels of Finnish women are significantly higher than those of their male counterparts, whereas German women are much less likely than German men to obtain a higher education qualification.

In almost all European countries, the decision to remain in the education system or to leave school on reaching the age of sixteen is largely determined by the social background: 'Data show that social origin is a factor which, to a large extent, determines the chances of young people to continue schooling or to drop out of school at a young age. In all countries except Finland, the percentage of young people prematurely leaving the educational system is far higher among those whose parents have a low

Employment opportunities for women

TABLE 1.7 Main courses studied by men and women in higher education, 2000

| | Women | | | | Men | | | |
|---|---|---|---|---|---|---|---|---|
| | Social sciences | Health and social work | Humanities | Teaching | Social sciences | Engineering | Computing | Health and social work |
| Finland | 26 | 32 | 12 | 8 | 19 | 46 | 9 | 8 |
| France | 43 | 10 | 19 | 8 | 31 | 28 | 20 | 4 |
| Germany | 18 | 37 | 14 | 13 | 24 | 29 | 13 | 16 |
| Italy | 36 | 18 | 22 | 7 | 37 | 26 | 9 | 16 |
| Netherlands | 31 | 30 | 8 | 22 | 39 | 20 | 8 | 12 |
| Spain | 38 | 16 | 10 | 16 | 32 | 27 | 14 | 6 |
| UK | 31 | 20 | 18 | 13 | 31 | 20 | 22 | 7 |
| EU-15 | 33 | 20 | 15 | 13 | 30 | 26 | 16 | 9 |

*Source*: Eurostat 2003c

level of education than among those whose parents are more educated and the differences are very significant' (Eurostat 2003b: 4). However, with the exception of Hungary, women have a much greater chance than their male counterparts of obtaining a qualification that is higher than that of their parents (their father, in fact). Women are systematically less likely to leave school before reaching the same level of qualification as their parents than are boys from the same social background.

The influence of education levels on women's labour market participation rates also depends on the kind of higher education qualifications they receive. As shown in Table 1.7, once they have entered higher education, women tend to qualify in the humanities, the social sciences and in the field of health and social work, while men tend to obtain degrees in engineering and in computer sciences. These gender-specific education choices obviously influence the places men and women occupy in the labour market after their studies (see below). However, the so-called 'adjustment rate' between the disciplinary field of study and the sector of the labour market varies considerably between countries and between disciplines:

> The frequency of discrepancies changes from one field of studies to the next. Young people who have followed a vocational degree course in the Humanities, agriculture or the 'hard' sciences are more likely to be employed outside their disciplinary field. For example, nearly two thirds of those who have left the educational system after vocational training in the Humanities have jobs that do not correspond to their degree subject. On the other hand, a far tighter connection is maintained between the course of study and subsequent employment after a degree in teaching or in the health/social work sectors. The extent to which vocational degrees in these fields provide employment-specific knowledge and skills no doubt plays a part here. Certain degrees specifically prepare students for specific careers (teachers or doctors in the case of education and health/social work), careers therefore that are only accessible with the appropriate qualifications, whereas others are wider in scope and do not prepare for specific careers. (Eurostat 2003b: 3)

This is an important factor to bear in mind when considering the employment outcomes of Women's Studies graduates in different EU member-states (Le Feuvre and Andriocci 2002b).

*Employment rates according to family situation* Once the question of education and qualification levels has been taken into account, it is obviously important to consider the influence of care activities on women's (and men's) labour market participation patterns. If we refer back to the typology developed by Pfau-Effinger (1993, 1999), it is clear that there has

33

been a significant increase over the past decade in the number of 'dual breadwinner' households:

> Within all the European Union member States for which there is available data, the relative proportion of couples in which both partners work has risen constantly since 1992. The fact that these households may have children does not necessarily mean that the women work less: in 2000, in six of the twelve member States studied, the percentage of couples with children in which both partners work was equal or superior to that of childless couples in which both partners work. In addition, the higher the woman's level of education, the more chances there are that both partners will be working, whether or not they have children. (Eurostat 2002d)

The data in Table 1.8 indicate the increase in the proportion of dual-earner households over the past ten years. The data refer to households where the reference person is in the labour market, is aged between twenty and fifty-nine years old, and is living with another person in the same age

TABLE 1.8 Changes in the distribution of households (with or without children) according to the employment patterns of both partners, 1992–2000 (%)

| | 1992 | | 2000 | |
|---|---|---|---|---|
| | Single-breadwinner households | Dual-breadwinner households | Single-breadwinner households | Dual-breadwinner households |
| Households without dependent children | | | | |
| France | 35.7 | 64.3 | 31.8 | 68.2 |
| Germany | 36.0 | 64.0 | 30.1 | 69.9 |
| Italy | 58.1 | 41.9 | 53.5 | 46.5 |
| Netherlands | 37.6 | 62.4 | 29.0 | 71.0 |
| Spain | 69.8 | 30.2 | 57.8 | 42.2 |
| UK | 23.7 | 76.3 | 20.9 | 79.1 |
| Households with dependent children | | | | |
| France | 40.1 | 59.9 | 36.0 | 64.0 |
| Germany | 44.9 | 55.1 | 39.7 | 60.3 |
| Italy | 57.6 | 42.4 | 53.6 | 46.4 |
| Netherlands | 52.4 | 47.6 | 32.7 | 67.3 |
| Spain | 68.1 | 31.9 | 56.3 | 43.7 |
| UK* | 36.6 | 63.4 | 29.8 | 70.2 |

*Field*: households in which the reference person is between twenty and fifty-nine years old, is working and living with a person who is also between twenty and fifty-nine years old.
* = 1999 data

*Source*: Eurostat 2002d

bracket. In all cases, there has been an increase in the number of dual-earner households between 1992 and 2000. The percentage of couples in which both partners work varies sharply from one member-state to another: 'In Greece, Spain and Italy, the proportion in 2000 was between 40% and 50% for couples with or without children, whereas two thirds or more of households in France, the Netherlands, Austria, Portugal and the United Kingdom were composed of "dual earners"' (Eurostat 2002d). The greatest change over this period concerns households with dependent children. The Netherlands has experienced a particularly large increase (+20 per cent) in the proportion of dual-earner households with children over this period. As we shall see below, this increase is partly due to the development of a 'male breadwinner/female part-time carer' model over recent years in this country. We can thus summarize this section as follows:

> Children's influence on the employment of couples differs according to the member states. The model in which both partners work is actually more widespread among couples with children than among couples without children in five member states. The percentage of couples in which both partners work is the same for both groups (with/without children) in Italy. The proportion of couples in which both partners work is less high among households with children than among those without children in six member states. The most substantial differences are recorded in Ireland (-10%), Germany (-10%) and the United Kingdom (-9%). The differences in employment situations between member states actually seems more pronounced than the differences observed between households with or without children. (Eurostat 2002d)

Since not all European women live in households composed of an adult couple, it is also interesting to consider the economic activity patterns of women living alone, either with or without children:

> At European Union level, the average rate of employment among 20 to 49 year old women living alone with a child under the age of 16 did not greatly differ from that of women living alone without children. However, this global similarity hides substantial differences between member states. Whereas in Denmark, France, Austria and Spain the rate of employment among women living alone hardly varied whether or not they had a child, in Germany, Ireland, The Netherlands, Finland and the United Kingdom, the percentage of those working was far less high among women with children than among women without children. It was equally less high in Belgium but the difference was more slight. In Greece, Italy, Portugal and to a lesser extent in Spain, the proportion of single working women was, on the other

hand, higher when they had a child than when they did not. The imperative necessity for single mothers to have an income therefore seems to take
precedence over the organizational problems posed by childcare. (Eurostat
2002c: 66)

*Part-time work* This rapid presentation of factors that influence the rates
and patterns of women's employment clearly illustrates the pivotal role
played by part-time work in all the current debates concerning women's
employment in Europe (Angeloff 1999; Fagan 2001; O'Reilly and Fagan
1998; Silvera 1998). Part-time employment is a non-standard form of employment that is highly feminized: approximately 80 per cent of part-timers
in the EU are women. However, within this general definition, it is useful
to emphasize the variability of part-time work within the EU. In the year
2000, fewer than 18 per cent of working women in Finland, Italy and Spain
were in part-time jobs, whereas one-third of working women in France,
approximately 40 per cent in Germany and the United Kingdom and two-
thirds of those in the Netherlands were working part-time (Table 1.9). For
men, part-time employment rarely exceeded the 10 per cent threshold,
except in the Netherlands where almost 22 per cent of men work on a
part-time basis.

The figures in Table 1.9 show the varying influence of children on
women's propensity to work part-time. In all the partner countries with
available data, the number of households where both partners work on a
part-time basis is negligible, as is the proportion of households where a
man working part-time lives with a woman working full-time. The main
options adopted in Europe are therefore either households where the
man works full-time and the woman part-time or households where both
partners work full-time.

TABLE 1.9 Average part-time employment rates by sex, 2002

|  | Women | Men |
| --- | --- | --- |
| Finland | 17.1 | 8.0 |
| France | 29.7 | 5.0 |
| Germany | 39.3 | 5.3 |
| Italy | 16.7 | 3.7 |
| Netherlands | 72.8 | 21.5 |
| Spain | 17.0 | 2.6 |
| UK | 44.0 | 9.4 |
| EU-15 | 33.7 | 6.3 |

*Source*: Eurostat 2003a

Without exception, the latter pattern is adopted by the majority of households without dependent children (Table 1.10), although in Germany, the Netherlands and the UK it is not unusual for women to work part-time, even when there are no children to be cared for. Likewise, in these three countries, most households with dependent children are organized along the 'male breadwinner/female part-time carer' model. In France, Italy and Spain, dual-earner households with dependent children are more likely to be organized around both partners working full-time.

TABLE 1.10 Distribution of households according to male and female working time patterns, 2000 (dual-breadwinner households)

| | Man part-time and woman part-time | Man part-time and woman full-time | Man full-time and woman part-time | Man full-time and woman full-time |
|---|---|---|---|---|
| **Households without dependent children** | | | | |
| France | 1.0 | 1.6 | 13.2 | 52.3 |
| Germany | 0.8 | 1.2 | 20.4 | 47.5 |
| Italy | 1.3 | 1.3 | 9.0 | 34.9 |
| Netherlands | 2.2 | 1.6 | 29.3 | 37.9 |
| Spain | 0.2 | 0.4 | 6.3 | 35.4 |
| UK | 1.1 | 1.6 | 21.2 | 55.2 |
| **Households with dependent children** | | | | |
| France | 1.2 | 1.1 | 16.3 | 45.4 |
| Germany | 0.6 | 0.7 | 32.9 | 26.1 |
| Italy | 1.3 | 0.9 | 13.0 | 31.2 |
| Netherlands | 2.3 | 1.3 | 52.9 | 10.8 |
| Spain | 0.2 | 0.4 | 7.5 | 35.6 |
| UK* | 0.7 | 0.9 | 40.0 | 28.6 |

*Note*: * 1999 data
*Source*: Eurostat 2002d

It should be remembered that dual-earner households with dependent children are less frequent in Spain and Italy than they are in France. It is interesting to note the very low proportion (10.8 per cent) of households with dependent children where both partners work full-time in the Netherlands, whereas this pattern is adopted by almost 40 per cent of households without dependent children. The effect of having dependent children on women's propensity to work part-time is also quite stark in Germany (21.4 per cent) and in the UK (26.6 per cent), whereas it is far more negligible in a country like France (6.9 per cent).

This analysis can be taken further with the data presented in Table 1.11

37

Employment opportunities for women

TABLE 1.11 Distribution of women (20–49 years and 50–64 years) between part-time and full-time employment, according to domestic responsibilities, 1998 (%)

| | | Finland | France | Germany | Italy | NL | Spain | UK | EU-15 |
|---|---|---|---|---|---|---|---|---|---|
| **Aged 20–49** | | | | | | | | | |
| with care responsibilities: | Part-time | 12 | 21 | 53 | 25 | 78 | 20 | 54 | 37 |
| | Full-time | 88 | 79 | 47 | 75 | 22 | 80 | 46 | 63 |
| without care responsibilities: | Part-time | 9 | 15 | – | 17 | 26 | 16 | 21 | 17 |
| | Full-time | 91 | 85 | – | 83 | 74 | 84 | 79 | 83 |
| **Aged 50–64** | | | | | | | | | |
| with care responsibilities: | Part-time | (7) | (20) | – | 35 | 74 | 26 | 49 | 36 |
| | Full-time | (93) | (80) | – | 65 | 26 | 74 | 51 | 64 |
| without care responsibilities: | Part-time | 6 | 20 | – | 25 | 62 | 21 | 40 | 28 |
| | Full-time | 94 | 80 | – | 75 | 38 | 79 | 60 | 72 |

*Note:* Figures in brackets are unreliable

*Source:* Eurostat 2002c: 161

which compares the working time patterns of women with and without care responsibilities in two different age brackets (twenty to forty-nine years and fifty to sixty-four years).

It is important to remember that Table 1.11 refers only to women who are in the labour market and that, in some EU member-states, a sizeable proportion of women with care responsibilities may be full-time house-wives. However, with this proviso in mind, we can analyse the impact of care on women's working time patterns in different countries. Taking the younger age cohort first, it is clear that having to care for a dependent person increases the rate of part-time work for women across the EWSI partner countries, but the degree of influence is highly variable from one country to another. Thus, on EU average, women are twice as likely to work part-time when they have care responsibilities than when they do not. This increase is however marginal (less than 10 per cent) in Finland, France, Italy and Spain, while it is significant in the UK (21 per cent) and very important in the Netherlands (52 per cent). A similar pattern can be observed for women in the older age group, but the influence of caring for a relative in later life on the adoption of part-time work is less important, notably because a larger proportion of women in this age group have already left the labour market (cf. Table 1.3).

It is therefore unsurprising to note that the reasons women give for having adopted a pattern of part-time work vary considerably from country to country (Table 1.12). In Germany, the Netherlands and the UK, women tend to refer to their domestic and care responsibilities in order to explain the fact that they work part-time, whereas in France and Spain the unavail-ability of full-time employment is more frequently cited as a reason for working part-time. Only in the Netherlands and the UK do more than a quarter of the women working part-time say that they are doing so by per-sonal choice. Alternative motives, combining paid employment and study or ill-health, are particularly important in Spain and in Italy. It should be pointed out that from 1983 to 1992, 56 per cent of all new jobs created within the EU were part-time. These new part-time jobs are not only impor-tant for women, they also affect men, since, over the same period, 54 per cent of the newly created jobs filled by a man were part-time jobs (against 56 per cent of newly created jobs taken up by women). However, in so far as the increase in the active population was mostly due to women, more than 75 per cent of newly created part-time jobs in Europe were taken up by women (Rubery et al. 1996: 20).

There is, however, no real consensus about the desirability of part-time work in the recent debates about women's employment levels in the EU (Le Feuvre 1997; Le Feuvre et al. 1999b).

TABLE 1.12 Main reasons given by women for adopting part-time employment, 2000

|  | France | Ger-many | Italy | NL | Spain | UK | UE-13 |
|---|---|---|---|---|---|---|---|
| Domestic and family reasons | 29 | 68 | 24 | 50 | 30 | 48 | 49 |
| Could not find alternative work | 44 | 12 | 22 | 11 | 38 | 11 | 18 |
| Personal choice | 14 | 10 | 12 | 27 | 6 | 28 | 19 |
| Other (study, ill-health, etc.) | 13 | 10 | 42 | 12 | 26 | 14 | 14 |

*Field*: those in salaried employment working at least fifteen hours a week.
*Source*: Eurostat 2000

Thus it is possible to identify a position that is highly favourable to the development of part-time work for women, particularly mothers. Under what is known as the 'reconciliation' argument, part-time employment is seen as an effective tool in helping women with dependent children to 'reconcile' the often contradictory demands of their jobs with 'their' domestic and care responsibilities. This position in favour of women's part-time work may, however, be related to two radically conflicting value judgements about the legitimacy of women's paid work in society. In a first case, the call for the development of more part-time jobs for women may be associated with the 'partial return' of women to the 'domestic home carer' role. Of course, the feasibility of this line of argument depends on women having a 'bread-winning' (male) partner available and therefore tends to value heterosexual marriage and a very traditional gender division of domestic work. However, the idea that more extensive availability of part-time jobs may actually help women to contest the 'male breadwinner/female home-carer' model has also been developed in some EU countries. In this case, it is argued that increasing the part-time job opportunities for women may actually help women to maintain a more continuous employment history, enabling them to avoid career breaks during their child-bearing years and may therefore help them to bypass the difficulties connected with maintaining their skill levels, one of the important problems facing so-called 'women returners'. This second argument in favour of women's part-time employment opportunities is often accompanied by calls for the state to impose the possibility for 'flexible' or 'family-friendly' working patterns on employers (Ellingsaeter 1999). Despite their major differences, both of the arguments in favour of women's part-time employment opportunities are usually associated with explicit demographic goals, since the ageing of the European population and the fall in fertility rates in many EU countries poses serious problems for the long-term viability of many social benefit measures, particularly regarding old-age pension rights (Ginn and Arber 1992).

Second, the available literature provides ample evidence of a critical perspective on women's part-time employment, which highlights the dangers of the development of part-time jobs for women within the EU. Some authors have even identified part-time work as the 'main source of discrimination against women' in the labour market (Bihr and Pfefferkorn 1996: 67). According to this perspective, part-time employment needs to be analysed in relation to the mechanisms of labour market 'flexibilization'. Part-time jobs are seen to offer the opportunity for employers to exploit their female labour force in order to increase productivity and competitiveness in the 'global market'. The stress is placed less on the opportunity for women to 'choose' their own working time arrangements in relation to their family circumstances, than on the role played by the development of part-time jobs in the deepening inequalities between different social groups with regard to employment. In this case, women's part-time work emerges as 'partial unemployment in disguise' (Maruani 2002) and is analysed as one of the major causes of the increase in the proportion of the so-called 'working poor' in EU member-states.

Not only do part-time jobs tend to be associated with high levels of employment insecurity, they also tend to command lower levels of pay and benefits than do full-time jobs and to be clustered in the least qualified sectors of the labour market (Angeloff 2000). Furthermore, working part-time may not only contribute to increasing the 'feminization of poverty' in contemporary societies, it also leads to severe financial difficulties for women in later life, since part-time jobs, associated with very low incomes, may lead to reduced retirement pension benefits for women (Ginn and Arber 1992). Theorists who adopt this critical vision of women's part-time work argue that it is, by definition, incompatible with the drive to increase 'equal opportunities', both between men and women and between different social categories of women. While recognizing the 'time famine' of working mothers, they argue that equality would be better achieved by the overall reduction of working time for men and women (thus increasing the opportunities for men to take a more equal share of domestic and care responsibilities) than by encouraging women and women alone to adapt their working time to their family circumstances (Méda 2001).

There are several explanations for the differences in the proportion of women in part-time employment in the various European countries. It is generally recognized that this non-standard form of employment results from the combination of economic and institutional constraints that prevent women from entering the labour market under the same conditions as men (Pfau-Effinger 1993: 386). However, any cross-national comparison of part-time work has to deal with the fact that, under a single concept (part-time work), we are actually confronted with very different social practices. In certain countries, part-time employment is synonymous with 'very short hours', whereas in others so-called 'part-time workers' may actually be working the equivalent of 80 per cent of a full-time job. Because of the cross-national variations in working time patterns more generally, it may be that a 'part-time worker' in one national context actually does longer hours than a 'full-time worker' in another country. Thus:

> Part-time work also reflects social norms and regulations; in some countries with high levels of part-time work there is a tendency for these jobs to be organised on a short-hours basis of less than 20 or even less than 10 hours a week, while in others with medium to high levels of part-time working – for example, Denmark, Sweden and France – most part-timers work more than 20 hours [ ... ] Part-timers working short and very short hours are more likely to be marginalized and less likely to earn a subsistence wage, reinforcing dependence on another wage earner, usually a man. Indeed, in Austria and the Netherlands those working less than 12 hours are not included in national definitions of the working population. (Rubery et al. 1999: 264)

Furthermore, whatever the country, the length of average working time for men and women varies according to their occupational status:

> In all countries men work longer hours than women but the difference is a result of the different levels of involvement of women in part-time work on the one hand and of men in long-hours work, either as self-employed or full-time employees on the other [ ... ] However, in practice the gender gap in average hours ranged from around 4 to 5 hours in all the Southern European countries and Luxembourg and in Austria and Finland to more than 12 hours in the Netherlands and the UK [1994 figures]. In Greece and Portugal the small gender gap rose out of long average hours for both men and women, with employed women in both these countries usually working more hours than men in Denmark and the Netherlands. In Spain, Italy, Luxembourg, Austria and Finland men had working hours similar to the European average but a relatively low incidence of part-time work for women resulted in a smaller gender gap. In the Netherlands and the UK the particularly large gender gap arose out of a high incidence of part-time work with very short hours for women. However, in the case of the UK, this was combined with very long hours for men, second only to Greece, reflecting

Le Feuvre and Andriocci | 1

the polarised pattern of working time in the UK, while the Netherlands has the shortest average hours for men as well as short hours for women. (Rubery et al. 1999: 256)

The economic and social consequences of part-time work are far from identical for all women in Europe. As already suggested, it is difficult to conclude as to the 'positive' or 'negative' of part-time work on gender equality in the labour market, because experiences vary so much between countries and between women of different social backgrounds within a given national context. It nevertheless remains the case that women are always first in line when it comes to designating the 'ideal part-time worker' and that promoting part-time work for women (mothers) is usually associated with a modified version of the 'male breadwinner/female home-carer' model. A number of recent research projects have highlighted the paradox of the 'reconciliation' argument in favour of women's part-time work (Junter-Loiseau 1999), since there is ample evidence to suggest that employers may develop particular forms of part-time work for women that are far from 'family friendly'. In many EU countries, the retail sector is often cited as an example where the increase in part-time jobs developed through evening, late shift and/or weekend working, which actually makes it harder rather than easier for mothers to combine employment with childcare responsibilities (Angeloff 1999, 2000). Even in better paid, white-collar occupations, part-time workers often experience negative effects on their promotion and training prospects. Furthermore, the limited cross-national comparative data available on this topic suggest that men living with women working part-time spend less time on domestic and care responsibilities than do men with partners working full-time (Barrère-Maurisson et al. 2001; Brousse 2000). While we have sought to draw attention to the dangers of an over-hasty analysis and simplification of the consequences of part-time work for women, it is nevertheless vital to understand that when women aspire to working part-time or when they declare themselves to be 'satisfied' with their part-time jobs, they do so within the structural constraints of the 'gender cultural model'. One of the major characteristics of these models in most EU member-states is the unequal gender division of domestic and care activities in the home. We therefore turn to a more detailed analysis of this aspect of women's employment opportunities in the following section.

*The sexual division of domestic labour and care* No serious analysis of women's labour market participation patterns can ignore the question of the sexual division of domestic labour and informal care activities. As a recent Eurostat report has noted:

Women are confronted, far more than men are, by the difficulties of reconciling their professional career and family responsibilities, whether through
childcare or care given to another dependent person. One must indeed note
that even if a significant amount of men devote time to their children, this
does not seem to have noticeable repercussions on their work. In the case
of women however, family responsibilities can mean the inability to work
altogether or the obligation of having to choose part-time rather than full-
time employment. (Eurostat 2002c: 55)

According to the 1998 European Household Survey, almost 40 per cent
of European women aged between twenty and forty-nine years spend part of
their day looking after children, while fewer than 20 per cent of men in the
same age cohort do so. Furthermore, '86% of women of this age cohort devote time to caring for other dependent people (disabled or elderly notably),
this percentage is twice as high as that of men. In all member states, the
proportion of women providing care is far greater than the proportion of
men' (Eurostat 2002c: 55). Thus 'approximately 80% of women between the
ages of 20 and 49 living in households in which there are young children
have care responsibilities – the percentage is higher in Denmark, Greece
and the Netherlands and lower in Portugal, the United Kingdom and France
– and that this proportion is at least 1.5 times higher to that of men living
in the same type of household' (ibid., p. 56).

Once again, the degree to which fathers participate in the care and education of their children shows considerable variation by country. Over 60 per
cent of fathers in Finland, Germany and the Netherlands do some kind of
childcare activities, whereas only a third of fathers are actively involved in
family life in France, Spain and the UK (Table 1.13). The precise definition
of 'care' activities used in Eurostat comparisons is rather imprecise and
would seem to include both passive supervision and more active interventions, such as bathing, feeding, entertaining.

However, as we have seen in the previous sections of this chapter,
mothers may be more or less intensively involved in the daily care of their

TABLE 1.13 Proportion of men and women (20–49 years) with children who
devote time to caring activities, 1998 (%)

| | Fin-land | France | Ger-many | Italy | NL | Spain | UK | EU-15 |
|---|---|---|---|---|---|---|---|---|
| Men | 62 | 37 | 73 | 54 | 89 | 34 | 35 | 49 |
| Women | 81 | 61 | 92 | 89 | 99 | 84 | 76 | 81 |

*Source*: Eurostat 2002c: 160

children, notably according to the degree to which the dominant national 'gender culture model' allows for the state or market provision of childcare facilities and/or for the mobilization of older generations in the provision of childcare services on an informal basis. From the data in Table 1.14, it would seem that childcare activities are highly 'privatized' in Germany and the Netherlands (i.e. they are carried out within the child's own home, principally by the mother), whereas other social partners (kindergartens, schools, child-minders, grandparents, etc.) are more likely to be involved in childcare in the other countries. However, overall it is clear that women spend more time looking after dependent members of their (extended) family than men: 'In eight of the eleven member states for which there is available data, women aged 20 to 49 and caring for children spend 45 hours a week, or more, doing so' (Eurostat 2002c: 57).

TABLE 1.14 Employment rate of men and women (20–49 and 50–64 years) according to whether or not they devote time to care responsibilities, 1998 (%)

| | Fin-land | France | Ger-many | Italy | NL | Spain | UK | EU-15 |
|---|---|---|---|---|---|---|---|---|
| **Aged 20–49 (childcare responsibilities)** | | | | | | | | |
| **Men** | | | | | | | | |
| Care | 83 | 88 | 92 | 93 | 97 | 87 | 87 | 90 |
| No care | 67 | 76 | 86 | 72 | 87 | 72 | 90 | 81 |
| **Women** | | | | | | | | |
| Care | 58 | 57 | 62 | 42 | 66 | 40 | 69 | 57 |
| No care | 67 | 65 | 82 | 51 | 88 | 48 | 81 | 69 |
| **Aged 50–64 (childcare responsibilities)** | | | | | | | | |
| **Men** | | | | | | | | |
| Care | (48) | 33 | 46 | 48 | 78 | (49) | (51) | 48 |
| No care | 50 | 58 | 65 | 54 | 62 | 61 | 73 | 63 |
| **Women** | | | | | | | | |
| Care | 37 | 33 | 32 | 20 | 36 | 11 | 39 | 29 |
| No care | 44 | 42 | 44 | 21 | 41 | 21 | 56 | 38 |
| **Aged 50–64 (responsibilities other than for children)** | | | | | | | | |
| **Men** | | | | | | | | |
| Care | 32 | (44) | (51) | 29 | 57 | 42 | 64 | 47 |
| No care | 50 | 58 | 65 | 54 | 62 | 61 | 73 | 63 |
| **Women** | | | | | | | | |
| Care | 45 | 30 | 16 | 16 | 39 | 13 | 53 | 29 |
| No care | 44 | 42 | 44 | 21 | 41 | 21 | 56 | 38 |

*Note*: Figures in brackets are unreliable
*Source*: Eurostat 2002c: 161

As we have already seen, taking care of dependent relatives (children or elderly parents) not only takes up more of women's time, it also has a decisive impact on the rate and pattern of their labour market participation, whereas the influence of care activities on men's employment rates is negligible:

> Whereas looking after children does not seem to have major repercussions on whether men under the age of 50 are employed or not, the situation is quite different for women. Indeed, across the EU, approximately 90% of men aged 20 to 49 with childcare responsibilities also had a job, whereas the percentage of those who do not have family responsibilities does not exceed 80%. Within the same age cohort, however, only 57% of women who say they care for children are employed as against 69% of those who do not have such responsibilities. (Eurostat 2002c: 59)

However, although men with caring activities are likely to be in the labour market, they also have to adapt their working hours to their family situation. As we have seen, they are less likely than their female counterparts to work part-time and are more likely to reduce the length of their working week: 'The length of the working week decreases for all those that have child care responsibilities: part-time employment for women, and reduced full-time for men' (Eurostat 2002c: 63). As shown in Table 1.15, men with caring responsibilities (or men who share part of the childcare burden of their households) also tend to reduce the duration of the time spent in paid employment as their caring load increases. However, since this reduction rarely leads to the adoption of part-time jobs (and since it concerns fewer men than women), it is far less visible from the employer's point of view and does little to challenge the belief that women (as mothers) carry

TABLE 1.15 Average length of working week for men and women, according to the time spent on childcare, 1998 (hrs)

| | < 14 hours/week spent on childcare | | 14–28 hours/week spent on childcare | | > 28 hours/week spent on childcare | |
|---|---|---|---|---|---|---|
| | Men | Women | Men | Women | Men | Women |
| Finland | 45 | 36 | 46 | 40 | 41 | 36 |
| France | 44 | 39 | 41 | 36 | 39 | 34 |
| Italy | 45 | 34 | 41 | 35 | 43 | 34 |
| NL | 45 | (33) | 41 | 25 | 33 | 19 |
| EU-15 | 45 | 37 | 42 | 36 | 41 | 33 |

*Note:* Figures in brackets are unreliable

*Source*: Eurostat 2002c: 66

the burden of care and that men (as fathers) are the primary breadwinners of the family. Such beliefs play an important role in the gender segregation of the labour market and determine to a large extent the kinds of jobs and the status of men and women on the European labour market.

*Horizontal and vertical segregation of the labour market* The different European labour markets are characterized by varying degrees of horizontal and vertical segregation by sex. The term 'horizontal segregation' refers to the fact that men and women tend to occupy different sectors of the labour market, while the term 'vertical segregation' refers to the fact that, whatever the occupations they carry out, men and women are unevenly distributed along the occupational hierarchy.

From the point of view of horizontal segregation, women tend to be disproportionately concentrated in the tertiary sector of the economy, while men work in the industrial sectors, although a significant proportion of women also work in manufacturing. Women are also overrepresented in public sector employment:

> In 2000, the employment of nearly half the women (48%) working in the EU was concentrated in four of the 60 sectors of activity of the two figure General Industrial Classification of Economic Activities within the European Communities – that is to say in health and social work, education, public administration and retailing – yet all these put together represented only a third of total employment. Approximately 17% of the women were employed in the health and social work sector alone and 18% were employed in teaching and the civil service. Over a third (35%) of working women were therefore employed in tertiary occupations in the public sector as compared with barely 15% of men (and 24% of the total workforce, men and women together). (Eurostat 2002c: 70)

Men's employment shows far less concentration. The four main sectors for men, building, agriculture, wholesale trade and transport, account for 25 per cent of the male workforce (and 8 per cent of the female workforce) (Eurostat 2002c: 70). Women are also more concentrated in fewer occupations than men:

> At EU level in 2000, approximately half of working women were employed in ten of the 130 standard occupational categories whereas the ten main professions for men accounted for less than 36% of the male labour force. In addition, the professions in question were very different for women and for men. Approximately 80% of the women working in the Union are employed, in some form or another, as shop or sales assistants, in cleaning

occupations and in domestic services to households (childminders, nannies, cleaners, etc.). These three occupational groups account for about 22% of the female labour force. (Eurostat 2002c: 72)

Despite the progressive increase in women's labour market participation, there has been little change to the horizontal segregation of the labour market over the past years: 'Neither the relative rates of occupational concentration of male and female employment, nor the specific fields in which men and women tend to work have undergone major changes these last years. They were therefore quite similar in 2000 to what they were in 1990, the main change being a relative decline in the importance of agriculture and the manufacturing industry, with regard to men's employment in particular' (Eurostat 2002c: 70). This horizontal and occupational distribution varies little from country to country.

The analysis of the professional concentration of the female labour force raises questions about the ability of the existing international classification systems to accommodate and adequately describe the occupational positions of women on the labour market. Because the jobs women occupy in the tertiary sector expanded much later than the industrial sector occupations that men have traditionally carried out, they are far more difficult to distinguish in the existing occupational classification schemes. For the purpose of the EWSI project, we used the ISCO-88 international classification system (see Chapter 8). It soon became apparent that this scheme provided a far more detailed distinction between jobs in the manufacturing sector than it provided for tertiary-sector occupations. One of the recommendations from the project concerns the need to develop new occupational classification systems that are sensitive to the different occupations carried out by women, not least because of the overwhelming predominance of the tertiary sector for women's employment in Europe (Dale and Glover 1989; Glover 1993).

Turning now to the question of vertical segregation, we can analyse two different dimensions to this question. First, we can compare the relative chances that men and women have of reaching the upper echelons of the occupational hierarchy in the course of their working lives. Second, we can compare the positions of men and women as regards self-employment and entrepreneurship. Both these dimensions of vertical segregation are important, since they determine the extent to which women can shape the organization of the labour market, and also the family–employment interface, in the years to come. The figures for 1998 show that there is still a long way to go before women break through the so-called 'glass ceiling' that limits their career prospects in Europe. Although the proportion of workers to reach management status depends on the internal structure of the labour market and varies considerably from one European country to another (ranging from 25 per cent in the UK to just 7 per cent in Italy), men are twice as likely as women to benefit from management status in almost all EU member countries. Thus, while 16 per cent of working men have management status, this is the case for under 9 per cent of working women. A similar gender gap exists for middle-management positions. On average, 17 per cent of working men occupy jobs with middle-management status, compared to 14 per cent of working women, although women dominate this category in Belgium, France and Finland (Eurostat 2002c: 78).

It is important to understand that vertical segregation stems from several different social processes. On the one hand, employers may be unwilling to promote suitably qualified women to positions of responsibility, in the belief that they will be 'hampered' by their disproportionate role in domestic and care activities. If this were the case, single women or women without children should be as successful as men in obtaining promotion. This may sometimes be the case, but it does not account for the very high levels of vertical segregation noted above. Second, women may themselves be less willing to apply for promotion, believing that the additional responsibilities will add to their time-pressured existence and will lead to conflict on the domestic front. They are generally less able to count on the support services of their partners, children and extended families than are their male counterparts. However, we have already seen that men who take on care responsibilities in the home are able to reduce their working hours and this does not seem to affect their ability to follow upwardly mobile career paths (Crompton and Birkelund 2000). Third, there is a relationship between the high levels of horizontal segregation of the labour market and women's underrepresentation at the top of the occupational hierarchy. Since women occupy a small range of occupations, they come into competition with each other (and with men) for a limited number of managerial positions. Finally, because of the high degree of horizontal segregation, women receive fewer rewards (in terms of promotion and working conditions) and less recognition for their skills and qualifications. This is partly because they occupy jobs which are seen as an extension of their domestic and caring roles and which are socially defined as being 'less qualified' than many of the highly masculinized sectors of the labour market (Kergoat 1982).

For many of these reasons, self-employment may offer more promising career prospects to women. However, once again, average figures for the EU member-states show that women are only half as likely as men to be self-employed (6 per cent of the female labour force, as compared with 10 per cent of the men, agriculture excluded): 'In practice, far less women than men are self-employed in the European Union and women in management positions or self-employed with employees are even more rare' (Eurostat 2002a: 1). Thus, in 2000, 'Close to 7.5 per cent of men employed in industry and services (excluding the agriculture sector) were listed as self-employed with employees, whereas the corresponding figures for women reached only 3%. The relative number of women in management positions is highest in Italy, where 8% of self-employed women have others working for them, but this clearly remains below the corresponding figures for men (15%). In all other member States, it is lower than 4%' (ibid., p. 2).

Thus, women are currently underrepresented among the entrepreneurs of the EU, while this category plays an important role in shaping the future of the European labour market, particularly in a context of intensive global competition and the risk of unemployment. Since women are among those hardest hit by unemployment, their ability to invest in the creation of jobs (for themselves and for other women) is one of the important factors for the future of gender equality in Europe.

*Unemployment rates and benefits* The fight against unemployment has been at the heart of European employment policies for many years. Although the rates of unemployment vary greatly according to country (from 5.1 per cent in the UK to 11.4 per cent in Spain in 2002), Table 1.16 shows that, with the exception of the UK and Finland, women's unemployment rate is always higher than the rate for men. The gender gap is particularly pronounced in Italy and Spain. These high levels of female unemployment persist, despite the fact that women are more likely to be working in the tertiary sector that has not tended to be hit by the large-scale redundancies that occurred in the industrial sectors.

Table 1.17 provides an overview of the proportion of young women in education, in the labour market and unemployed in 2001; it also provides some indication of the inactivity rates of young women once they leave the education system. The figures show that in Germany, Hungary and Italy, between a third and a quarter of women in the twenty-five to twenty-nine age bracket have left the labour market and are not registered as unemployed: they are what remains of the 'female home carer' model in these societies. In the remaining countries, this status accounts for fewer than 20 per cent of women aged between twenty-five and twenty-nine.

It should, however, be remembered that interpreting and comparing unemployment data across countries is somewhat problematic. Contrary to men, women who leave the labour market do not necessarily consider themselves unemployed. In the welfare state regimes based on the 'male breadwinner/female home-carer' model, working mothers are generally

TABLE 1.16 Male and female unemployment rates, 1993–2002 (%)

| | 1993 | | | 1997 | | | 2002 | | |
|---|---|---|---|---|---|---|---|---|---|
| | F | M | Total | F | M | Total | F | M | Total |
| Finland | 14.4 | 18.1 | 16.3 | 13.0 | 12.3 | 12.7 | 9.1 | 9.1 | 9.1 |
| France | 13.2 | 9.7 | 11.3 | 13.7 | 10.2 | 11.8 | 9.9 | 7.8 | 8.7 |
| Germany | 9.4 | 6.5 | 7.7 | 10.4 | 9.1 | 9.7 | 8.0 | 8.3 | 8.2 |
| Hungary | – | – | – | 8.1 | 9.7 | 9.0 | 5.1 | 6.0 | 5.6 |
| Italy | 14.5 | 7.5 | 10.1 | 16.1 | 8.9 | 11.6 | 12.3 | 7.0 | 9.1 |
| NL | 7.5 | 5.4 | 6.2 | 6.6 | 3.7 | 4.9 | 3.0 | 2.5 | 2.7 |
| Slovenia | – | – | – | 7.1 | 6.8 | 6.9 | 6.4 | 5.7 | 6.0 |
| Spain | 2.41 | 15.5 | 18.6 | 23.4 | 13.1 | 17.0 | 16.5 | 8.1 | 11.4 |
| UK | 7.6 | 11.9 | 10 | 5.8 | 7.7 | 6.9 | 4.5 | 5.7 | 5.1 |
| EU-15 | 11.4 | 9.1 | 10.1 | 10.2 | 8.9 | 10.0 | 8.6 | 6.8 | 7.6 |
| US | 6.5 | 7.1 | 6.8 | 5.0 | 4.9 | 4.9 | 5.6 | 5.9 | 5.8 |
| Japan | 2.6 | 2.4 | 2.5 | 3.4 | 3.4 | 3.4 | 5.1 | 5.5 | 5.4 |

*Sources*: Eurostat 2002e, 1999

defined as a 'social problem'. Thus a woman who loses her job or decides to leave the labour market at a given time during the course of her adult life and who has difficulty finding another job may either be considered (and may indeed consider herself) as a 'housewife' or as an unemployed person. Once again, the 'standard' statistical distinctions between the 'working population in employment', the 'unemployed working population' and 'inactive' adults proves far less effective in measuring women's exclusion from the labour market than in understanding the position of men.

We have seen in the previous parts of this chapter that the different systems of social protection cover the risks of job loss in a variety of manners. Like the other components of the social protection system, the rights of the unemployed have often been constructed on the basis of the 'male breadwinner/female home-carer' model. In the countries in which this model remains dominant, the right to receive unemployment benefit is often granted only to people who have enjoyed a continuous employment history, with a minimum amount of working hours. Women who have taken a voluntary or enforced 'career break' or who have worked part-time have a great deal of trouble in fulfilling the standard, legal unemployment benefit requirements. Furthermore, in certain countries, only the unemployed who are seeking full-time employment are recorded in national statistics. The case of the UK is particularly enlightening in this respect. At least up until the mid-1990s, one of the conditions that had to be fulfilled by job-seekers was that of being 'immediately available to work'. Furthermore, since a

Employment opportunities for women

TABLE 1.17 Distribution of young women (15–29 years) according to education and employment status, 2001

| Age group | In education | | | | | Not in education | | | | Total |
|---|---|---|---|---|---|---|---|---|---|---|
| | Students in work-study programmes | Other employed | Un-employed | Not in the labour force | Sub-total | In employment | Un-employed | Not in the labour force | Sub-total | |
| **Finland** | | | | | | | | | | |
| 15–19 | a | 14.3 | 7.2 | 68.7 | 90.2 | 6.0 | 1.6 | 2.1 | 9.8 | 100 |
| 20–24 | a | 23.5 | 4.5 | 31.2 | 59.2 | 27.9 | 5.0 | 7.9 | 40.8 | 100 |
| 25–29 | a | 18.4 | 2.1 | 9.8 | 30.3 | 46.6 | 8.1 | 15.1 | 69.7 | 100 |
| **France** | | | | | | | | | | |
| 15–19 | 3.7 | 0.5 | n | 90.9 | 95.3 | 1.2 | 1.8 | 1.7 | 4.7 | 100 |
| 20–24 | 6.5 | 5.8 | 0.7 | 43.6 | 56.6 | 27.6 | 8.7 | 7.1 | 43.4 | 100 |
| 25–29 | 1.7 | 4.9 | 0.4 | 5.3 | 12.3 | 62.3 | 9.9 | 15.5 | 87.7 | 100 |
| **Germany** | | | | | | | | | | |
| 15–19 | 17.0 | 4.3 | 0.6 | 67.5 | 89.3 | 5.3 | 1.3 | 4.0 | 10.7 | 100 |
| 20–24 | 13.2 | 6.0 | 0.3 | 17.7 | 37.2 | 44.1 | 4.1 | 14.6 | 62.8 | 100 |
| 25–29 | 1.1 | 4.1 | 0.2 | 5.3 | 10.7 | 64.6 | 4.7 | 20.0 | 89.3 | 100 |
| **Hungary** | | | | | | | | | | |
| 15–19 | a | 0.4 | 0.3 | 85.2 | 85.9 | 6.1 | 1.6 | 6.3 | 14.1 | 100 |
| 20–24 | a | 5.1 | 0.3 | 31.5 | 37.0 | 38.5 | 3.7 | 20.8 | 63.0 | 100 |
| 25–29 | a | 5.2 | 0.2 | 4.8 | 10.2 | 51.3 | 3.7 | 34.8 | 89.8 | 100 |

| | | | | | | | | | | |
|---|---|---|---|---|---|---|---|---|---|---|
| Italy | 15–19 | n | 0.7 | 1.0 | 78.1 | 79.8 | 7.7 | 4.7 | 7.8 | 20.2 | 100 |
| | 20–24 | n | 3.3 | 2.1 | 36.7 | 42.3 | 30.4 | 11.9 | 15.4 | 57.7 | 100 |
| | 25–29 | n | 3.8 | 1.4 | 13.8 | 19.0 | 47.0 | 10.2 | 23.8 | 81 | 100 |
| Netherlands | 15–19 | m | 40.2 | 5.9 | 36.6 | 82.7 | 13.8 | 1.2 | 2.2 | 17.3 | 100 |
| | 20–24 | m | 22.0 | 1.3 | 12.1 | 35.4 | 53.4 | 2.3 | 8.9 | 64.6 | 100 |
| | 25–29 | m | 2.5 | 0.1 | 1.9 | 4.5 | 77.3 | 3.1 | 15.2 | 95.5 | 100 |
| Spain | 15–19 | 0.3 | 2.7 | 1.9 | 76.9 | 81.8 | 8.7 | 5.5 | 4.0 | 18.2 | 100 |
| | 20–24 | 0.7 | 7.2 | 3.2 | 38.2 | 49.3 | 32.8 | 10.0 | 7.9 | 50.7 | 100 |
| | 25–29 | 0.4 | 6.9 | 2.7 | 8.5 | 18.4 | 53.8 | 10.0 | 17.9 | 81.6 | 100 |
| UK | 15–19 | 3.2 | 29.6 | 2.7 | 36.1 | 71.5 | 18.5 | 3.9 | 6.1 | 28.5 | 100 |
| | 20–24 | 2.9 | 15.1 | 0.8 | 15.1 | 33.9 | 46.9 | 3.9 | 15.2 | 66.1 | 100 |
| | 25–29 | 1.3 | 9.9 | 0.5 | 4.0 | 15.8 | 61.4 | 2.9 | 19.9 | 84.2 | 100 |

*Source:* <www.oecd.org/els/education/eag2002>

1989 change in legislation, any person who has already accumulated more than thirteen weeks of unemployment and who turned down a job offer for reasons related to the kind of work, the working hours, pay or geographical location, ran the risk of losing his or her benefit (Hegewisch 1995). In a country where public childcare facilities are notoriously lacking and where private systems of childcare are very expensive, it is extremely difficult for British mothers to qualify as 'officially registered unemployed', since their 'availability' to work is often conditioned by access to informal childcare networks and to the precise location and pay levels of any job offer. Further-more, even when they do manage to register, there is evidence to suggest that British women are far less likely to obtain unemployment benefit than their male counterparts, since this requires a two-year minimum continu-ous employment history, with wages that exceed the minimum threshold of social contribution payments. In 1994, one-third of all women working in the UK (and two-thirds of those in part-time jobs) had incomes below that level (ibid., p. 14). At least part of the explanation for the 'exceptional UK case' with regard to gender differences in unemployment rates prob-ably lies in these institutional rules, rather than in lower labour market exclusion rates for women than for men.

Moreover, in several countries, unemployment benefit (particularly when paid on a long-term basis) is means-tested. This can prove problematic for women if it is the household rather than the person's individual income that is taken into account. If they live with a relatively well-paid (male) partner, women may lose their own rights to unemployment benefit. On the other hand, when the male partner loses his job and becomes eligible for unemployment benefit, his wife's income may be deducted from his entitlements. Research has shown that these social policy measures may encourage the wives of unemployed men to 'voluntarily' leave the labour market, in order to maximize household resources, their own income be-ing lower than the unemployment benefit entitlements of their husbands (European Commission 1996b: 4).

For all these reasons, the extent of women's unemployment within the EU is clearly greater than that reported in official statistics (Maruani 2002). Some research has suggested that the term 'underemployment' provides a better picture of the labour market access problems faced by women, since it enables all kinds of 'marginalized' employment statuses to be taken into account. This term applies to all those who are excluded from the official unemployment statistics for the reasons outlined above, but also covers women in part-time employment who wish to work full-time (European Commission 1996a: 6). This concept provides insight into the fact that, when they face difficulties in finding a job, women are clearly more likely than men to 'disappear' from the official unemployment statistics without necessarily having found a job.

The transition towards inactivity is particularly pronounced in countries where women usually adopt a discontinuous employment pattern. Thus, at the beginning of the 1990s, a study found that in Germany, Belgium, Italy and the Netherlands, over a third of the women who were registered as unemployed for under a year had actually become full-time 'housewives' by the time their situation was reviewed. This can be explained both by difficulties in gaining recognition for their 'unemployed' status as wives and mothers, but also by the fact that, particularly in countries where there are high levels of short-duration part-time jobs for women, the marginal financial benefits gained from working are lower for women than for men. This brings us to the question of pay differentials in the European labour market.

*Wage differentials* Since 1995, women's average earnings have increased more than men's in most of the EU member-states, but this increase is weak and women's average earnings clearly remain lower than those of men in all countries. According to 1995 income statistics, the average earnings for women in full-time employment in the industrial and service sectors of the EU only corresponded to 75 per cent of men's earnings. Despite strong variations between the different countries, women's average earnings represented more than 85 per cent of men's average earnings in only four countries (Belgium, Denmark, Luxembourg and Sweden). At the other extreme, in three countries (Greece, the Netherlands and Portugal), 'women's average earnings only just reached 70% of those earned by men' (Eurostat 2001b). The data presented in Table 1.18 indicate slightly different wage differentials than those cited above. This is due to the fact that some national statistics include workers only in the industrial and manufacturing sectors, whereas others also include all or part of service sector employees. Also, some countries include the wage levels of part-time workers, whereas others include only full-time staff in their calculations. Cross-national comparisons of wage differentials by sex are therefore extremely difficult (Elliott et al. 2001). However, from 2002 onwards, Eurostat will produce harmonized data sets for all EU member-states.

Not only do women receive lower levels of remuneration than their male counterparts, they also represent a majority of the so-called 'working poor' in Europe. They are more likely to be receiving very low incomes from employment, not only because they are more likely to be working part-time, but also because they are employed in the least well paid sectors of the labour market. Overall, about 15 per cent of all workers in the EU (16.5 million

TABLE 1.18 Gender wage differentials, 1994–99 (women's gross average hourly wage as percentage of men's gross average hourly wage)

| | 1994 | 1996 | 1998 | 1999 |
|---|---|---|---|---|
| Finland | – | 83 | 81 | 81 |
| France | 87 | 87 | 88 | 88 |
| Germany | 79 | 79 | 78 | 81 |
| Italy | 92 | 92 | 93 | 91 |
| Netherlands | 77 | 77 | 79 | 79 |
| Spain | 90 | 86 | 84 | 86 |
| UK | – | – | – | 78 |
| EU-15 | – | – | – | 84 |

*Source*: Eurostat 2003a

people) receive a salary that is below 60 per cent of the average mean salary in their country (Eurostat 2000). Women represent 77 per cent of the poorly paid in Europe, i.e. twice their proportion in the labour force. This does not necessarily mean that this proportion of women live below the poverty line – 'In almost half the cases, a low wage received by one household member is "compensated for" by a higher wage received by one or several other people within the household' (ibid., p. 1) – but this 'income compensation effect' obviously has repercussions on the degree to which women can earn a subsistence income and on their ability to escape from dependence on a 'breadwinning' male partner, particularly in cases of domestic violence and abuse (Hanmer 1990; Jaspard and l'équipe Enveff 2001).

*Continuing education and training* In recent years, the European Union has made access to continuing education one of the priorities in the fight against unemployment and in the promotion of economic development and competition in a global market. The degree to which 'life-long learning' is integrated into personnel management policies in companies obviously varies by country, by economic sector and according to the size of firms. According to the Continuing Vocational Training Survey carried out in 2000–01, over 50 per cent of private sector employees in Sweden, Denmark and Finland had access to company-funded training programmes in 1999, compared with just 25 per cent of staff in Spain and 17 per cent in Portugal (Eurostat 2002c: 88).

With the exception of Finland, women working in the private sector are less likely than their male counterparts to benefit from continuing education programmes once they are in employment. However, because of the high degree of horizontal segregation of the labour market, women fared better in the most highly feminized sectors of the labour market. The highest rates of staff training are found in companies with 250 employees or more, while women tend to be overrepresented in small or medium-sized firms. However, data from the 1999 Household Panel Survey, which includes public sector employees, show that women in the twenty-five to forty-nine age group were more likely than their male counterparts to have received continuing education and that, in Finland, Italy, Spain and the UK, women in this age group were more likely to have followed a training programme that was directly related to their jobs than men in the same age group. At the same time, women also lead the field in extra-professional educational programmes – such as evening classes – that are not directly vocational in nature (ibid., p. 88). These figures confirm the importance of the initial 'training gap' between men and women when they leave full-time education (see Table 1.6) and the importance of enabling women to catch up with men through an extensive network of continuing education programmes in all EU countries.

In conclusion to the second part of this chapter, we need to stress the continuing inequalities that characterize women's access to and experience of the labour market in the EU. Despite significant national variations, the expectation that women will continue to take responsibility for domestic and care activities throughout their adult lives clearly shapes their employment expectations, aspirations and experiences in many different ways. In the following and final part of the chapter, we will turn to the potential influence of Women's Studies training on promoting equal opportunity policy measures across the EU.

### Potential impact of Women's Studies training on equality of opportunity in employment in the EU

The results of the EWSI project presented in the other chapters of this book enable the real and potential impact of Women's Studies in promoting gender equality in employment and in other spheres of social life to be analysed in some detail. This section will simply provide some general comments and suggestions for future action.

Despite the various degrees of institutionalization of Women's Studies and varying course contents offered in different partner countries (Griffin, ed. 2002), Women's Studies teaching can be unambiguously associated with increasing levels of awareness about the persistence of gender inequalities in contemporary Europe and elsewhere in the world. We have seen in the first part of this chapter that the different 'gender cultures' identified within the EU provide a template for the everyday lives of men and women in a given national and historical context. When a person is born into a society organized entirely on the differentiation of the social functions that are allocated to men and women and on the systematic devaluing of whatever comes to be designated as 'women's work' (Héritier 1996), it is extremely difficult to break away from the gender stereotypes that lead men and women to act in different ways (Bourdieu 1990; Haicault 1993). This differentiation process not only permeates institutions and structural, organizational aspects of society, it also influences the way people think about themselves and their role in society. By placing the analysis of different 'gender cultures' in historical perspective, Women's Studies teaching provides a vital first step in broadening horizons and enabling social change to become even 'thinkable'. It serves to 'deconstruct' the most engrained beliefs about the differences between men and women and therefore opens up new possibilities for the future. In all the EWSI project partner countries, Women's Studies students and graduates stress the importance of their course in providing 'awareness' of gender inequalities and also in making alternative social arrangements appear possible (see Chapter 5). This awareness is merely the first step in the process of social change set in motion by Women's Studies. Subsequently, it would seem that these lessons enable students to develop several individual and collective strategies for change within the specific 'gender contract' or 'gender culture' of their own society.

First, whatever 'gender culture' they have been brought up in, Women's Studies students and graduates unanimously reject the 'male breadwinner/ female home-carer' model which has left a more or less indelible mark on the experience of previous generations of women in their country. Although, given their qualification levels, one would expect women from our study sample to show high levels of labour market commitment, it is still nevertheless the case that Women's Studies students and graduates adopt something of a vanguard role in comparison to their similarly qualified compatriots. Moreover, even where full-time, continuous employment patterns have long been adopted by women and have become the dominant societal norm (e.g. Finland), Women's Studies students and graduates still demonstrate a certain capacity for innovation. They reject the perceived social pressures to behave like 'surrogate men' (for example, by adopting long working hours, at the expense of other interests) and attempt to invent life projects for themselves and for men that have more intrinsic meaning than work alone. Second, Women's Studies students and graduates demonstrate unusually high commitment to social change. Although they rarely believe that their Women's Studies courses play a direct role in helping them to find a job, they are convinced that the content of their courses has altered (or will alter) the way they carry out their work.

On the one hand, they acquire the self-confidence that enables them to consider leaving the 'beaten track' of women's employment, as defined in their own country. The international mobility opportunities offered during Women's Studies courses undeniably open up new personal and professional horizons for the students (see Chapter 4). But even those women who do not or cannot take advantage of these opportunities appreciate the way in which the cross-national comparative aspects of Women's Studies enable them to gain a better understanding of the diversity of women's experiences, both across Europe and throughout the world. This newly gained self-confidence is important for their employment aspirations and expectations in several ways. First, the mere feat of getting a university qualification can represent a specific labour-market asset, particularly in countries where women have long been underrepresented in higher education institutions. Endowed with higher qualifications than most women of their generation, Women's Studies graduates can enter new occupational fields and/or adopt career patterns from which they were previously *de facto* excluded. It is particularly important to note the large proportion of 'mature' students on Women's Studies courses in many of the EWSI partner countries. For women who had to leave school at a relatively young age and for those who have taken an extended 'career break', Women's Studies clearly enhances 'life-long learning' opportunities.

Second, although, with the notable exception of academe, the EWSI data provide no conclusive evidence of Women's Studies directly helping women into the least feminized sectors of the labour market (since most Women's Studies courses have been created within the 'traditionally feminine disciplines' of each national higher education system), nor indeed of helping them to break through the 'glass ceiling' imposed on their career progression over time, there is plenty of evidence that Women's Studies has helped graduates to modify their professional experiences (see Chapter 4). The knowledge acquired through Women's Studies subsequently enables students and graduates to develop a 'gender sensitive' worldview. They are equipped for life with what many of them call their 'feminist glasses' (van der Sanden and Waaldijk 2002). These 'glasses' make them particularly sensitive to discriminatory practices, whether these are directed at themselves or towards other women or even other marginalized groups. Their awareness and knowledge about the multiple discrimination mechanisms that operate in the labour market enable them to encourage the widespread adoption of more egalitarian principles in their workplace. In addition, this desire to 'work differently' tends to direct them towards occupations or sectors that are directly connected to women's well-being and/or to the promotion of gender equality. In countries where the institutionalization of equality policies has provided specific job opportunities, a considerable proportion of Women's Studies graduates move into equality policy implementation jobs. Unfortunately, these employment opportunities are available only in a small number of EWSI project partner countries. What is particularly striking is the ability of Women's Studies graduates to introduce gender equality issues into all sectors of the labour market (see Chapter 2).

Third, the skills that Women's Studies students and graduates have developed come into evidence in the way in which they envisage their 'work–life integration' strategies. To begin with, their Women's Studies training provides them with ample understanding of the 'reconciliation' difficulties that often lie ahead. Contrary to other women of their generation, they are better able to pre-empt the tensions they will almost inevitably experience at some point in their lives. We have already seen that, with very few exceptions, Women's Studies students and graduates intend to enter the labour market and to spend a large proportion of their adult lives in employment. However, they do not resemble the somewhat negative 'career women' archetype, ready to sacrifice all the other aspects of their lives – love, partnerships, motherhood, personal growth and citizenship – to their professional 'success'. Far from adopting the 'work-centred' pattern that is usually associated with 'male breadwinners', Women's Studies students and graduates put a great deal of energy into the development of new, more diverse models of professional and personal 'success'. When they plan to live with someone or to have children, most of them do so with the idea of breaking away from the more differentiated 'gender cultural models' we have outlined above. They aspire to a 'well-balanced' life that implies that both partners/parents should have the opportunity to experience the satisfaction of a successful career and the satisfaction of a fulfilling relationship with loved ones, friends and children. In other cases, the self-confidence gained through Women's Studies teaching also enables some women to distance themselves from the dominant models of marriage and family life and to develop new lifestyles (celibacy, homosexual relationships, living with friends, living as a couple, but in separate homes, sharing childcare with a partner and/or friend; see Chapter 5).

Thus, thanks to Women's Studies, these young women become 'agents of social change'. They confirm that their Women's Studies training has equipped them to promote gender equality in a wide range of social arenas including, but not exclusively, in employment. This involvement in equality relies on their enhanced ability to 'decode' the 'gender culture' norms of their society, to develop pro-equality discourses and to invent new ways of building their relationships with men and with other women (including their own parents).

## Conclusions

In this chapter, we have sought to explore the potential influence of Women's Studies on European women's employment aspirations, expectations and experiences. In the first part, we presented a theoretical framework which suggests that the issue of gender equality in employment is woven into a much wider and complex social reality. We have shown that women's employment patterns – and the changes that they have undergone since the 1960s – must be analysed in relation to the wider 'gender culture model' which determines the positions of men and women within a given societal context.

In the second part, we presented and analysed some of the major characteristics of women's employment in contemporary Europe. With the help of recent statistical data on women's employment patterns, we illustrated the complexities of the 'work–life integration' process, described the trans-European characteristics of the progression of women's employment rates, and identified the specific characteristics of women's employment in each of the EWSI project partner countries. When presenting cross-national comparative data, we also stressed the need to consider diversity within and not only between EU member-states. From this point of view, we have seen that higher education plays a major role in increasing women's employment rates. The labour market behaviour of women with a university degree is far more similar across Europe than are the employment rates of less well qualified women. However, the influence of motherhood on women's employment rates and patterns varies significantly between countries. Some of the EWSI project partners are characterized by quite a strong 'male breadwinner/female home-carer' model, where women either give up paid work altogether or reduce their working hours during their child-bearing/rearing years. Other EWSI partner countries are governed by a 'dual breadwinner/state carer' model. However, even in those countries where women tend to remain in the labour market throughout their adult life, maintaining women's employment rates is often achieved through various forms of 'underemployment' of which women's higher than average unemployment rates and their above average rates of part-time work are the most important elements (Maruani 2002).

This chapter also illustrates the degree to which the 'part-time question' acts as an extremely powerful pointer to the nature of the dominant underlying 'gender culture model' in a given national context (O'Reilly and Fagan 1998). This is particularly important at a time when the promotion of part-time jobs for women has been presented as an effective policy option for promoting gender equality in the labour market. We tend to disagree with this idea and believe that the massive development of part-time work for women (mothers, in fact) may actually play a major role in maintaining or even creating gender inequalities in employment and in society at large. In many EWSI partner countries, the increase in women's part-time work explains the substantial proportion of women among the 'working poor' of the European Union. Furthermore, part-time work rarely enables women to obtain the subsistence incomes that provide the base-line for transforming the 'male breadwinner/female home-carer' model of gender relations.

In the third part, we outlined some of the most important contributions of Women's Studies training to the promotion of gender equality in employment. These issues are obviously developed further in the other chapters of this book. Although there is no direct relationship between gaining a Women's Studies qualification and maintaining high female employment rates (helping women to gain a degree would seem to be more important in this respect than gaining a qualification in a particular subject area), we have nevertheless identified some of the major influences that Women's Studies may have on women's employment aspirations, expectations and experiences in Europe. The results of the EWSI survey clearly show that Women's Studies training enables women to become active 'agents of social change' (Griffin 2003b). Indeed, the effectiveness of EU and member-state-level equal opportunities policies would seem to have much to gain from the expertise of Women's Studies graduates. First, in a context where overt and blatant gender discrimination is often seen as a 'thing of the past', Women's Studies students are equipped to identify the more subtle, structural and cultural mechanisms that produce inequality today. Second, they are also convinced that specific measures to combat gender inequalities are vital to the future of the EU. Third, they are equipped with a 'gender sensitive' worldview that enables them to understand the complexity of the factors that contribute to maintaining or reducing, and sometimes even reinforcing, gender inequalities. Fourth, they are personally, professionally and politically committed to enhancing women's rights and promoting equality. Last, their rather 'a-typical' education choices and employment experiences (different kinds of self-employment or job-creation) have given Women's Studies students the relatively rare ability to be socially reflexive and inventive.

Not only do Women's Studies academics possess considerable untapped expertise on the question of gender discrimination and inequalities, they also play an important role in awakening students to the inequalities they face in the labour market and in their personal lives and in providing the knowledge and skills required to make equal opportunities policies more effective in the future. Whether or not they enter jobs that are directly related to the application of equal opportunity measures, the remaining chapters of this book show quite clearly that Women's Studies graduates and students possess specific skills and motivations and that these should be more directly harnessed to serve the equal opportunity objectives of the EU and member-states in the coming years. The results of the EWSI project provide extensive evidence of the multiple ways in which Women's Studies graduates navigate their own way through a generally discriminatory social system and create new ideas and practices – what could be called micro-innovations – in their everyday lives. They represent essential allies for any attempt to transform gender relations and promote equality in employment in the EU of the twenty-first century.

## 2 | Equal opportunities in cross-European perspective

ISABEL CARRERA SUÁREZ AND LAURA
VIÑUELA SUÁREZ

This chapter deals with the institutionalization of equal opportunities in the UK, Finland, the Netherlands, Slovenia, Hungary, France, Germany, Italy and Spain, the nine countries represented in the EWSI project on the findings of which the present book is based. It also analyses the perception that Women's Studies students have of equal opportunities, and of the relationship between equal opportunities, Women's Studies and employment. The findings from the project are here presented in four sections: the first summarizes the different processes of institutionalization of equal opportunities in the nine countries, pointing out specific historical factors in their development and evaluating the role played by the European Union; the second describes the perceptions and experiences of Women's Studies students on equal opportunities policies and their effectiveness; the last two analyse equal opportunities and their relationship with employment and with Women's Studies.

At the start of the project, we gathered data on the institutionalization of equal opportunities and of Women's Studies in the nine countries involved. While the results of our study might have seemed relatively predictable from these (higher institutionalization, and therefore better effectiveness, in Northern Europe, a certain level of knowledge and interest in equal opportunities on the part of all Women's Studies students), our comparative perspective and the information offered by interviewees made conclusions less straightforward, showing that policies in all countries share certain shortcomings (particularly a disappointing lack of enforcement), and that cultural differences affect the implementation of general European Union directives or gender policies, even in apparently EU-integrated or gender-conscious countries. As a consequence, the conclusions and policy recommendations offered by partners in the project coincided on many points, as this chapter will show.

### Processes of institutionalization of equal opportunities

The process of institutionalization of equal opportunities in Europe is marked by the historical context after the Second World War, the political evolution of each country between 1945 and 1975, and their different trajectories since 1975, declared the International Year of Women, and following the major political changes in the European continent. Two additional factors in individual country histories which have direct effects on the institutionalization of equal opportunities policies are the establishment of democratic governments and the date of entrance into the European Union.[1]

Our research showed that *formal* equality has been achieved in all nine countries, and that three ways of legislating on equal opportunities are used for this purpose: the national constitution, an equality act, or inclusion within another set of laws and regulations (Silius 2002: 505). Some countries included the principle of equality in their constitutions in the second half of the 1940s, but this did not automatically lead to the implementation of equal opportunities. In reality, the process of applying this principle to the rest of the legal bodies took much longer, and although initial steps towards equality in legislation were taken in many countries during the 1950s and 1960s, it was the second wave of the feminist movement in the 1970s that marked the beginning of continued action towards equality, with policies on women understood in terms of equality rather than protection. The UK, the Netherlands and Germany all show significant development in this decade. In 1975 the UK introduced the first legislation (the Sex Discrimination Act and Equal Pay Act) and the first institution (the Equal Opportunities Commission) at national level. The second half of the 1970s also saw the first moves in the Netherlands, with the Equal Payment Act (1975) and the 'Anders Geregeld' report (1978), an inventory of all Dutch legislation found to be discriminatory by sex or marital status, which was a starting point for legal changes. The first equality institutions were also set up at the time: an Emancipation Commission and a National Committee for the International Year of Women in 1974 and, in 1977, a State Secretary on Emancipation. As for the Federal Republic of Germany, several legal reforms for equality took place between the 1950s and the 1970s (First Equal Rights Act in 1957, reform of the Matrimonial and Family Law Act in 1977) and the process continued during the 1980s (European Union Adaptation Law of 1980).

For France and Finland, the 1980s were more relevant than the previous decade. In France, the Roudy Act of 1983 moved the law from an approach based on the protection of women (as wives and mothers) to an approach that aimed at promoting gender equality in all spheres of society. French equality organizations developed from the mid-1960s, but the nomination of Yvette Roudy as Minister of Women's Rights in 1985, even if only for one year, is a landmark (see Le Feuvre and Andriocci 2002a). For Finland, the period of development of equal opportunities legislation was the late 1980s, with an Equality Act passed in 1987, although from the 1960s there had been social policy legislation that promoted women's equality, and the first institution, the Council for Equality, had been created in 1972.

Four of the project partner countries – Spain, East Germany (GDR), Slovenia and Hungary– did not have a democratic government after the Second World War. Among these, Spain presents a special case. Under a dictatorship from 1939 to 1975, with a highly discriminatory legislature and society, Franco's death in 1975 led to the beginning of democracy and to the rapid development of equal opportunities legislation. The 1978 constitution introduced the principle of equality and, subsequently, in a matter of a few years, many legal changes were accomplished. In 1983, the socialist government established the National Institute for Women's Issues, which coordinates action and defines national policies. In contrast to the Spanish case, the histories of the GDR, Hungary and Slovenia were inflected by their socialist period. The ideology of the socialist states had aimed at integrating women into the labour market. Although the focus was not on equal opportunities, social policies tried to provide the conditions for women to work in paid employment, particularly childcare facilities and social and material support for mothers. In this sense, democratization post-1989 brought negative consequences for women, since the entrance into a market economy meant a backlash against certain socio-political measures that had favoured women. In fact, after unification, the stronger labour market integration of women in the eastern federal states played an important role for equal opportunities in Germany as a whole.[2]

The European Union seems to have played an important role in promoting and (to a lesser extent) homogenizing equal opportunities in Europe. Article 119 of the Treaty of Rome, and its revision in Article 141 of the Treaty of Amsterdam, come across as key points for the subsequent development of equality legislation in Europe. EU decisions are nationally binding for the member-states, but they have also inspired changes in other countries. Many of the steps taken towards equality, especially regarding legislation, have developed to a significant extent out of European initiatives: directives, resolutions, recommendations, action plans (Griffin, ed. 2002). However, given the diversity of backgrounds and EU entry dates of the nine countries involved in this project, the European impact varies. In the case of Finland, for example, it was feared that the EU influence would result in a backlash, since the country perceived itself as 'if not the most equal, the second best after Sweden' (Tuori 2003: 7), and thought that it had more to offer than to gain. In practice, though certain decisions by the European Court of Justice have supported this idea, the EU has had a positive impact on equal opportunities implementation in all countries. Hungary and Slovenia (in early 2004 not yet members of the EU) have developed equal opportunities in their own legislative bodies and established equality institutions, even if their degree of institutionalization is low. They used EU initiatives as models for this purpose. In Slovenia, the Equal Opportunities for Women and Men Act, conceived as an umbrella law, was adopted in 2002 with the aim of bringing the entire area of equal opportunities for women and men in line with the EU (see Bahovec et al. 2002). In Hungary, the issue of equal opportunities was included in the discourse of the Socialist Party during their election campaign 'in a EU enlargement framework, with the simple message that accession requires not only sewage systems and motorways but gender equal opportunities'; the delegation of the EU in Budapest also included equality in their PR campaign, organizing a road show entitled 'Hungary and Enlargement: Equal Opportunities. What Does the EU Offer Women?' (Juhász 2003: 7). The enlargement of the EU seems to be raising great expectations regarding the development of equal opportunities in Hungary, for example in the creation of jobs that would require gender expertise; as one interviewee commented, change is already happening: 'You can positively detect a change and I think our Europeanisation, if we can talk about it, plays a very important part in it' (ibid., p. 10).

Most interviewees underlined that a fundamental issue for the implementation of equal opportunities is the degree of interest in the subject taken by the political parties in power. The direct impact of politics on women's lives was shown in the UK report which discussed the varying degrees of institutionalization of equal opportunities at a local level: 'This has widespread implications for women since all manner of provision disproportionately affecting women, from child care and nursery provision, to other forms of care support, enforcement of anti-discrimination legislation etc. is dependent upon the political configuration of the local council where women live. Thus where a woman lives will quite literally make a difference to many of the major issues in her life' (Griffin and Hanmer 2002: 13).

The background data reports from the project suggested that left-wing governments are more sympathetic towards equal opportunities and promote measures further than conservative ones. The UK, France and Spain are examples of countries where, in recent periods of conservative rule, the European Union was crucial in guaranteeing the development of equality and the protection of previous achievements. The European Union was also a fundamental source of funding for equality institutions or schemes at the national level, providing the resources to continue with plans despite the political profile of the national government. This notwithstanding, national governments have the means of delaying the accomplishment of the equal opportunities policies developed by equality institutions, since in all countries the latter are usually advisory bodies with the power to 'persuade' governing bodies, but no enforcement power.

Using the background data gathered from each country, Harriet Silius evaluated the level of institutionalization of equal opportunities and of Women's Studies in the partner countries and compared it to one of the initial hypotheses of the project. This had presupposed that there existed a relationship between the degree of institutionalization of equal opportunities and that of Women's Studies, and that these had an impact in women's professionalization (Silius 2002: 512, 514). Silius's analysis showed the following results (see Table 2.1).

TABLE 2.1 Degree of institutionalization of equal opportunities and of Women's Studies in nine European countries

| Country | Equal opportunities | Women's Studies |
| --- | --- | --- |
| Germany | High | High |
| Netherlands | High | High |
| UK | High | High |
| Finland | Medium | High |
| Italy | Medium | Low |
| Spain | Medium | Low |
| France | Low | Low |
| Hungary | Low | Low |
| Slovenia | Low | Low |

*Source*: Silius 2002: 512 and 514

As shown in this Table, both degrees of institutionalization are high in the UK, the Netherlands and Germany, and low in Slovenia, Hungary and France. In contrast, there was a discrepancy between them in Finland, Italy and Spain. The results of this Table seem to relate to the individual histories explained above, the political will of recent governments and the effects of EU directives. While the UK, the Netherlands and Germany have long histories of equal opportunities development and democracy, as well as a long relationship with the EU, other countries such as Slovenia or Hungary are at the moment working towards formal equality. In the case of Italy and Spain, the degree of institutionalization of equal opportunities is quite high if we take into account its development in a very short period of time. France offers a peculiar case, since its low levels of institutionalization were not obviously predictable. The universalism of its discourse of *égalité* appears to have been an obstacle for the development of equal opportunities policies specifically directed at women, and for the establishment of recognized forms of Women's Studies (Le Feuvre and Andriocci 2002a). Finland offers a similar explanation for an unexpected medium level of institutionalization of equal opportunities, due to the gender-neutral character of Finnish equal opportunities (Silius and Tuori 2003).

In general, the institutionalization of equal opportunities seems to come prior to the institutionalization of Women's Studies. However, as explained in the background data reports (Griffin, ed. 2002), both types of institutionalization spring from the same source: the feminist movement and the commitment of specific women to effecting change in women's lives.

### (Un)equal opportunities in practice: the views of Women's Studies students

In spite of their different processes and degrees of institutionalization, all nine countries seem to face similar difficulties when it comes to implementing equal opportunities, to going beyond the erasure of gender discrimination in law. The interviews carried out in each country provide us with information on Women's Studies students' knowledge of equal opportunities and on their experiences regarding (un)equal opportunities. Rather unexpectedly, if we consider the diversity of their national backgrounds, the responses showed a great degree of similarity. A major point in common, mentioned by all interviewees, was that equality is far from being achieved in practice, despite the relevant policies.

*Knowledge and understanding of equal opportunities* The question 'What do you understand by "equal opportunities"?', asked in the interviews, rendered far more complex responses than anticipated. The questionnaire responses had indicated that relatively high percentages of students thought that their understanding of equal opportunities had changed after their Women's Studies training (see Table 2.2) and that, as a result, they had become more involved in equal opportunities (see Table 2.3).

The qualitative data which resulted from interviews, however, offered a different picture from the questionnaire responses. The answers of interviewees ranged from a first reaction of complete silence (Spain) to a high degree of knowledge and conceptualization of the term (Germany). In between, different kinds of replies were offered, with many discussing the concept through a mixture of personal experiences, political opinions and specific issues present in the public debate through the media. The variety of answers can sometimes be traced to the differing equality discourses in each country, which range from explicitly women-focused conceptions to those based on gender neutrality (see Silius 2002: 503–5).

69

TABLE 2.2 Changes in understanding of equal opportunities among past and current Women's Studies students (%)

| Country | Past students | Current students |
|---|---|---|
| Finland | 89 | 97 |
| France | 71 | 87 |
| Germany | 86 | 81 |
| Hungary | 54 | 84 |
| Italy | 54 | 62 |
| Netherlands | 78 | 92 |
| Slovenia | 74 | 88 |
| Spain | 74 | 72 |
| UK | 72 | 84 |

*Source*: Frequency tables, EWSI project, 2003

In all countries, the interviewees who displayed the most accurate understanding of equal opportunities were those who had been directly in contact with equality work, either through employment (in social services or equal opportunities institutions) or through research. Since Spain and Germany represent two opposite poles, we shall describe their responses in more detail. However, it must be noted that in both cases there were exceptions among the interviewees, not all Spanish students being unaware of the term or all German ones highly informed

The lack of specific equal opportunities knowledge among Spanish interviewees seems surprising in a country we had found to have a medium degree of institutionalization of equal opportunities. Yet most interviewees admitted that they had never paid much attention to the issue of equal

TABLE 2.3 Percentage of Women's Studies students reporting greater involvement in equal opportunities following their training (%)

| Country | Past students | Current students |
|---|---|---|
| Finland | 54 | 71 |
| France | 76 | 59 |
| Germany | 66 | 58 |
| Hungary | 64 | 70 |
| Italy | 81 | 85 |
| Netherlands | 79 | 84 |
| Slovenia | 70 | 88 |
| Spain | 72 | 57 |

*Source*: Frequency tables, EWSI project, 2003

opportunities or reflected on the term. In many cases it was obvious from the answers that students were talking about equal opportunities explicitly for the first time during the interview. A literal reading of the expression 'equal opportunities' was the most common response: 'My idea is that we should all have the same opportunities. But I don't know much about what is being done' (Carrera Suárez and Viñuela Suárez, 2003a: 5). While we must keep in mind that most interviewees were PhD students, as this is where Women's Studies tends to be located in Spain, and that such curricula were not job-oriented,[3] it still seems to reflect an obvious gap in disseminating policies, even to 'naturally' interested recipients.

Among the German interviewees we found the opposite case. Not only were they fully aware of the term equal opportunities, they were also able to engage in a discussion of details. Thus, they distinguished between the terms 'promotion of women', 'equal rights' and 'mainstreaming', and problematized their meanings. The high degree of understanding and knowledge demonstrated by German students seemed to be the result of several factors: the presence of related issues in the media (an Equality Act had been discussed in Parliament, although unsuccessfully), the presence of equal opportunities in the university, the important role of the Commissioners for Women's Affairs and, of course, the personal interest of the students interviewed. However, it must be said that some of these elements also exist in other countries where the knowledge of equal opportunities was less thorough, so that the German case seems to show particularly effective dissemination of policies.

An important feature regarding the understanding of equal opportunities was the fact that interviewees did not restrict the term only to gender, but talked about it in a broader sense which included ethnicity, economically disadvantaged groups, sexual orientation and disability. They frequently questioned the way in which current equal opportunities policies applied only to differences between the sexes, thus making other types of difference invisible. As was stated in the Finnish report, 'this conception about the relationship between the sexes is very strongly heterosexual. The woman of equal opportunities is very clearly a heterosexual woman and a woman who would like to have children' (Tuori 2003: 10). However, some interviewees also expressed the fear that a misuse of the concept of equal opportunities could even lead to the disappearance of gender differences and result in a general masculinization. This was a key issue for Italian interviewees who mentioned it as a 'hidden danger' behind the concept of equal opportunities. German interviewees also expressed a concern, arguing that 'women should not strive to follow the male professional model' (Schmidbaur et al. 2003: 10).

71

However, when moving from an understanding of equal opportunities to the naming of specific policies, the awareness of interviewees levelled off for all countries, and became much more limited. Again, Germany was the exception, together with the Netherlands. In these two countries the interviewees were able to mention some equality measures, such as the organization E-Quality and the Stimulating Measure Daily Routine or the successful Aspasia programme in the Netherlands, while German students talked about their participation in activities organized by the affirmative action office of their university or the use of special offers of counselling, for instance by the Ministry of Labour; they were also aware of plans to promote equality in the public service and, especially, of equality policies in their own county of residence. In contrast, for Finnish interviewees, for example, the issue of equality 'did not necessarily (or hardly ever) lead to a discussion on policies on equal opportunities' (Tuori 2003: 7).

In all countries there were references to measures such as positive action, quotas or non-sexist language in job advertising. These actions seemed to be more visible to students, and probably to society in general, as a result of their presence in the public sphere. In the Hungarian report this presence was explicitly considered a key point in the students' knowledge of equal opportunities: 'gender equality is generally speaking not in the public discourse, so many interviewees could not answer the questions concerning equal opportunities' (Juhász 2003: 7). One conclusion to be drawn from this is the crucial importance of visibility in action for equal opportunities. Not only is it essential to disseminate the existence of policies, but also to generate a public debate that will enable their implementation. Visibility is a precondition for effective results.

The public presence of equal opportunities is therefore crucial, although it can also have its perverse effects. While visibility makes policies more susceptible to being discussed and implemented, it can also produce or reinforce the widespread idea that equality has already been achieved. Students stated how they were forced to fight actively against this belief, and how it led to their categorization as 'raving feminists'. This was especially true for countries where the equality discourse tends to be 'gender neutral', such as France or Finland. The Slovenian report also included a comment on the role of the media in the dissemination of this lie: 'Another interviewee [believed] that it is the media that create the illusion of equal opportunities and women's freedom while in reality what society above all expects from a woman is for her to be a mother and housewife' (Drglin et al. 2003: 9).

Judging by the interviewees' answers, dissemination is far from effective in Europe. The degree of institutionalization of equal opportunities

72

achieved to date is not matched by a similar degree of knowledge of equal opportunities, since, with the already mentioned exception of Germany and to a lesser extent the Netherlands, Women's Studies students from all the countries had serious difficulties in articulating answers to specific questions.

*Formal equality versus real equality* Despite their different degrees of institutionalization, the nine European countries here represented have tried to erase the traces of gender discrimination left in their legal system, set up equality institutions and promote government action. However, our qualitative data show that formal equality has not led to equality in practice, not even in countries with a high level of institutionalization. The opinions of the students on this issue were supported by the fact that, while they may not have been familiar with experiences of equal opportunities, they could all describe experiences of discrimination, which led most of them to express negative views regarding the effectiveness of policies and legislation. In fact, when asked about equal opportunities, many students commented instead on the 'unequal' opportunities they had observed or suffered in their lives. The expression 'equal opportunities' brought to mind their experience of discrimination rather than positive action.

Interviewees talked about discriminative practices in all social spaces, from family to employment, and at all stages of their lives. British and French students provided examples of discrimination from an early age, and of its consequences. They described different treatment at home ('In my family, there were always things that I wasn't allowed to do and that my brother could do. So I was pretty aware of the inequality issue, inequality compared to what my brother could do, just because I was a girl'; Le Feuvre and Andriocci 2002b: 12) and at school, where they were encouraged into 'feminine' professions such as nursing or secretarial jobs, while boys were channelled into university education if they got good marks (Griffin 2003a: 13). Inequalities seemed only to grow in later stages, since 'it would appear that the career advice given to young women throughout the course of their secondary school education imposed even more limited horizons on their future than did their parents' (Le Feuvre and Andriocci 2002b: 8). These experiences of discrimination at such an early age provoked in some women a sense of frustration, besides leading to later gender inequalities in the workplace (Griffin 2003a: 13). A Finnish interviewee elaborated on this issue: 'So as a child I took for granted that women are inferior to men, because in a way it was evident – at school and everywhere it could be read between the lines – that men were leaders and women were not' (Tuori 2003: 7–8). Students described situations of inequality also later in

73

their lives, especially in the workplace and in the domestic space, as we shall discuss below.

It came as no surprise, therefore, that interviewees found equal opportunities policies ineffective. They did recognize and value the work being done and the achievements, but they found legislation useful only in cases of flagrant, direct discrimination, and held that it does not deal effectively with indirect cases because, as stated in the UK report, 'equal opportunities legislation [ ... ] is easily ignored or circumvented' (Griffin 2003a: 7). This can also be seen in the delays in the implementation of equality laws (see Griffin, ed. 2002). In interviews from all countries, equal opportunities measures were described in terms such as 'cosmetic', 'too weak', 'symbolic', 'insufficient', 'just a piece of paper', 'only political correctness' or, as a Spanish interviewee put it, 'the naming of things changes, but things don't. There's a lack of content and an excess of form' (Carrera Suárez and Viñuela Suárez 2003a: 7). Interviewees were often suspicious of the actual goals of equal opportunities policies, and thought that they did not undermine the structures that sustain discriminatory situations. They saw the moves towards equality as superficial action aimed at giving patriarchy 'a prettier face'. One Italian interviewee stressed this point: 'As I see it, the discourse of equal opportunities is seriously flawed in that it does not undermine the dominant model' (Barazzetti et al. 2003: 11). As gender-conscious students, many thought that the practices of equal opportunities policies lack depth of understanding of gender and power relations.

This perception of ineffectiveness was paralleled by a feeling of detachment from institutionalized policies, which might explain the lack of knowledge and interest in equal opportunities action, legislation or institutions. It is true, as was shown in the UK report, that institutionalization led in some cases to an 'invisibilization' or misuse of equal opportunities. This in turn made more visible the work of women's NGOs or informal women's networks, which the students generally felt more comfortable in approaching. In Italy especially, equal opportunities were understood as being closely related to an institutional and political apparatus where the connection with society and women's real problems was lost. In contrast, women's associations operating at ground level were valued positively as places where useful action was taking place. The same was observed in France, where awareness of the ineffective equal opportunities policies, and of the lack of political will to amend this, made women who are interested in working on equality turn 'to the voluntary sector and grass-roots women's organization [rather] than to institutional settings' (Le Feuvre and Andriocci 2002b: 12).

Interviewees who had a direct relationship with equal opportunities institutions held a different view. As an example, we quote a Spanish woman who had worked in a regional equality institution but was also involved in a feminist NGO, speaking about the need to combine both types of action:

Equality institutions are, I don't know how to put it [ ... ] they are necessary. They are spaces from which I think many things can be done. Women can be educated, women's associations can be educated, studies and research can be promoted, important things can be disseminated, it's possible to contribute to social opinion [ ... ] But it is very hard to reach the social realities. Because there's also a bureaucratic and administrative structure that must be set up [ ... ] I think that Institutes [for women's issues] must promote the idea that they shouldn't have all the responsibility regarding women's issues and that equality does not depend only on institutes, that they won't solve all the problems. What they must do is generate a network inside the political institutions but also taking into account the associations, so the whole thing sinks in and expands. I think that's what they intend to do but it's very hard, isn't it? And all the Plans for Equal Opportunities and the European directives, it's all a network that we can't abandon because then it's a space that all women lose, it's a lost space. (Carrera Suárez and Viñuela Suárez 2003a: 8–9)

Students also expressed their own opinions on what was needed to implement equal opportunities successfully, and often showed a thoughtful understanding of the complexity of gender issues. They saw equality as a process of deep social change and stressed the importance of gender training as a fundamental tool to achieve this goal. They pointed towards education as a key area from which to alert young people to discrimination (not only gender-related but in the broader sense mentioned above) and to awaken in them a desire to challenge it. They also advocated the introduction of compulsory equality measures for economic and social agents, and the development of more accurate tools for the evaluation of the effectiveness of equality measures.

## Equal opportunities and employment

The processes of institutionalization of equal opportunities, carried out in all countries through changes in legislation, are mostly related to the participation of women in the labour market. Action was taken to promote women's training, to assure them better opportunities in accessing jobs, to promote women to decision-making posts, to overcome horizontal segregation and to conciliate work in paid employment with family responsibilities, mainly through better conditions for parental leave and childcare facilities. These issues have been dealt with in all countries with varying results. The limited effectiveness of the measures becomes evident when we consider that most countries have been developing equal opportunities policies for more than twenty years, but women's situation in employment continues to be one of inequality, while traditional gender roles have changed very little. Harriet Silius described this discouraging picture of women in the labour market: 'Insecure and fixed-term work is more frequent among women than among men today. Part-time work has increased, especially during the last 20 years. Nowhere do equal opportunities exist in the labour market. Even if positive developments have occurred, the pay gap is still around 20–25% in spite of different wage policies and starting levels. In many countries the pay gaps have been stable during the last 25 years' (Silius 2002: 503).

*Experiences of discrimination (and the difficulties of fighting against it)*
Most of the interviewees who were working or had worked in paid employment had experienced some kind of gender discrimination in accessing employment, or in the workplace, or in their job conditions. German students spoke of the glass ceiling and how decision-making posts were occupied by men who act as gatekeepers against women's promotion. UK students also described how men were progressing in their careers more easily and faster than women: 'We started getting men coming into the profession [midwifery]. And all of them without exception went to the top of the tree [ ... ] fast track men were getting top flight jobs whereas the women who had slogged were being left behind and I found that infuriating' (Griffin 2003a: 6–7). This interviewee also stressed the feeling of anger that followed from her awareness of that form of discrimination and the impossibility of fighting against it. Some of the French students detailed experiences of sexual harassment:

> I was working as a newspaper journalist and the chief editor was this really awful guy, fat and ugly, with a beer-gut, who used to try and charm his way round all the young women working there, including me. I'll always remember the way he harassed me, right up until the day I hit back. After that, he gave up on me, but he didn't give me any more assignments either. So you really got to understand how things worked there quite quickly. That guy oppressed me. He thought he was going to sleep with me and 'in exchange' give me more work assignments. That's how I analyse the situation today, but even at the time, I knew that it wasn't right for him to dominate me like that with his body and his power, I was sure of that. (Le Feuvre and Andriocci 2002b: 6)

By far the most frequently recurring issue affecting employment was motherhood. Women from all countries expressed their concern about their chances of combining a professional career with a family. As a reaction, there were two broad groups: those who chose not to have children to avoid the risk of problems in their working life, and, those who, as the Hungarian report put it, 'fear a good career and children are not compatible, and therefore go for the children' (Juhász 2003: 5). This fear is justified, given the negative impact of motherhood on women's employment in all countries, either in accessing – 'when taking employment women are sometimes required to sign a pledge that they will not have children within a certain period of time' (Drglin et al. 2003: 10) – or in the course of their working life – 'I'm trying to move into an academic department, not having an awful amount of luck [...] I do feel the terms and conditions are very different for people like me [a mother with two children] than they are for other people. I've got to go that extra mile that other people just don't have to' (Griffin 2003a: 2).

It is striking that, after decades of equal opportunities legislation and policies, women still find it so hard to negotiate between the public and the private spheres. This testifies to the fact that traditional gender roles are deeply engrained in society and in women's minds. Women are considered, and still consider themselves to be, responsible for domestic life and care activities, and feel obliged to choose between family and employment. The low percentage of men who make use of their right to parental leave confirms this social feature, and proves that equality legislation is not effective enough to promote social changes unless accompanied by other kinds of measures. This should be taken into account when developing policies for conciliating work and family life, which mostly seem to try to help women to take on more easily the double burden of domestic and public life. As one interviewee said, 'women have stepped into the public sphere, but they haven't got rid of domestic responsibilities' (Carrera Suárez and Viñuela Suárez 2003a: 6).

The weakness of equal opportunities measures in the context of employment does not only stem from this contradiction, but also from the structure of the labour market itself. Insecure employment (fixed-term and part-time, which affects mostly women), as well as high percentages of unemployment (in general, but higher for women in particular)[4] prevent women from taking legal action against discrimination. The presence of mostly indirect discrimination, legally hard to prove, is another crucial factor inhibiting action. A French interviewee provided a good example of this:

> I started working as a shop assistant and I was put on the men's counter of a department store, where I spent a good part of the day on my hands and knees adjusting the length of men's trousers. You can imagine, that's a pretty good way of misogyny in action. They always put female students to do

that job, to kneel down at the feet of men. When the clients came with their wives, you also got a good feel of gender relations. I didn't say anything at the time and I ended up leaving one day just like that. It was totally unbearable, but you couldn't really defend yourself, because you needed the job and you needed the money. (Le Feuvre and Andriocci 2002b: 8)

The length of a legal process, its expense, the lack of social support and the fact that it might lead to difficulties in finding another job add to the understanding of why most interviewees recount experiences of discrimination but none talked about formal action against it. In such instances the role of equality institutions could be decisive, but they need the power and resources to offer the victims of discrimination the support they lack.

Public employment seems to be more sympathetic towards women than the private sector. More objective access procedures lead to a higher presence of women in the public sector and the fact that it is permanent employment (in certain countries especially in the case of civil servants) provides greater self-confidence and a more active stance against discrimination. It also seems more conciliation-friendly work, and commitment to the accomplishment of equal opportunities policies seems to be higher in the public than in the private sector. However, this did not apply strictly to all countries: in Finland, for instance, public employment has recently become more insecure, with a high number of short-term contracts. In the private sector equality measures are fewer in number and seldom implemented, monitored or evaluated. The opinions and experiences of Women's Studies students coincided with this, though they talked about having suffered discrimination in both sectors.

Finally, in some interviews there was reference to what we have called the 'myth of social work'. Interviewees said that they had not suffered discrimination in employment because they worked in a field (social work) where it did not exist. This claim was probably based on the fact that the percentage of female social workers is very high, which provides a women-friendly environment, and that it is a socially accepted job for women. The sector, however, is feminized and therefore undervalued, and represents an extension of traditional female care activities. Gender discrimination might be less apparent in the field but social work is inscribed in a whole structure of relationships that is highly discriminative towards women (most of them working in the services sector, underrepresented in decision-making posts, with a wage of around 25 per cent less than men). The complex structure of the patriarchal system is hard to decipher even for students with a higher than average degree of gender consciousness, not only regarding employment issues but, as will be seen, in all spheres of life.

*Equal opportunities jobs* The number of students working in the field of equal opportunities was not as high as might have been expected. Also, as stated in the French report, the different understandings of what working in equal opportunities meant among interviewees made it difficult to pinpoint the exact number of students in this field. 'From the interview data we get the feeling that the past students adopt a fairly broad definition of "working in equal opportunities". Although their job titles do not explicitly mention an equal opportunities brief, they tend to consider themselves to be working in this area as long as they have the possibility to introduce women's or gender equality issues in their work' (Le Feuvre and Andriocci 2002b: 51).

Although many students stated that they would have liked to work in the field of equal opportunities, and also felt capable of carrying out such work, only a few knew about the jobs offered. This should make us reflect on the importance of providing information on employment in equal opportunities if we consider it to be a career path for Women's Studies. In Finland, only the students already working in equal opportunities expressed interest in this type of employment, and many of them considered themselves a 'lucky exception': 'So one reason for me getting this job was that I had Women's Studies training. But it is an extreme case, because it could be said that this is an organisation which deals exclusively with women's questions' (Tuori 2003: 32). Their views implied that they did not expect to go on working in the field. In general, we must stress that equal opportunities jobs are not secure employment and that, looking at our data, most of them are not occupied by Women's Studies experts. This seems striking, as Women's Studies students have gender expertise that should make them the first choice for employers seeking equal opportunities candidates. However, in some cases such students were explicitly avoided, as happened in the recruitment of one of the first equal opportunities officers for a French regional council, when the person recruited was to be as 'neutral' as possible, as the initiative had met with much resistance within: the post was therefore given to a psychology graduate who had no gender expertise whatsoever. Aside from their political implications, cases like these may also be related to the low degree of visibility of Women's Studies in most countries, and the need to foreground graduates' skills (see Chapters 3 and 4 in this volume).

## Equal opportunities and Women's Studies: Women's Studies graduates as agents of social change

*Equal opportunities in universities* The institutionalization of equal opportunities in universities differs across the various countries. In the

UK, France, Finland, Germany, the Netherlands and Italy there are equal opportunities offices, or their equivalent, in universities. Although their reach varies (they are far from generalized, for instance, in France), where they exist they constitute a nucleus from which equal opportunities policies are promoted. In the case of France, plans for equal opportunities in universities are agreed directly with the appropriate national bodies. In the UK during the 1980s many universities had equal opportunities officers, often academics with an interest in Women's Studies; in German universities the affirmative action office was cited by interviewees. In Finland all universities have equality committees that provide statements, organize training and develop equality plans. Emancipation commissions have been set up in Dutch universities at various levels and were from the 1980s nationally organized in the consultive body LOEKWO. The National Coordination of the Equal Opportunities Committees of the Italian Universities was created in 1998, and a year later the figure of the Delegate of the Rector for Gender Studies and Equal Opportunities Policies was created. In France the inter-ministerial Action Plan for Equality in Education (25 February 2000) aimed at the introduction of equal opportunities in the development contracts of universities, which, in some cases, involved the creation of an equal opportunities office. However, this has taken place so far only in a few universities due to the efforts of specific women involved in Women's Studies.

Such institutionalization helps to make equal opportunities visible in the university context, although, as stated in the report from the UK, sometimes it turns into a routinization and, therefore, an 'invisibilization' of equal opportunities work, as well as its detachment from user groups (Griffin 2003a: 12). In Hungary, Slovenia and Spain no such thing exists, Spain being the only EU country of this project where equal opportunities does not have an official presence in universities, although slow steps are being taken by individual institutions.

*Theory and practice: the missing link* The relationship between Women's Studies and equal opportunities offered a variety of responses from interviewees. Though not in all cases, Women's Studies was mostly considered a theoretical subject while equal opportunities was seen as a political and social issue. Therefore many students did not see the relationship between the two, which makes sense if we consider the low degree of knowledge that most interviewees had of equal opportunities policies. Significantly, the lack of connection to women's real lives that students criticized in equal opportunities was also expressed regarding Women's Studies: 'I found the approach too intellectual, too theoretical. In class, no one ever made the link between the theory and the practice' (Le Feuvre and Andriocci 2002b: 7). 'The greatest disappointment with WS was that at times it became very abstract and I wanted to solve these kinds of small problems, like for example, why people are unequal or why a woman gets smaller wages than a man. And for that I wanted practical tools' (Tuori 2003: 11).

In Hungary this issue was raised when discussing the opposition between academic life and activism: 'I think the university women who do very good and important work in this field are blue dahlias. They are very few. Obviously they would need outside and inside support, but they leave out a lot of possibilities, how to create connections with the real world, with the outside world, the world of women. By this they actually harm themselves too, because they lack outside support or they remain unknown' (Juhász 2003: 10).

Though less common, there were also other views on this issue. One Spanish interviewee explained how she understood the relationship between theory and practice:

> You must do that [the active and practical aspect] later on your own. The place for activism, for street action, is not the doctorate programme. The relationship between women's groups and the doctorate could be a good thing, but I approached feminism from the groups and through the street, and then I got into theory. So I have both points of view and connecting them is easy for me. Of course, it's true that what you read in the books is one thing and what we experience every day as women is another. I know both things and I don't think that the doctorate is the place to work on the daily life issues; there are other places for that. If the doctorate goes into the streets, then where are you going to learn the theoretical framework? You can't go to a women's group with theoretical issues because they won't understand you, but you can use what you have learnt and apply it to that specific situation. (Carrera Suárez and Viñuela Suárez 2003a: 3)

Although the 'missing link' between theory and practice in equal opportunities policies and legislation was confirmed by the disadvantaged position of women in social and economic life, as well as by students' own experiences, in the case of Women's Studies training there seemed to be a discrepancy: after criticizing the highly abstract character of their Women's Studies courses and expressing the need for 'practical tools', all students gave long accounts of how useful they found the knowledge acquired during their training, showing that there actually is a link between Women's Studies theory and women's everyday lives.

*Women's Studies training as a tool to promote equal opportunities* The first step towards fighting inequality is gaining consciousness of its existence and its forms, being able to recognize it and understand how it works. This might seem an obvious remark, but the ineffectiveness of equal opportunities policies is often related to this fact. As explained, equality legislation is useful in overcoming direct discrimination, but the experiences of our interviewees were mostly of indirect discrimination, more subtle and harder to perceive. This has serious consequences for women, since it leads to feelings of frustration, of misunderstanding and of guilt. Women suffering from indirect discrimination seriously lack self-confidence.

Students spoke of having confronted and solved a great deal of these negative features through their Women's Studies training, which was, for many, an 'eye-opening experience' and, for others, the place where they found a confirmation of their previous ideas, and, importantly, the tools to systematize them. First of all, this training developed their critical thinking and changed their view of society. The theoretical tools of Women's Studies and feminist theory provided them with a better understanding of the world and its power relations, raising students' gender consciousness: 'women [who are] alone think something must be wrong with them, when actually it is the existing system they have a problem with, which is natural. They suddenly realise that everyone has a problem with that, and they understand they are normal' (Juhász 2003: 27). This remark reminds us that identifying gender discrimination is not as easy as it may appear. It also highlights the contradictory position of women in a society which, on the one hand, encourages them to develop their own desires and aspirations, and convinces them that they are already liberated in a gender equal world, and, on the other, has this propaganda contradicted by their lived experiences, by the obstacles they find and by the expectations that society actually has of them. The understanding of the concealed mechanisms of patriarchy helps Women's Studies students to cope with these contradictions in three ways: first, discrimination or sexism does not come as a surprise or shock; second, it becomes easier to cope with and, third and more importantly, women no longer understand it as a personal problem (Tuori 2003: 21). Following from their newly acquired vision of society and of their place in it, Women's Studies students stressed a feeling of empowerment and a significant increase in self-confidence.

Thus, there are key aspects of Women's Studies training that enable students to promote social change and that provide the apparently 'missing link' between theory and practice. Their new understanding of gender relations not only helped students personally, but gave them the desire to change things, to become active in society and intervene in the discriminatory relationships observed in their own environments. They became more alert towards discrimination and, through the knowledge acquired in Women's Studies, they felt able to oppose it, even though, in some cases, their ability and commitment was not rewarded by success and they ended up quitting the job: 'I was there for three years, just three years, and then I left. There were only five employees. And I was downright mobbed [harassed] by the boss. I was very successful. My courses were always full. I had a constant stream of team-mates, developed good adult education programmes. But he launched into such a competition with me [ ... ] I couldn't take it anymore' (Schmidbaur et al. 2003: 4–5).

It must be stressed again, however, that action against discrimination consisted of developing personal strategies against it, not using the existing equal opportunities resources. Not a single one of the interviewees in any of the nine countries talked about having started legal procedures, despite the fact that they all had felt discriminated against at some point.

Students consistently reported feeling the impact of Women's Studies training in all spheres of their lives. They became active in promoting equality for themselves and for others in all personal and social contacts. In the domestic space, for example, students tried to challenge and renegotiate the traditional heterosexual partnerships, especially the domestic division of labour (see also Chapter 5). This was a difficult and painful task that, in some cases, led to the end of the relationship: 'And of course, sharing domestic chores is still the nub of the problem. As feminists, we say that if you want equality at work then you must have equality at home. The problem is that's very, very difficult to get, that kind of equality, as a woman, even as a feminist, even with strong feminist convictions' (Le Feuvre and Andriocci 2002b: 1–2). However, 'there was a general feeling that a better understanding of macro-level gender relationships improved the quality of those partnerships that survived the Women's Studies watershed' (ibid., p. 56). Making changes in domestic structures often found the resistance of men who were not willing to lose their privileges or who felt at a loss with the personal changes experienced by women after their training. This seems to indicate that the process towards 'real' equality must promote a consciousness of gender structures also in men, or it will remain uncompleted and will transfer only a sense of incomprehension to them. Changes in men's attitudes were reported as hard to achieve, though sometimes they did take place. Nevertheless, women were very aware of their responsibility as 'equality agents' and those who had children tried to bring them up in a non-sexist environment. Many also declared their personal commitment to promoting equality in their working environment, in the way they carried out their work: using non-sexist language, not putting up with sexism or, when possible, introducing gender issues into their jobs. This was especially important for teachers, who tried to create gender awareness in their pupils and, in some cases, also in colleagues and bosses.

One fundamental aspect mentioned by all interviewees was the promotion of solidarity among women, which was considered a fundamental tool in the struggle against discrimination: 'we had problems with a chief editor a few months back, I was working for this big company [ ... ] the young women working there, under 30 years old, were being harassed – sexual and moral harassment – and they were in a real panic, not knowing what to do, too afraid to make a complaint for fear of losing their jobs, blaming themselves for what was happening. I had to wake them up to the reality of it all, to work on them not feeling guilty' (ibid., p. 9). In this line, Women's Studies students were also aware of the usefulness of belonging to a women's network and many of them still benefited from those established during their training.

*Introducing equal opportunities in the curricula of Women's Studies* Many interviewees stated that Women's Studies training had not prepared them to work on equal opportunities, but the issues just analysed contradict this argument. The changes they experienced in their daily lives and in their perception of the world provided them with a fundamental basis for any kind of job, but particularly for a job related to equal opportunities. It is clear, though, that there is no specific training in this direction in most Women's Studies curricula.

The issue of whether Women's Studies is the place for equal opportunities training is a complex one. While the theoretical knowledge that Women's Studies provides is basic for such a job, it is also true that more specific knowledge is required. It seems, however, that these two types of knowledge are not usually provided together, as practitioners of both seem to follow separate paths. If we consider how Women's Studies students are able to promote equality in their environments despite their ignorance of equal opportunities, it seems obvious that this kind of training should be a basic requirement for equal opportunities workers, and, conversely, equal opportunities training would make Women's Studies students excellent professionals. Since only some Women's Studies students are interested in finding a job in this field, it should not become the main curriculum focus. Nevertheless, the scant knowledge that most Women's Studies students have of equal opportunities was surprising, as one would expect them to be better informed and more interested in the mechanisms available. After all, equal opportunities knowledge might be a useful tool, not only in their daily lives, but also as a path into paid employment.

These considerations suggest at least a compromise solution: during their training, it would seem sensible to inform Women's Studies students of the equal opportunities resources available and the kind of institutions which provide aid if required. Career orientation, including information on employment options in the field of equal opportunities, and where to acquire specific knowledge, seem equally advisable. This would result in a twofold strategy, not only informing Women's Studies students of professional opportunities, but also promoting the visibility and value of the expertise of Women's Studies students.

Many students thought of equal opportunities as a 'light' version of feminism. In fact, when feminism was discussed in interviews, those students who did not declare themselves to be feminists claimed instead to be in favour of equal opportunities for women – 'I'm very much an equal opportunities person' (Griffin 2003a: 2) – thus establishing a separation between the two terms and implying that equal opportunities is a more socially accepted position than feminism. This was seen as inconsistent by some students, who talked about how they had female friends who would not call themselves feminists though they agreed with the main issues of feminism:

I see that very often. They don't want to be feminists but then, in their lifestyle, they can't deny that they are feminists because they reject the traditional roles and have feminist thoughts. They want to be independent and they want to decide and they say that they won't admit this and that from a man, things that were admitted before. So that's a feminist lifestyle, no matter if they don't want to admit it. (Carrera Suárez and Viñuela Suárez 2003a: 8)

Such attitudes were seen as derived from the negative and stereotyped social representation of feminists. The Hungarian report listed the main features of this well-known stereotype: 'a feminist is ugly, or takes no care of her beauty, she is a lesbian, frigid or pretends to be, she is against the traditional family, would like to produce tube babies on a conveyor belt, she hates men, is aggressive to men and would like to wipe them from the earth, she also hates beautiful women because she herself is ugly and sexually dissatisfied' (Juhász 2003: 31).

In contrast, feminist students did not believe in equal opportunities because they considered it a political use and manipulation of feminism. This came up in many interviews, where equal opportunities institutions were seen as part of a 'State feminism' that did not really seek social change but only political profit (female votes) without aiming at subverting patriarchal structures. The use of the term 'equal opportunities' instead of 'feminism' in public and political discourse can thus be understood as a strategy to make demands for women while circumventing the negative stereotype of feminism, or, in a less charitable reading, as a debasement of feminist ideology, using its demands for other purposes.

## Conclusions

Our comparative study of the institutionalization of equal opportunities and its relation to Women's Studies and to employment in the nine European countries detailed in the introduction seems to have produced useful, if not always optimistic, information. Background data show that legal steps towards equality have been taken in all countries, but the implementation of equality policies is perceived as ineffective by most students, whichever their country of origin or its degree of institutionalization. While our research produced a diversity of results in terms of institutionalization and students' knowledge or use of equal opportunities resources, it presented great similarities on the subject of (in)equality experiences in women's everyday lives and employment, a fact which should draw our attention to procedures and to the measurable effects of policies.

Briefly put, the common points in reports from all countries were the certainty on the part of the students that gender equality is far from being achieved, the sense of ineffectiveness of equal opportunities policies and legislation, the need for an exchange of knowledge and for communication between equality institutions and Women's Studies, and the importance of Women's Studies students as agents of social change.

One of the causes of the ineffectiveness of equal opportunities policies identified through this report is their low visibility. Women's Studies students were too often surprisingly unaware of the institutional actions taken towards equality. If this is the case for students who are gender conscious, interested in women's issues and active in promoting equal opportunities themselves, it is very probable that such a lack of awareness will be accentuated in general society. More widespread knowledge would aid the effectiveness of equal opportunities, with resources more clearly taken advantage of, and it should also establish a dialogue between institutions and society to favour implementation and new development of policies.

Most recommendations from students and research partners in the project aimed at bridging the existing gap between theory and practice, both in equality policies and in gender pedagogy. There is a clear need for better dissemination of equal opportunities policies and resources, to Women's Studies students and women workers in particular, but also to society in general. This seems to require a combined effort, involving local authorities, NGOs and educational institutions, as well as equal opportunities and social agents. It was emphasized that equal opportunities and Women's Studies topics should be introduced at all levels of education, combining specific courses with a mainstreaming approach. Feminist commitment was still found to be crucial, since social movements like the second wave of feminism, and, more recently, individual action (in universities, for instance) were behind many initiatives and advances.

The strong emphasis found in the interviews on the difficulties of conciliating the public and private spheres, and the non-permeable structure of the labour market for women, showed the distance between theory and practice, and prompted the suggestion of involving men in the process through specific programmes.[5] Since, on the other hand, a clear shortcoming of equality institutions is their lack of sanctioning power, recommendations included enforcement measures in the field of employment, and particularly in the private sector, where policies have been generally less effective. The UK report suggests annual gender audits on pay and on gender structure of hierarchies, in both the public and private sectors, which should include action plans and timelines for improving gender inequalities (Griffin 2003a: 17). The monitoring and evaluating of the effectiveness of equal opportunities policies and plans by gender equality experts, with the results of the evaluations made public and used for further action, was also seen as a step towards efficiency.

The lack of Women's Studies training among equal opportunities officers and decision-makers was perceived as a major problem, as social change cannot be effected without a deep understanding of gender relations. Women's Studies students proved themselves capable of fighting discrimination and promoting equality, but their gender expertise was not sufficiently used or called for in equal opportunities jobs. This was due, sometimes, to the fear of hiring someone 'too' gender conscious, a fear related to the negative stereotype of 'radical' feminists, but, perhaps more relevantly, it reflected the low visibility of Women's Studies students and their specific skills in the labour market, including the apparently obvious field of equal opportunities. Since, on the other hand, some students were themselves unaware of their skills, even when they described the fundamental learning acquired and its applied use in their jobs, career orientation also seems a priority.

Results suggested a need for further exchange of knowledge and closer interaction between social institutions and universities: students need to be better informed of equal opportunities action and of related jobs, universities must highlight and reinforce their own positive action, while, on the other hand, Women's Studies training clearly needs to be promoted as a basic requirement for equal opportunities workers and gender training should be provided to other professional groups, particularly those

Equal opportunities

working in the field of human resources, education or the civil service. This combined action and a more comprehensive approach to gender structures should favour a better identification of discriminative features and the effective development and implementation of equal opportunities policies. The expertise acquired through Women's Studies training has proved to be of great importance to the accomplishment of this goal and should be taken into account in promoting a change in social structures and in attitudes towards women.

**Notes**

1  France, Germany, Italy and the Netherlands are founding members; the UK joined in 1973, Spain in 1986, Finland in 1995 and Hungary and Slovenia in 2004. More extended contextual information on each country can be found in Griffin, ed. 2002.

2  This process is described in more detail in Mazari et al. 2002: 393–426.

3  This is now changing, as most applications for recognition of studies, including PhD programmes, demand specific employment information and career focus.

4  Unemployment rates of women and men in the EU in 2003 (%).

| Country | Women | Men |
| --- | --- | --- |
| Finland | 8.9 | 9.2 |
| France | 10.6 | 8.3 |
| Germany | 8.9 | 9.6 |
| Hungary | 5.5 | 6.0 |
| Italy | 11.7 | 6.8 |
| Netherlands | 3.9 | 3.5 |
| Slovenia | 7.1 | 6.1 |
| Spain | 15.9 | 8.2 |
| UK | 4.4 | 5.5 |
| EU-15 | 8.9 | 7.2 |
| EU + accessing countries | 10.0 | 8.2 |

*Source*: Eurostat

5  Germany offered the 'Fatherhood and career' project, run by the union service of workers ver.di, as a successful example (Schmidbaur et al. 2003: 13).

# 3 | The institutionalization of Women's Studies in Europe

## GABRIELE GRIFFIN

In most European countries[1] the institutionalization of Women's Studies in the academy via the Social Sciences and Humanities[2] occurred as a response to, and in conjunction with, the women's liberation movement of the late 1960s and 1970s.[3] It was driven by feminists whose political activism provided the basis for many of the issues – such as women's relation to the state, to their bodies, to employment and participation in public life, to culture, to science and knowledge (production) – that subsequently became the focus of feminist research, Women's Studies modules and courses in and outside of universities (see Threlfall 1996). As indicated below, while in some European countries such as the UK and Germany, these feminists often were activists as well as teachers, in others feminist teaching was institutionalized by women academics who did not simultaneously engage in grassroots political activism. A shared concern for all, though, was the recognition that gender is a foundational category of both experience and knowledge, shaping women's and men's lives in significant and different ways (see Bowles and Klein, eds 1983; Humm 1989).

Utilizing both the background data from the EWSI project[4] and the empirical data collected as part of that project, I shall explore two issues in this chapter: the institutionalization process of Women's Studies in Europe on the one hand, and the impact of that institutionalization on the other.

### The institutionalization process of Women's Studies in Europe

The EWSI project revealed that, in general, six phases of institutionalization can be observed in most European countries (Silius 2002). These phases are neither necessarily sequential, nor do they occur in exactly the same order, or to the same degree in all European countries.[5] They are:

- The activist phase: individual optional modules begin to appear within traditional disciplines though most Women's Studies-related work is carried out outside the academy.
- The establishment phase: generic and thematic Women's Studies modules[6] are introduced; interdisciplinary co-teaching units are established.

- The integration phase: Women's Studies modules become part of the core compulsory provision of traditional disciplines.
- The professionalization phase: Women's Studies degree programmes are introduced and Women's Studies staff including professors are appointed.
- The disciplinization phase: department-like centres for teaching, research and documentation are established.
- The autonomy phase: Women's Studies functions like any other discipline with the same accreditation, funding, and degree-awarding rights.

As our project showed, nowhere in Europe is this process complete, and although Women's Studies is very well established in many north-western European countries such as Germany, the Netherlands, Finland, Sweden and the UK, it still operates nowhere on a par with more traditional disciplines. Thus in the UK, for example, it is not accepted as a discipline by the HEFC (Higher Education Funding Council) which means that it is not, or only as part of other disciplines, assessed in the TQA (Teaching Quality Assessment exercise) and in the RAE (Research Assessment Exercise).[7] This has implications both for the status and the funding of the discipline. Apart from the UK, only one or two universities in Germany, and universities in Sweden, can award undergraduate degrees (BA/BSc) in Women's Studies. But unlike Finland, Germany and the Netherlands, the UK has not benefited from state feminism in the form of endowed chairs or endowed PhD studentships in Women's Studies. While the UK thus has many autonomous[8] named undergraduate and postgraduate degree programmes in Women's Studies, it lacks the state support Women's Studies has enjoyed in countries such as Germany as part of traditional disciplines.

The degree of institutionalization of Women's Studies may be measured in terms of the following indicators:[9]

- the number of (endowed) named chairs/professors and lectureships in the field
- the existence of autonomous or faculty-based Women's Studies centres or departments
- the academic standing of the staff involved
- the existence and range of degree-awarding under- and postgraduate programmes
- the number of disciplines involved in Women's Studies
- the amount and kind of funding (temporary or structural) available
- the research capacity of the discipline
- the recognition of the discipline by the various key decision-making

bodies relevant to higher education in a given country such as education ministries, higher education funding authorities etc.

In terms of these indicators, Women's Studies has not achieved full disciplinary status in any European country to date, and the degree of its institutionalization across the European countries is variable (see Table 3.1).

TABLE 3.1 Degree of institutionalization of Women's Studies in selected European countries

| Finland | High |
|---|---|
| Germany | High |
| Netherlands | High |
| UK | High |
| Spain | Medium |
| France | Low |
| Hungary | Low |
| Italy | Low |
| Slovenia | Low |

*Source*: Silius 2002

It is important to note that comparable degrees of institutionalization of Women's Studies in various countries do not have the same meaning when it comes to how that institutionalization manifests itself. Thus, the UK has significantly more degree programmes awarding BA/MA/PhDs in Women's Studies than any other country in Europe but it has neither endowed chairs nor endowed studentships such as are available in Germany and the Netherlands, for example. The institutionalisation of Women's Studies in both France and Italy is low, not least because the women's movement was strongly anti-institutional. In France this same anti-institutionalism is augmented by little university autonomy in the creation of new curricula which have to be agreed by the Ministry of Education every four years (Le Feuvre and Andriocci 2002a), and by the specific history of the concept of *égalité* which proclaims a universal, gender-neutral subject, thus precluding the possibility of the recognition of gender difference and, for instance, positive action. A similar scenario regarding the concept of equality exists in Finland (Tuori and Silius 2002) but this has not prevented the relatively high degree of institutionalization of Women's Studies there, fostered by a greater degree of flexibility in study patterns and by modularity. Hungary and Slovenia have low levels of institutionalization of Women's Studies because their pre-1989 status as member countries of the Eastern bloc in Europe enshrined women's equality in the law, if not in the countries'

91

cultures, because they had no women's movements, and because feminism was viewed as a Western concept (see Bahovec et al. 2002; Gazsi et al. 2002; Part VII of Griffin and Braidotti, eds 2002a; Barazzetti and Leone 2003). The project thus shows that contextual factors and country-specific histories play a key role in the institutionalization of Women's Studies.

We found that a number of other factors can either further or hinder the institutionalization of Women's Studies (see Table 3.2). These factors impacted on the project partner countries (see Table 3.3). As Table 3.3 indicates, no two European countries show the same pattern of factors influencing the institutionalization of Women's Studies. Thus, the anti-institutional attitudes of the women's movement made the institutionalization of Women's Studies more difficult in Germany, France and Italy than in Finland or the Netherlands, for instance (Barazzetti and Leone 2003). But even though this was the case, the outcomes for these countries in terms of Women's Studies institutionalization were very different. For while many Women's Studies modules were established within traditional disciplines in Germany, which overall has a high degree of institutionalization of Women's Studies, for instance, this did not occur in France where additional factors such as the lack of university autonomy in developing curricula and the socio-cultural embeddedness of the concept of *égalité* make positive action for women virtually impossible (Le Feuvre and Andriocci 2002a). Absence of state support for Women's Studies did not preclude its rapid establishment during the 1980s and 1990s in Britain because the UK's market-led educational system allowed staff to establish courses in response to student demand. By the same token, of course, absence of student demand or insufficient arousal of student demand can lead to the

TABLE 3.2  Factors impacting on the institutionalization of Women's Studies

| Factors *furthering* Women's Studies institutionalization | Factors *hindering* Women's Studies institutionalization |
| --- | --- |
| High degree of university autonomy in developing curricula | Little university autonomy in developing curricula |
| Modularity/flexible degree structures | Rigid disciplinary structures |
| Support from or neutrality of women's movement towards institutionalization | Anti-institutional attitudes of the women's movement |
| State support for Women's Studies | Absence of state support for Women's Studies |

*Source*: Silius 2002

TABLE 3.3 Factors impacting on Women's Studies institutionalization by country

| Countries | Factors impacting on Women's Studies institutionalization |
|---|---|
| Finland | • High degree of university autonomy in developing curricula<br>• Flexible degree structures<br>• Neutrality of women's movement towards institutionalization<br>• Some state support for Women's Studies |
| France | • Low university autonomy in developing curricula<br>• Rigid disciplinary structures<br>• Anti-institutional attitudes of the women's movement<br>• Absence of state support for Women's Studies<br>• Importance of concept of *égalité* |
| Germany | • High degree of university autonomy in developing curricula<br>• Rigid disciplinary structures<br>• Anti-institutional attitudes of the women's movement<br>• State support for Women's Studies |
| Hungary | • Low university autonomy in developing curricula<br>• Rigid disciplinary structures<br>• No women's movement<br>• Absence of state support for Women's Studies |
| Italy | • Some degree of university autonomy in developing curricula<br>• Rigid disciplinary structures<br>• Anti-institutional attitudes of the women's movement<br>• Absence of state support for Women's Studies |
| Netherlands | • Some degree of university autonomy in developing curricula<br>• Rigid disciplinary structures<br>• Neutrality of women's movement towards institutionalization<br>• Some state support for Women's Studies |
| Slovenia | • Low university autonomy in developing curricula<br>• Rigid disciplinary structures<br>• No women's movement<br>• Absence of state support for Women's Studies |
| Spain | • Some degree of university autonomy in developing curricula<br>• Rigid disciplinary structures<br>• Women's movement limited under Franco's regime<br>• Absence of state support for Women's Studies |
| UK | • High degree of university autonomy in developing curricula<br>• Flexible degree structures/modularity<br>• Neutrality of women's movement towards institutionalization<br>• Absence of state support for Women's Studies |

*Source*: Griffin, ed. 2002

Institutionalization of Women's Studies

demise of courses and whole disciplines as has been evident in the UK since the early 1980s (see Griffin 2003c).

One factor which is beginning to bite regarding the institutionalization of Women's Studies is the Bologna process which requires European Union member-states to refigure their higher education degree structures into a division of BA, MA, PhD as is already the norm in Britain. However, different European countries, unfamiliar with the three-year compulsory undergraduate degree structure and its postgraduate *Überbau* of MA and PhD (but not a habilitation), are interpreting this restructuring process in different ways, and utilizing the opportunity to streamline their degree provision such that in the Netherlands, for instance, various Women's Studies programmes have now been closed down as the discipline is concentrated in specific institutions and centres. Women's Studies institutionalization thus remains the quintessential feminist subject-in-process.

Apart from context-specific factors, Women's Studies has had a difficult time establishing itself within the academy in Europe because of the characteristics of the discipline[10] itself. Thus it is:

- A single-sex subject[11] that promotes women within predominantly secular, co-educational cultures that do not practise very overt forms of gender segregation.
- An overtly political discipline with a transformative agenda[12] focused on gender relations driven by one gender (women) in cultures and institutions dominated at the managerial and decision-making levels by another gender (men)[13] and by the notion of objective, uninvested knowledge which the discipline explicitly refutes.
- An interdisciplinary subject in educational structures that are still for the most part very rigidly monodisciplinary.[14]

The current situation of Women's Studies in Europe might thus be described as follows:

- An absence or near absence of Women's Studies in higher education institutions in some countries, especially Southern and Eastern ones (e.g. Greece, Portugal, Slovenia, Hungary) where, however, efforts are being made to establish the discipline.
- The existence of individual Women's Studies modules and courses within traditional disciplines is probably universal in Europe now but mostly without those modules coalescing into a Women's Studies degree.
- In many of the north European countries there are now some named degree routes in Women's Studies, either at undergraduate or at postgraduate level, or both.

- Many European countries have feminist research centres both inside and outside the academy.

- There are many female academics working on Women's Studies topics but in only a small number of European countries has this resulted in the establishment of Women's Studies departments.

- In some countries such as the UK, Norway and the Netherlands, with long histories of institutionalization, we are beginning to see a withdrawal from named degree routes into a position of mainstreaming, i.e. of reintegrating Women's Studies into other, traditional disciplines.

Overall, then, the institutionalization of Women's Studies across the various European countries remains uneven and frequently underdeveloped. This has implications for the discipline, for Women's Studies staff and students, and I shall address some of these now.

### Some consequences of the uneven development of the institutionalization of Women's Studies across Europe

One of the first impacts of the relatively low levels of institutionalization of Women's Studies in many countries in Europe is that the discipline lacks visibility (Barazzetti and Leone 2003). Most students in our project, in fact, took Women's Studies not as a degree in its own right but as modules in other, traditional disciplines as Table 3.4 indicates. The column entitled 'Course dates' in this Table shows the earliest dates when the students interviewed commenced Women's Studies courses, and indicates the period of course participation from which the majority of interviewees stemmed. This reveals that Women's Studies came to the fore across Europe from the second half of the 1970s, gaining momentum in some countries (Finland, France, Germany, Italy) during the 1980s, and in others during the 1990s (Hungary, Slovenia, Spain).

Table 3.4 shows that the vast majority of students interviewed in the project took Women's Studies modules as part of another discipline, mostly in undergraduate degrees. This continues to be the academic reality for Women's Studies students across Europe. One of its implications is that it is very difficult to track students who have taken such modules since these modules will be subsumed in official data as part of the traditional disciplines of which they form a part. It could be argued that the establishment of feminist or Women's Studies modules in traditional disciplines constitutes a desirable mainstreaming effect, particularly where such modules form part of the compulsory core provision of a discipline. This is undoubtedly the case, and Women's Studies has been particularly successful in changing the canon of Social Sciences and Humanities disciplines. However, the visibility of the discipline also depends on its establishment

TABLE 3.4 Percentage of respondents undertaking particular kinds of Women's Studies courses

| | | Course dates | PhD | MA** | BA** | Modules in other undergraduate disciplines | Other |
|---|---|---|---|---|---|---|---|
| Finland | Past students | 1980; 65% from 1995 | – | 21 | – | 77 | 2 |
| | Present students | 1993; 66% from 1998 | – | 17* | 44 | 38 | – |
| France | Past students | 1987; increasing from 1993 | 2 | 43; 6* | – | 45 | 4 |
| | Present students | 1994; 73% from 2000 | – | 13; 7* | 3 | 75 | 1 |
| Germany | Past students | 1981; 62% from 1991 | 4 | 2; 23* | 4 | 53 | 13 |
| | Present students | 1988; 51% from 2001 | – | 2; 5* | 37 | 38 | 19 |
| Hungary | Past students | 1990; 53% from 1999 | – | 2* | 4 | 63 | 31 |
| | Present students | 1995; 64% from 2001 | – | – | – | 77 | 22 |
| Italy | Past students | 1974; 40% from 1999 | 5 | 16; 7* | 7 | 23 | 42 |
| | Present students | 1984; 2% from 2001 | 8 | 19; 2* | – | 49 | 21 |
| Netherlands | Past students | 1976; 58% from 1991 | – | 4; 4* | 21 | 61 | 11 |
| | Present students | 1979; 57% from 1999 | 7 | 11 | 24 | 65 | 4 |
| Slovenia | Past students | 1992–2002 | – | 6; 8* | 6 | 62 | 16 |
| | Present students | Mostly from 2002 | 6 | 18* | – | 74 | 2 |
| Spain | Past students | 1995; 64% from 1998 | 40 | 5/10* | – | 12 | 33 |
| | Present students | 1998; 79% from 2002 | 8 | 2* | – | 48 | 41 |
| United Kingdom | Past students | 1975; 67% from 1991 | 1 | 50 | 16 | 18 | 6 |
| | Present students | 1990; 63% from 2000–02 | 17 | 12; 5* | 24 | 36 | 13 |

*Notes:* * Modules are part of another discipline    ** This terminology (BA/MA) is used here to distinguish between under- and postgraduate courses; the process of the adoption of this terminology across EU member countries dates only from 2002

*Source:* Quantitative data, EWSI project, 2003 <www.hull.ac.uk/ewsi>

TABLE 3.5 Sources of information about Women's Studies (according to questionnaire respondents) (%)

| Country | University | | School | | Friends | | Women's organizations | |
|---|---|---|---|---|---|---|---|---|
| | PS* | CS** | PS | CS | PS | CS | PS | CS |
| Finland | 89 | 86 | – | 3 | 9 | 9 | 2 | 3 |
| France | 80 | 90 | – | – | 12 | 4 | 4 | 6 |
| Germany | 88 | 87 | 2 | 4 | 5 | 6 | 5 | 3 |
| Hungary | 98*** | 100 | – | – | – | – | – | – |
| Italy | 64 | 72 | 2 | 2 | 18 | 14 | 14 | 8 |
| NL | 71 | 82 | 13 | 2 | 8 | 10 | 4 | 2 |
| Slovenia | 70 | 94 | 14 | – | 12 | 4 | 4 | – |
| Spain | 65 | 75 | – | – | 12 | 14 | 23 | 8 |
| UK | 65 | 68 | 5 | 13 | 21 | 12 | 3 | – |

*Notes*: *PS = past students   **CS = current students   *** Figures do not always add up to 100% as a small percentage in some countries cited 'other sources'
*Source*: Quantitative data reports, EWSI project, 2003

as a discipline in its own right with the same degree of autonomy, funding etc. as other disciplines. This is one of the greatest hurdles that Women's Studies continues to face.

Since Women's Studies is not taught in schools (though some women's history is taught in Dutch secondary schools, for example), students tend to come across the subject by chance once they are at university. Some students, particularly past students who worked as feminist activists prior to taking Women's Studies courses, learnt about these courses in women's organizations. This is reflected in their sources of information about Women's Studies (see Table 3.5).

Most students, as Table 3.5 illustrates, come across Women's Studies while at university. This has implications for market-led university systems such as the UK where the ability to attract students on to a course is critical for the survival of the course; if the discipline is invisible, attracting students is difficult. It is also felt in countries where attracting students on to courses is not a priority. As one French student described it: 'The first time I ever heard anything about Women's Studies was in my first year of Sociology. There was this core course on social inequality [ ... ] as soon as I heard [lecturers] talking about masculine domination, that triggered something inside me, it was really strong, and that just sort of got me interested, so when it came to choosing the final year degree options, I took the Women's Studies option, because of that class' (Le Feuvre and Andriocci 2002b: 33). Another French interviewee described the process as follows: 'in the first year, there was this one lecture on gender relations, I went twice, the second time I even took a friend [ ... ] In the second year, we had this group project to do [ ... ] so we chose to work on the social construction of femininity [ ... ] As soon as I was given the opportunity to develop those kinds of questions, I did. In the third year, I didn't hesitate at all' (ibid.). Such 'conversion experiences' are not uncommon. Our interviews indicated that many students, once they embarked on Women's Studies courses, found these highly stimulating and wanted to continue with the subject. The progression from coming across the subject by chance to making a deliberate commitment to it was not unusual among interviewees, and led to a high level of desire to pursue the discipline at postgraduate level as I shall discuss below.

'Conversion' to the subject, particularly where it is not well institution-alized, was often effected through individual academic staff with Women's Studies interests who inspired students. One Hungarian PhD student, describing how she became involved in Women's Studies, said:

Absolutely accidentally [ ... ] I had never heard the word women's history or anything like it. I had no opinion about feminism, if anything, it was only negative. The very first day, when the students arrived [at the Central European University, Budapest, history MA programme], they didn't know anyone, a welcome party was organised for the teachers and the students. At this get-together a rather peculiar looking woman came up to me, she had a strip of hair dyed blue [ ... ] I had no idea if she was Hungarian or American, you see everyone spoke English there. She immediately asked me what my topic was, who I was. She asked everyone, mind you. Then I said well this and that, 1956, and then she said, then you will write the history of women in 1956. She said [that] to me, and then she dashed away for a semester in Vienna [ ... ] Thus a relationship started [ ... ] One thing follows the other, you dig yourself into something which you enjoy immediately. (Juhász 2003: 9)

Another Hungarian student reported something similar: 'First about my background. I graduated from ELTE [state university in Budapest] in art history, and the first time I heard about the existence of the *gender* topic was in 1997 from O.D. Under O's influence, that was the time when such essays started to appear, *Thalassa* [a philosophy journal] had a feminist issue [ ... ] then, I don't know, *Cafe Babel* [a cultural journal] had a Body issue, then the book edited by F.E. in the winter of 1998–99, so when this whole business started going, I was already consuming all of it' (Juhász 2003: 10). Such influences by individual women characterize much of the institutionalization enterprise of Women's Studies. To the extent that the

TABLE 3.6 Reasons for taking Women's Studies (% of questionnaire respondents)

| Country | Personal interest | | Awareness of gender discrimination | | Academic interest in subject | | Gaining a qualification | |
|---|---|---|---|---|---|---|---|---|
| | PS* | CS** | PS | CS | PS | CS | PS | CS |
| Finland | 98 | 97 | 73 | 60 | 80 | 66 | 4 | 0 |
| France | 77 | 86 | 67 | 60 | 80 | 80 | 39 | 16 |
| Germany | 93 | 97 | 91 | 96 | 93 | 79 | 22 | 24 |
| Hungary | 69 | 65 | 36 | 22 | 56 | 34 | 13 | 2 |
| Italy | 94 | 87 | 60 | 87 | 40 | 44 | 7 | 20 |
| NL | 92 | 100 | 89 | 80 | 78 | 86 | 11 | 8 |
| Slovenia | 82 | 67 | 58 | 49 | 62 | 74 | 20 | 15 |
| Spain | 90 | 64 | 80 | 67 | 71 | 70 | 23 | 50 |
| UK | 86 | 91 | 65 | 74 | 63 | 74 | 54 | 57 |

*Notes*: *PS = past students    **CS = current students (2002)
*Source*: Quantitative data reports, EWSI project, 2003

move from individual to collaborative effort is achieved, Women's Studies develops anchorage in academe. However, where the discipline relies entirely and continuously on individual effort, not only is it vulnerable to 'disappearance' when the person in question moves (see Griffin 2002) but over time fatigue can set in, resulting in the (re-)absorption of feminist scholars in traditional disciplines as has occurred in the UK.

A different effect of the invisibility of the discipline (though other issues such as lifecycle stage, for example, play a role here) is that students do not connect it with subsequent employment.[15] Instead, they tend to take it for personal reasons, because of an awareness of gender discrimination, or because they are, or become, interested in the topic (see Table 3.6).

These findings are not specific to this study. A project conducted by Maryanne Dever and Elizabeth Day (2001) from the Centre for Women's Studies and Gender Research at Monash University, Melbourne, involving four Women's Studies centres each in Australia, the United Kingdom, and the United States of America also found that 'career and vocational issues do not appear to feature prominently in students' initial reasons for selecting the major [ ... ] Women's Studies students indicated overwhelmingly (between 70% and 90%) that their primary reason for enrolling in the field was "interest in the subject", a trend largely replicated in the control groups from other humanities and social science majors' (Dever and Day 2001: 56). Indeed, 'fewer than 5% of students in the various Women's Studies programs surveyed listed "career prospects" as the principal motivating factor in their enrolment decision' (ibid.). This project's data confirmed these findings (see Table 3.6), with the low percentages of respondents taking the subject who sought to gain a qualification in it explained by the lack of opportunity in most European countries of doing so.[16] However, it should be noted that there were significant variations between countries regarding these expectations. These can be explained by a number of factors which vary from country to country and include general levels of women's employment in the countries concerned (i.e. high or low), age and employment experiences of the respondents, and the visibility of Women's Studies and degree of institutionalization of equal opportunities in a given country.

Since the academy is ruled by an ideal of objective, uninvested knowledge (see Bourdieu and Passeron 1977; Bourdieu 1984), the notion of taking a subject out of personal interest is apt to relegate that subject to the status of a leisure pursuit. Although there have significant challenges to that ideal,[17] it still drives public perceptions including those of the Women's Studies students themselves. One Finnish student for example said: 'We felt we were not supposed to say [ ... ] that we are in a Women's Studies group because [...] in other seminar groups you might not get the same kind of attention if it became known that "you are one of those Women's Studies freaks", and so what you do does not have to be taken seriously' (Tuori 2003).

Such perceptions could make some students even decide not to take the subject, for fear of damaging their subsequent career, particularly in academe, as demonstrated by this Italian interviewee:

> When I did my doctorate, although I was very keen on these studies [Women's Studies], I made a universal and neutral choice [ ... ] I got a neutral qualification as a philosopher [ ... ] By doing this, I was playing it safe, in order to be recognised by the scientific community and be viewed less suspiciously as regards my feminist interests. It was as if my making such a powerful choice guaranteed a sort of seriousness and a scientific status [...] I believe that if I had chosen a more eccentric subject for my research dissertation, or anyway a subject that was far from shared certainties, I would have been more penalised. (Brazzetti et al. 2003: 26)

This interviewee articulates the idea that certain disciplines are 'universal and neutral', i.e. project the notion of an uninvested knowledge, while others are at the very least 'eccentric', lacking 'shared certainties'. Such a position reinforces traditional, indeed outmoded, assumptions about the nature of knowledge and the academy which Women's Studies has challenged since its inception. The fear expressed by the student, that taking Women's Studies might impair her career prospects, was not borne out by our data (see Griffin 2003a) as Chapter 4 in this volume indicates. Rather,

Women's Studies students fare like other Social Sciences and Humanities students in the employment market, are more likely than other Social Sciences and Humanities students to enter postgraduate education, and a high proportion (over 60 per cent) enters professional employment in their first post-education job.

One might argue that taking Women's Studies is a high-risk educational strategy since not only does it have the characteristics enumerated above (single-sex orientation; overt transformative political agenda) but it also seems not to lead to specific forms of employment. One French interviewee, for instance, said:

> It took me four years to get a tenured position. I already had the *Agréga-tion* [the most prestigious teaching qualification]; I had plenty of teaching experience. Of course, I also had my Doctorate. I had loads of publications, I hadn't yet published a book, but I had lots of articles. I really found that I was paying a high price and I'm absolutely sure that it was the topic of my doctoral dissertation – the history of the women's movement – that led to the repeated rejections; all my publications were on that theme [...] I had lots of friends who were in a similar position to me, who were applying to academic positions after their Ph.D., and [those who had worked on something else] didn't have such a hard time, it took them two years at the most to get a position. But of course, I can't prove that it was because of my thesis topic. (Le Feuvre and Andriocci 2002b: 28)

The time taken by this student to secure her tenure is in fact not significantly different from what someone in another discipline might expect. However, she firmly links it to her thesis topic – a topic that does not appear particularly controversial. Here we have an example of the ways in which Women's Studies students can internalize a state of embattle-ment such as the discipline is constantly exposed to and view themselves as embattled even when this cannot be said to be the case in comparative terms. It is undoubtedly true that there are few jobs in academe across Europe with a specific Women's Studies designation (see Chapter 4 in this volume for a further discussion of this issue) but in the UK, for instance, it has been recognized that gender expertise is valuable in many traditional Humanities and Social Sciences disciplines because the topics dealt with in Women's Studies are of interest to many women and men. Hence, many jobs advertised in those subjects ask for gender expertise as one of their preferred areas of specialism. Our research also showed that not only do a disproportionate number of undergraduates with Women's Studies train-ing relative to other similar subjects go on to do postgraduate work but they also occupy a wide variety of professions and a very high percentage (around 60 per cent) enter professional jobs straight away (Griffin 2003b). Indeed, satisfaction with Women's Studies courses is very high indeed among students (see Table 3.7), showing that the subject stimulates and challenges them, answering their interests and needs.

TABLE 3.7 Percentage of questionnaire respondents reporting satisfaction with their Women's Studies course

| Country | Past students | Current students |
|---|---|---|
| Finland | 98 | 100 |
| France | 92 | 100 |
| Germany | 96 | 97 |
| Hungary | 98 | 94 |
| Italy | 94 | 91 |
| Netherlands | 100 | 100 |
| Slovenia | 98 | 98 |
| Spain | 100 | 96 |
| UK | 98 | 99 |

*Source*: Quantitative data, EWSI project, 2003

This satisfaction, *inter alia*, leads to progression to postgraduate work: 'At first, my interest was limited to some readings, or to going to some meetings. Then, at the association, I started attending some study groups. After that, I started thinking about doing a PhD course in Women's Studies. At that point, my own, informal experience was joined by a recognised, more academic one: a PhD in women's history in Naples' (Barazzetti et al. 2003: 14).

This move into postgraduate work is very important because, as Eurostat data show, there is a very close correlation between the level of women's educational attainment and their labour market participation rates (see Table 1.4 in this volume). As Le Feuvre and Andriocci suggest in Chapter 1, country-specific contexts begin to play much less of a role in women's labour market participation as women progress along the educational scale. At the highest level, the country-specific differences between the Netherlands, the country with the highest labour market participation rate for women with higher education (84.9 per cent), and the lowest, Italy, with 77.0 per cent, is only about 8 per cent, whereas the difference between those with only primary education in Italy as the country with the lowest participation rate (32.8 per cent) and Finland with the highest (64.9 per cent) is more than 30 per cent. Women's Studies ability to inspire its students to prolong their education is thus one of the most important contributions the discipline makes to facilitating women's participation in the labour market. Indeed, our research found that women taking Women's Studies very much want to participate effectively and fully in the labour market (Griffin 2003b). It is also the case that women remain underrepresented at postgraduate level, including in the supposedly more 'feminine' disciplines (OECD 2002a, 2003), and Women's Studies contributes to redressing that balance.

Women's Studies postgraduates, as will be discussed further in Chapter 4 of this volume, want to work predominantly in three areas: feminist research/academe; women's NGOs/the voluntary sector; and equal opportunities. These are the arenas where they think they can most meaningfully apply the knowledge they acquired on their degree course. All three sectors are of course responses to, and have come about as a function of, the women's liberation movement; they constitute a professionalization of Women's Studies knowledge (Silius and Tuori 2003). They are also beset by difficulties including in academe the increasing casualization and flexibilization of the labour force, poor pay and lack of career prospects in the voluntary sector, and last, but not least, the absence of a demand for gender expertise as part of the job specification of equal opportunities employees which is the case in many countries (see Carrera Suárez and Viñuela Suárez 2003a, and Chapter 2 in this volume). Women's Studies knowledges and skills[18] are, however, useful in a wide range of professions. As one French interviewee put it: 'I work in logistics for a private company, nothing to do with women or equality as such, but I can assure you that I use the knowledge acquired through the DESS every single day in my job' (Le Feuvre and Andriocci 2003: 60). In saying this, this interviewee, as well as others, focused on the content of her Women's Studies training, rather than on the transferable skills she had acquired. Interviewees, in fact, had plenty to say about both, but their investment, inevitably, was in the content of their studies rather than the skills referred to just now. This is partly because these contents respond to their life experiences and enable them to understand the contexts in which they operate better.

Changes in students' understanding of personal relations as a consequence of doing Women's Studies will be discussed in greater detail in Chapter 5 of this volume. A key issue is that just as the women's movements addressed women's needs in all areas of their lives during the 1970s,[19] so Women's Studies in the academy continues to speak to those needs and to effect transformative understandings in its students. A British student, for instance, reported: 'I realized that [...] I was going to have to make some very hard decisions and hard choices in my life in order to achieve the things we were talking about in theory on the Women's Studies course [...] I became stronger and maybe a little bit more aggressive' (Griffin 2003a: 58).

Another British student said: 'I think [the Women's Studies course] was the catalyst because I started having counselling while I was doing the course because I just wasn't happy with how I was feeling in myself and so it was kind of you know hearing someone else do something to make something change, makes you think, well, OK, I can change something' (ibid., p. 57) This student described herself as having been a 'typical housewifey kind of person even although I wasn't married'. She was living with her boyfriend and, as a function of her changing disposition, 'I just stopped being that woman overnight, and I still kind of question all the time if it is really my turn with the washing up, so that kind of little mould of a woman that I thought I was going to be, I'm not' (ibid.).

This questioning of conventional gender roles which many of the interviewees across the European countries described as an effect of doing Women's Studies is a heritage of the women's movement from which Women's Studies arose. Such impacts notwithstanding, one of the effects of the institutionalization of Women's Studies across Western Europe has been the increasing divorce of Women's Studies as an academic discipline from political activism and grassroots movements. I was very struck by the comments made by one Indonesian student attending an MA course in Women's Studies in the UK in 2002, who talked about her surprise at the curriculum she was confronted with. This is what she said: 'Indonesia is still struggling with education, with poverty, with working conditions and some things like that [ ... ] and in Women's Studies in Indonesia there's always discussion about poverty, inequality, marriage, how Indonesia is [ ... ] in the classroom [in the UK] we don't talk about that [ ... ] we talk about self-identity and things like that that we haven't the laxity at home to talk about [ ... ] there's a lot of self-indulgence' (Griffin 2003c). What this student identified was in a sense a trend in certain Women's Studies curricula, particularly in Northern and Western European countries, and much influenced by Anglophone agendas, towards a culturalization of Women's Studies, away from certain material conditions that shape women's lives and towards what one might describe as sublimated knowledges. The Indonesian student on this postgraduate degree was left with the impression that poverty, working conditions, education are all no longer issues for or in Women's Studies in north-west European countries but this is clearly not the case. We know that the material conditions of women across all European countries remain worse than those of men. We know all about the glass ceiling, the pay gap, the poverty trap, the uneven distribution of wealth, domestic and care labour between the sexes. National labour surveys and OECD statistics endlessly parade these realities before us. We know it and, I would argue, it has become the mantra of a certain kind of experience of disempowerment, a sort of midlife crisis in Women's Studies. This is what one French Women's Studies student said:

> Sometimes I feel as if I'm trying to do the splits. I mean, I come out with things that I really, really believe in, the gender analysis framework, and at the same time, from a critical point of view, I don't have any practical solutions to offer, nothing. I mean, I know things aren't working right as they are, but at the same time I don't have an alternative solution to offer [ ... ] That makes me quite sad. You can see that things aren't right and, at the same time, you can't find any simple solutions, that's the problem really.
> (Le Feuvre and Andriocci 2002b: 38)

This is a serious issue for Women's Studies. My sense is that in some Women's Studies courses in some north-western European countries, agendas with clear, transformative subtexts and making claims for changes in women's actual lives have receded into the background in favour of theoretical investigations that mark Women's Studies as part of the pantheon of conventional university disciplines, facilitating its place at the high table of the academy through both high theorization and a concomitant depoliticization, a focus on politically uncontentious knowledge. This is part of a much wider issue, namely the question about what constitutes politically contentious knowledge today. We live in an age where, certainly within most European countries, only the extreme right is viewed as having anything politically contentious to say. The left, post-1989, has lost its political bite. It is only in the last few years that the new anti-globalization movements have begun to make themselves felt in any degree at all. We now live in an age where movements and micro-radical formations have a much greater sense of their political power than the average voter who stays at home and no longer feels the urge to exercise his or her political right. Certain forms of depoliticization have bitten deep, and this is evident in current university politics.

Women's Studies' contested position within the academy has traditionally, if I may use that word, rested on the assumption of its overt politics, its ideological commitment to social change. But it has also grappled with its intersectional position between activism and academy, and, as it has become significantly institutionalized, it has moved towards the academy, leaving certain forms of activism behind. Nowhere is that more evident than in the results of our project. A Hungarian interviewee, for instance, described her experience of the relation between the academy and activism as follows: 'Academic life is separate from activist life. And as I see it [ ... ] there are some who see it as an opportunity to get money from abroad, and build their own careers. It doesn't occur to them to spread this, and involve others. On the contrary, if they involve others, they might be a danger to their own advancement' (Juhász 2003: 15). Another Hungarian interviewee stated: '[Women's Studies] had very little to do with activism [ ... ] There are no professors who are interested in this' (ibid., p. 14).

This issue relates also to the question of work placements as part of Women's Studies degrees. One might have expected that Women's Studies courses offer or require work placements in women's organizations as part of their content. However, as Table 3.8 shows, very few women on Women's Studies courses across Europe are required to undertake work placements.

TABLE 3.8 Percentage of past and current Women's Studies students required to undertake work placements during their Women's Studies training

| Country | Past students | | Current students | |
|---|---|---|---|---|
| | Obligatory work placement | Voluntary work placement | Obligatory work placement | Voluntary work placement |
| Finland | 5 | – | – | – |
| France | 59 | – | 22 | – |
| Germany | 37 | – | 26 | – |
| Hungary | 1 | – | – | 8 |
| Italy | 17 | – | 19 | – |
| Netherlands | 35 | – | 30 | – |
| Slovenia | 18 | – | – | – |
| Spain | 8 | – | – | – |
| UK | 9 | – | 2 | – |

*Source*: Quantitative data reports, EWSI project, 2003

Where numbers of obligatory work placements are high, as is the case for France, this is a function of the kind of course attended (Le Feuvre and Andriocci 2002b); in other words, a bias in the sample. We also think that some respondents confused the category 'work placement' – an in-course requirement – with working for a living while studying. Irrespective of these reservations, it is quite clear that few students were required to undertake any form of work placement, and, if anything, the trend is declining. Theory and practice thus no longer have to be actively bridged as part of the academic study of Women's Studies. All too often now we opt for socially integrative rather than socially transformative knowledge. I would argue that whereas the process of institutionalization has transformed feminist academics, I am no longer certain that feminist academics have transformed the academy. This is still different in some of the Eastern European countries. Gender Studies students at Warsaw University, for example, have to do a work placement in a women's NGO (non-governmental organization) as part of their degree course. The foremost women's NGO in Hungary, NANE, an organization focusing on violence against women, provides Women's Studies training in exchange for work in the NGO. But such connections between the academy and activism have become increasingly weakened or are in fact non-existent in many European countries now.

When (in our project) we asked Women's Studies students across Europe about the impact which taking Women's Studies had on them, many, especially from the Nordic countries but also from Holland and to some extent the UK and Germany, described it as an 'identity project', and the identity that they referred to was in many ways a privatized, individual one. A French student said: 'One of the really amazing things I found on the [Women's Studies course] was that you could at last say openly that you were homo, that you were attracted to other women, without being judged or criticized. I think that [the course] helped me to come to terms with my homosexuality' (Le Feuvre and Andriocci 2002b: 75). The notion of Women's Studies as an identity project is, on one level, unproblematic since – in 1960s and 1970s parlance, to quote one of the key tenets of the women's movement – 'the personal was/is the political', but the question one might want to ask is, is the personal still the political, or is the personal now just that, a personal identity project whose interrelation with the political realities surrounding it are at best unclear and at worst non-existent? To what extent and in what ways are we still making the connection between the personal and the political? Among the Women's Studies students we interviewed there was a clear sense of the experience of a gap between theory and lived reality, expressed in recognitions such as the fact that equal opportunities legislation has failed to deliver equality for women (this is discussed in greater detail in Chapter 2 of this volume). The interviewees all paid tribute to the levels of gender awareness they acquired on their courses but simultaneously articulated their sense of the limited or even non-existent power they felt to change anything. I want to suggest that somewhere along the line we – and by 'we' I mean those who teach Women's or Gender Studies – have lost sight of the fact that to effect social change you need not only an analysis (that analysis is now well established and flourishing) but also tools to effect such change. We are much better at providing the analysis than the tools for change. This is a dilemma in a context where change is still needed as much now as it was when Women's Studies was first established. I want to suggest that it is time for us to take stock, to sit back and think again what it is that we want our students to take away from their studies. What theories, what practices, what concerns do we want them to engage with? How do we want to see them engage with the socio-political realities in the changing European and global world around them? How do we as feminist academics need to engage with the socio-political realities around us? These are questions Women's Studies needs to address.

## Some conclusions – future agendas

The institutionalization of Women's Studies as a discipline across European countries has progressed steadily, if unevenly. As other chapters in this volume as well as this one make clear, Women's Studies has significant impacts on the lives of those who take it, both professionally and personally. This has implications for its institutionalization. We would argue that the European Union should use the Bologna process to encourage the establishment of Women's Studies as a fully recognized independent discipline at under- and at postgraduate level in all European Union countries, as well as continuing to encourage its mainstreaming in traditional disciplines. All national governments should facilitate the establishment of Women's Studies as a fully recognized discipline at under- and at postgraduate level by including it as a discipline for all assessment and funding purposes, and supporting it, within the overall framework of their university systems, with endowed chairs and studentships.

One issue for Women's Studies is that it is not taught at school level, yet the majority of European citizens do not progress to tertiary education. It is therefore important that those who deliver primary and secondary education are aware of gender issues, both in their own practice and in the wider socio-economic context. National governments and ministries of education should therefore ensure that Women's Studies forms part of all teacher education curricula, and that it is integrated into primary and secondary education curricula so that changes in gender roles can be addressed at the educational levels to which all European Union citizens have access.

The project showed that students on modular degrees or on modules in traditional degrees that are interdisciplinary in character are difficult to track. We therefore recommend that the European Union and national governments agree common processes for keeping such data so that student aggregation around interdisciplinary areas can be tracked and analysed more effectively. Moreover, during the project we found that with the exception of the UK, universities in no other country kept exit data for students, which made it difficult to track students by discipline. The European Union and national governments therefore and additionally need to agree common processes for keeping data so that the transition from training to employment can be tracked and analysed more effectively.

Women's Studies impacts not only on women's professional lives but equally powerfully on their personal lives (see Griffin and Hanmer 2003, and Chapter 5 in this volume). They become change agents both in their private lives and in their working environments. Overall, we found that for those who committed themselves to Women's Studies, the benefits were enormous and varied (Griffin 2003b). Women's Studies remains a challenging discipline in every respect; the need for change in women's lives is as powerful as it was in the 1970s – therein lie both the opportunities and the issues for Women's Studies staff and students.

## Notes

1  Here I refer to the countries that participated in the EWSI project (Finland, France, Germany, Hungary, Italy, Slovenia, Spain, the Netherlands, the UK) as well as to other European countries such as Belgium, Greece, Norway that did not participate.

2  Among the key disciplines promoting Women's Studies were Literature, Sociology, History and Philosophy.

3  Countries such as Hungary and Slovenia, that is Eastern European countries, tended not to have a women's movement at that time for complex and diverse reasons (see Part VII of Griffin and Braidotti, eds 2002a). This also means that the institutionalization of Women's Studies in those countries occurred either much later or not at all (see Griffin, ed. 2002).

4  These have been published both on the project website and in separate book format (Griffin, ed. 2002).

5  For more specific details of the differences across the European countries see Griffin, ed. (2002).

6  Typical titles for such modules would be 'Introduction to Women's Studies'; 'Feminist Methodologies'; 'Feminist Theory'; 'Sexuality and Identity'; 'Women's Writing'; 'Issues in Women's History'.

7  See Griffin (2002b).

8  By 'autonomous' I mean 'not embedded in another discipline'.

9  See Braidotti et al. (1998); Barazzetti and Leone (2003), for a discussion of these indicators.

10  The issue of whether or not Women's Studies constitutes a discipline has been a matter of debate since its inception. The arguments for and against have been well rehearsed (see the 'Introduction' in Bowles and Klein, eds 1983 for details of these debates). It is clear that different and contradictory positions among feminist academics on this issue have contributed to the uneven development of Women's Studies as a discipline across Europe.

11  With the exception of Nordic countries such as Norway and Sweden, Women's Studies in Europe has been taught mainly by women to women. Even in those Nordic countries, very few men are located in Women's Studies. During the late 1980s and the 1990s men engaged in critical masculinity studies and in sexuality studies such as Jeff Hearn and Ken Plummer became involved

in related topics but, unlike Women's Studies in the USA, Women's Studies in Europe continues to be a female-centred enclave.

12  Many of the (early) textbooks on Women's Studies, especially from the USA, reflected this incendiary politics with titles such as *Feminist Scholarship: Kindling in the Groves of Academe* (Dubois et al. 1987), *Teaching to Transgress* (hooks 1994), and *Stirring It: Challenges for Feminism* (Griffin et al., eds 1994).

13  In *Failing the Future* (1998), feminist academic Annette Kolodny discusses the impact of feminists' failure to move into the management structures of higher education in order to effect institutional change.

14  The EU regards this monodisciplinarity as one reason for the lack of certain kinds of policy-oriented research in Europe and has made the better understanding of how such monodisciplinarity works and is maintained a research priority in its Framework 6 for research. This issue will be the object of investigation of a research project with the acronym RESEARCH INTEGRATION, coordinated by Gabriele Griffin, University of Hull.

15  This is not particular to Women's Studies. Many undergraduates have no very clear idea about what they want to do professionally following their training at the point of entry into the university (see Le Feuvre and Andriocci 2003).

16  As indicated above, Women's Studies is still predominantly taught in modules within other, traditional disciplines such as Sociology, Literature, etc.

17  See, for example, Hartsock (1998), Alcoff and Potter, eds (1993) and Harding (1987).

18  See Barazzetti et al. (2003), Bianchi et al. (2003), Silius and Tuori (2003) and Griffin (2003b) for a more extended discussion of the impact of Women's Studies training on women's employability.

19  It is perhaps worth remembering here that 'The Seven Demands of the Women's Liberation Movement' in Britain were:

The women's liberation movement asserts the right of every woman to a self-defined sexuality and demands:

1. equal pay
2. equal education and job opportunities
3. free contraception and abortion on demand
4. free 24–hour nurseries, under community control
5. legal and financial independence
6. an end to discrimination against lesbians
7. freedom from intimidation by the threat or use of violence or sexual coercion, regardless of marital status. An end to the laws, assumptions and institutions that perpetuate male dominance and men's aggression towards women. (Feminist Anthology Collective 1981: 4)

# 4 | The professionalization of Women's Studies students in Europe: expectations and experiences

HARRIET SILIUS

This chapter reports on the relation between Women's Studies training and employment, based on data from the EWSI project. It deals with the employment expectations and experiences of Women's Studies students, their employment outcomes after training, and the professionalization and professionalism of graduates[1] in the nine European project partner countries: Finland, France, Germany, Hungary, Italy, the Netherlands, Slovenia, Spain and the United Kingdom. The impact of Women's Studies training on its students' employment is discussed through the concepts of professionalization and professionalism. Until now there has been no systematic knowledge concerning the impact of Women's Studies training in Europe or of the situation of Women's Studies graduates in the labour market. The project shows that there is a positive relation between a high degree of institutionalization of Women's Studies training and of equal opportunities policies in a country, and the impact of Women's Studies training on women's employment. First, we suggest that the expectations and experiences of Women's Studies training direct Women's Studies graduates into specific employment fields and modes of working. Second, we found that the form and content of Women's Studies training in the different countries affects the ways graduates perform work. Third, we argue that the recognition or visibility of Women's Studies training in relation to employment is important. Fourth, we indicate that Women's Studies training implies new modes of professionalization and professionalism in a wide range of occupations.

Women's Studies programmes became part of university-level education in many European countries in the 1980s. The extent of institutionalization of Women's Studies as an academic subject within European university education, however, varies considerably (see Chapter 3 in this volume). A high degree of institutionalization, however, does not mean that the position of Women's Studies in the academic system is similar to the position of older subjects or disciplines. Women's Studies is a newcomer on the academic scene. The position of Women's Studies training in the countries with a low level of institutionalization of Women's Studies also varies. In

France, Italy and Spain, students have had the chance to do Women's Studies training for decades, while training in Hungary and Slovenia is both scarce and basically a twenty-first-century phenomenon. In the latter two countries, most Women's Studies graduates' experiences of Women's Studies training are mainly from abroad.

The institutionalization of equal opportunities shows similar heterogeneity. In countries with a high level of institutionalization of equal opportunities (Silius 2002: 512), such as Germany, the Netherlands and the UK, there is already a labour market in equal opportunities. In Finland, Italy and Spain this market is quite limited and in France, Hungary and Slovenia this particular field is only slowly emerging.

Women's Studies students predominantly pursue university education in the Humanities and Social Sciences. European university education is heterogeneous in these fields. The Bologna process will probably reduce this heterogeneity in the future. On the European continent, the two-tier BA/MA system has been rare and students often study up to seven years in order to gain the equivalent of a British Master's degree. In countries which have restricted access to university education, for example Finland, it is not unusual to take up to three years after leaving school before one gets accepted into a university. In such countries, university students often have labour market experience before university education. In two-tier systems, labour market experience often falls between the tiers. Additionally, in many countries university students have to work part-time during university education to support themselves. In most cases, however, this work experience is seldom highly qualified. This means that Women's Studies graduates are roughly between twenty-one and thirty years old when they enter the labour market for their first qualified job. Their experiences of working life vary both quantitatively and qualitatively.

The institutionalization of Women's Studies into academia also affects how much and in which ways students can pursue Women's Studies. A modular structure of university education (for example in Finland, the UK and the Netherlands) increases the amount of available courses in Women's Studies. Special programmes – whether generic, as in the UK, or integrated, as in Germany – offer possibilities for specialization in gender issues. If generic courses are offered or the supply of Women's Studies courses in general is high, students are less dependent on particular teachers and supervisors. In countries with a low level of institutionalization of Women's Studies or a limited supply of training, the options and choices available to students are much more connected to individual teachers and temporary circumstances.

In the nine European countries discussed here, university education in

Women's Studies, humanities and the social sciences seldom leads to qualifications for a specific occupation.[2] In some cases, however, students receive specialist training, for example when completing a Master's course in Gender and Health, Ethnicity or Social Work or the French DESS-programme in Social Policy and Gender Relations. This applies to some extent also to PhD training. In most countries and cases in this study, however, Women's Studies graduates have a generalist education. A specialist education, on the one hand, opens possibilities for a career in the field of equal opportunities and gender issues. A generalist education, on the other hand, often lacks explicit labour market orientation. The Humboldtian view of university education, valorizing non-labour market orientation, has been very strong, at least on the European continent, though not in the UK. These features strongly influence expectations towards the labour market as well as the outcomes of university education among Women's Studies graduates (cf. Bianchi et al. 2003). In general, the relation between Women's Studies training, a degree in Humanities or Social Sciences, and the future position in the labour market is much looser than between, for example, legal education and the legal profession. This implies that the university degree, the certificate, often has a more important role than the actual content of the education.

In many countries on the European continent, university education in the Humanities or the Social Sciences leads to jobs that are part of the civil service. In France, Italy and Spain, the civil service includes universities as well as other parts of the educational system. In order to be a university teacher one has to pass state examinations at different levels in addition to the university degree. Becoming a civil servant requires an intellectual investment in order to become eligible, and offers permanent employment. Guaranteed permanency is no longer the case in Finland, Germany or the Netherlands, although many jobs which are relevant for this study, among them university positions, belong to the civil service sector, not least in these countries.

## Research questions and methodology

This chapter examines four questions in connection with Women's Studies training and employment.[3] First, I ask what kind of expectations and experiences current and past Women's Studies students have, and I look into the actual outcomes in the labour market. Second, I explore the professionalization process, especially in connection to the academic profession, equal opportunities and NGOs. Third, I examine in more depth the professionalism of Women's Studies students. How do they perform their work? Fourth, I study the discourses on work and career. How do graduates talk about their jobs? These questions are motivated primarily by the lack of research-based knowledge of the impact of Women's Studies training on students' employment. Also the changes in the European labour market, including the aim of creating a knowledge-based society, open up questions about graduates with Women's Studies training. Are they different from other graduates? Finally, the changes in the European university education system, put forth by the Bologna process, make the impact of Women's Studies training highly relevant since lessons can be drawn from the development of that discipline.

This chapter is based on material from three comparative reports of the EWSI project. They address:

- the relationship between Women's Studies training and women's employment expectations (Bianchi et al. 2003)
- employment outcomes following Women's Studies training (Drglin et al. 2003)
- the professionalization of Women's Studies graduates in Europe (Silius and Tuori 2003)

In addition, national qualitative data reports and survey data are used.[4] The survey data raised some validity issues (see Chapter 8 in this volume). For instance, some questions were misunderstood, perceived or answered quite differently in the nine countries, and there were problems of translation and difficulties with transferring national data into a common resource of data. One of the major problems with the samples was that outside the UK, universities usually do not keep a record of graduates' current addresses: who is or used to be a Women's Studies student is not recorded. It is therefore not possible to know the size or characteristics of the entire population. Because of this, past students were usually approached in one of three ways: (i) by asking for participants on electronic lists or equivalent; (ii) by distributing questionnaires in university settings where students could be reached; and (iii) through snowballing. Current students were reached when taking part in courses. Interviewees were chosen among women who had taken part in the survey, with the aim of creating a group of interviewees representing different groups of Women's Studies students.[5] Because of this method of sampling, it is likely that interested and active Women's Studies students are overrepresented in the interview studies in comparison to a random sample. It is also evident that dropouts are missing. These problems are, however, reduced by the fact that the report writers were exceptionally well informed about the situation in their country thanks to their long experience and deep knowledge of the field (see also Chapter 8 in this volume).

The aim of this chapter is to draw a general picture and to point out similarities and specificities. The chapter uses a comparative method. This implies an additional validity issue. Because it summarizes a huge amount of material, nuances get hidden and complex contexts are simplified. To compress also implies further generalization and the universalizing of multiplicities. As a methodological approach, discourse analysis is used in order to identify the students' ways of talking about employment. The jobs that we discuss were mainly identified on the basis of the survey.

## Expectations and experiences of Women's Studies training

Women's Studies training can be regarded as a professionalization process in which students' expectations and experiences concerning employment develop. The relationship between Women's Studies training and job expectations involves several aspects. First, the different national contexts shape both expectations as well as experiences. Contexts include the labour market situation and how women perceive it. Second, the interaction between expectations and experiences develops and changes over time (Drglin et al. 2003: 6). Whether a respondent is a current student, has recently graduated, or has a long work history makes a difference. The national qualitative reports[6] reveal that the point in your lifecycle at which you enter Women's Studies training is also important. Because few students actually have a very long work history, the results that are presented below mainly refer to Women's Studies graduates with a relatively short working life.

Specific job expectations are rare among Women's Studies graduates in the nine countries (Bianchi et al. 2003: 25). Most students have vague expectations, they study in generalists' programmes, which also have a weak labour market orientation. A past Dutch student summarized the typical way of seeing the relationship between Women's Studies and employment: 'Of course it is vague. Women's Studies doesn't lead anywhere according to people and you will not be able to earn money with it regarding employment perspectives. You start when you are 18 and you do not become a lawyer or physician. You choose for the insecure regarding money and perspective' (van der Sanden 2003: 16).

In countries with Women's Studies specialist programmes (France, Germany and the UK), however, expectations are clearer. Such programmes sometimes offer work placements (France, Germany, Slovenia), something that sharpens job expectations. The general characteristics of the academic labour market for university graduates in the Social Sciences and Humanities are, however, strikingly similar, although for different reasons, in all nine countries: Women's Studies graduates compete for jobs that are open to graduates of any discipline.[7] Of importance is the degree itself (PhD, MA or equivalent), the title, the credentials (Bourdieu and Boltanski 1975). A

higher degree, a broader education, personal development are highly valued: 'I was interested first of all in doing an MA [...] I just wanted to do some
more studying and it seemed logical to go to a higher degree [...] I didn't
want to do something that was just purely a teaching qualification. I wanted
to do something that was slightly different [...] teaching can get very narrow
and I just wanted to broaden my life experiences really' (Griffin 2003a: 30).

Our findings show that Women's Studies training produces significant
changes in the students' subjectivity (see also Chapter 5 in this volume).
Attending Women's Studies training widens students' view of the world,
thus leading women to question taken-for-granted gender hierarchies,
for example (Bianchi et al. 2003: 6). In all countries, Women's Studies is
a specific learning experience, due both to the content and form of the
subject. The negative side of the experience seems to be a pessimistic view
of women's career chances in the labour market and of possibilities of
finding jobs where gender expertise is valued. Bianchi et al. (ibid., p. 61)
therefore conclude that there is a tendency among Women's Studies graduates to play down the impact of Women's Studies on employment. Women's
Studies has a predominantly theoretical orientation in all countries under
scrutiny. This in turn leads to two different outcomes. On the one hand,
students get better theoretical but less practical training than in some other
programmes. On the other hand, students also perceive Women's Studies
as rather abstract knowledge.

The positive effects of the training include the search for self-fulfilment,
a desire to transform one's quality of life, and a need to build and live meaningful relationships in everyday life (ibid., p. 7). These effects contribute to
a strong work orientation among the students: they take participation in
the labour market for granted. This implies that Women's Studies students
seek a specific combination of working and private life. The dream life of
Women's Studies students is as follows: the job recognizes their gender
expertise; the job environment is compatible with this expertise; it offers
sufficient pay to conduct a modern, mobile and culturally rich life; and
it takes fully into account the need for reconciliation of work and family
life. Although this might be the dream, the students in our project were
quite realistic, perhaps because of their pessimistic expectations. Thus, in
practice they water down their ideals. If self-fulfilment through paid jobs
is not possible, they go for voluntary sector jobs, continue their education,
take care of small children or choose a job that is well paid and therefore
offers high-quality non-working-related conditions.

For many students, Women's Studies is a different experience from other
types of academic training. Several factors shape this experience. Among
them one can mention the close connection between the content of the

training and the students' own (earlier) experiences; innovative teaching methods focusing on team-work, learning by doing together – i.e. the collective group experience – and a women-friendly atmosphere; openness towards new modes of thinking, and an unorthodox relation to mainstream education.[8] According to the results of the qualitative studies, the experience of Women's Studies training affects the students' cognitive insights, their way of behaviour and their personal relationships. I use 'experience' in a Scottian way (Scott 1992) to describe a continuously changing process of forming and interpreting what we perceive, feel and know. One example of this process is the narration of experiences through utterances in interviews. Bianchi et al. (2003: 7) show that Women's Studies training is the tool through which a meaningful relation can be established between three different dimensions: the expression of one's subjectivity, the centrality of the gender dimension and self-fulfilment through jobs. They argue that at least for some women looking for future academic jobs (as, for example, the Spanish, the German and the Hungarian reports reveal), self-fulfilment means a freer time schedule, opportunities to travel to conferences and workshops, summer schools, the 'hype' of networking to create new possibilities of self-achievement. In a nutshell, the enjoyable 'eternal student' lifestyle, as opposed to the lifestyle of settled members of the same age groups. Experiences are not only positive: students become frustrated, pessimistic (perhaps even cynical) and have trouble coping with negative reactions to Women's Studies among students from other disciplines as well as among their friends and relatives. In the long run, however, the negative experiences, when overcome on the personal level, can be used in working life, as we shall see in the discussion about professionalism.

### Employment sectors for Women's Studies

The survey and interview studies indicate that past Women's Studies students entered a variety of professions (see Le Feuvre 2002). These included, according to Drglin et al. (2003: 12–13), equality adviser, representative for an association, secretary, project manager, editor, office manager, researcher, social worker, journalist, archivist, policewoman, museum guide, librarian, planning officer of a programme at university, lecturer, midwife, teacher, childcare worker, coordinator, architect, psychologist. In some countries, graduates also had jobs in NGOs. Other students continued their studies, working on their Master's degree or doctorate. Some recent graduates were looking for work, participating in voluntary work, or creating a family.

Past Women's Studies students held a wide range of occupations. For instance, in the Netherlands, looking at the current jobs of past students interviewed, ten women ended up in the public sector, five in the private sector, while the other women are working for an association, a church-institution, as a free-lancer, looking for work, and labour disabled. There are two women who next to their job have their own business [...] Many women are (sometimes next to their paid labour) actively engaged in voluntary work that is related to Women's Studies/emancipation/feminism, for instance editorial work for a feminist magazine or working in a meeting project with foreign women. (van der Sanden 2003: 20)

Half the German interviewees (the other half continued their education) 'work[ed] in various fields. Five respondents [were] active in union-sponsored continuing and adult education, with four offering courses in Women's and Gender Studies. Two graduates [were] doing social work on women's projects. One graduate [was] a commissioner for women's affairs, while for another equality politics [was] one among a number of concerns addressed in her work. Two graduates [were] employed in jobs having no direct relation to Women's or Gender issues' (Schmidbaur et al. 2003: 41).

In Slovenia,

a few of the interviewees [were] employed in fields directly connected to Women's Studies (School of Social Work, Association Against Violent Communication, Women's Counselling Centre, the Peace Institute, Women's Studies Centre at Educational Institute). On the other hand, students taking a master's or doctoral degree in the field of Women's Studies also expected to change jobs: 'When I have finished this [doctorate] I will certainly look for another job. Because this [what I'm doing now] is pure clerical work.' Some of the Slovene postgraduate students interviewed are unemployed. ( Drglin et al. 2003: 39)

Drglin et al. (2003: 18) conclude that 'Women's Studies training influences the kind of work women look for although many of them did not establish a direct relationship between Women's Studies and employment. The reported actual impact of the subject was however higher than the expected impact among the past students. The longer-term impact of Women's Studies training on employment would actually seem to be greater than the students themselves realise.'

Women's Studies graduates predominantly end up in five employment sectors: research and education, equal opportunties, civil society, journalism and information, and the social and health sector.

## Women's Studies training as a professionalization process

The most popular job among past Women's Studies students is the academic profession. I use the term 'profession' for university teachers and researchers. I do not regard these jobs as one single profession, nor do I see these positions as homogeneous. On the contrary, university teachers and researchers often have different interests and, for example, do not necessarily belong to the same unions or professional associations. The academic profession has a long history of male domination and masculine values (ETAN 2000; Husu 2001). In the lower ranks, however, especially in the Humanities and Social Sciences, women form a substantial part of the staff. As civil servants in the majority of the countries in this study, they do not share the characteristics of the liberal professions in these countries. But university teachers and researchers to a large extent create the content of their work, use scientific as well as tacit knowledge, and develop new knowledge. In this sense they are highly professionalized and their expertise can be seen as a very specific professionalism. They do share some characteristics of traditional male-dominated professions. By the creation of new disciplines such as Women's Studies, new borders, hierarchies and specialisms emerge in academia. This process (Silius 2002: 509; Witz 1992) can certainly be regarded as a typical female professional project.

Earlier research on professionalization has been limited because of its dominant Anglo-American context and male-centredness. Many studies in the sociology of the professions started with a view of a profession typical for an Anglo-American context. In other contexts, however, the divide between the professions and other occupations is less clear-cut. The relationship between the professions, the state, the educational system and the market also varies across countries due to different societal contexts. Because of the importance of the context, some scholars today avoid the concept of professionalization (Benoit 1994; Freidson 2001; Evetts 2003). Feminist scholars have revealed the masculine construct of the very idea of profession (Crompton 1987; Silius 1992; Witz 1992; Davies 1996). Others have criticized the ideological implications of traditional theories of professions concerning gender, class and race, for example (Allen 1987). Feminist critiques have mainly focused on two aspects. First, theories of professions have neglected the implications of the former's masculine position. Second, these theories have not been applicable to women-dominated professions. Features which have been considered important for professions such as status, rewards, autonomy, closure, strategies and education, operate differently in women-dominated and men-dominated professions. Thus, the concept of profession and its derivations such as professionalization are multidimensional concepts with different meanings in different societies and contexts.

In addition to the academic profession, I shall discuss the ways Women's Studies graduates have professionalized their expertise in the field of equal opportunities and in civil society. Finally, I shall investigate upward occupational mobility as a specific form of professionalization. It implies the transfer from occupations requiring less education (nurse) to occupations which require high-level university education (university teacher in nursing).

*The academic profession: the most popular career* An obvious result of the project interviews was that one desired trajectory after completing undergraduate studies is to continue with a postgraduate degree. In some of the countries (Spain) the sample consisted predominantly of past and present PhD students, a fact which influences the results. The large proportion of women interested in continuing with Women's Studies in academia and in some cases also outside academia in research institutes, educational centres etc. is due in part to the way students were selected. One can hypothesize that students with research interests who are also more committed to Women's Studies were keener to answer the questionnaire and to show interest in the interview. Thus, past and present students with interests in research and teaching are probably overrepresented. Women also opted for research because Women's Studies offers interesting topics to them. It is, however, apparent that Women's Studies arouses more interest in students for research than there exist possibilities. A Dutch past student explained: 'Women's Studies trains you for scholarship, which is a good thing. You can't lower your standards, but the result is that you want to be a scholar and then it turns out that there is no place' (van der Sanden 2003: 24).

The conditions of academic careers are different in all the countries involved in the project. Centralized university education, rigid disciplinary boundaries and lack of funding limit the size of the academic Women's Studies profession in many countries, whether there exist specific positions in Women's Studies or not. Discrimination occurs (Giacometti 2002). In the establishment phase of Women's Studies institutionalization (cf. Silius 2002: 509) feminist research outside universities plays an important role. In 2004 this is the case in Hungary and Slovenia, for example.

One important division is between countries where Women's Studies is mainly integrated into other disciplines and those where autonomous Women's Studies departments exist. According to the background reports (Griffin, ed. 2002), a high degree of integration (e.g. Germany) tends to imply more jobs than a high degree of autonomy (e.g. Finland). One might argue further that funding systems are of great importance, explaining the amount of positions in Women's Studies in the Netherlands and the UK. Finland, Germany, the Netherlands and the UK have the highest number of jobs in Women's Studies and in these countries the interviewees express concern about the lack of funding for PhD training and the scarcity of university positions. Where opportunities exist, expectations seem to increase. A Hungarian interviewee said that she wanted to stay in her profession as a historian, while a German past student originally aspired to the sciences. 'I always wanted to do something scientific,' she claimed, 'already from a very young age.' She had a great admiration for women professors but found they had to pay an extremely high price. 'The pressures on these women even today are unbelievable,' said the German interviewee (Schmidbaur et al. 2003: 39–40). The quote reveals a discrepancy between aspirations and reality. In addition, it suggests that Women's Studies graduates long for free and independent work, while everyday university life sometimes frightens them. An additional obstacle is that interdisciplinarity, as well as Women's Studies as a field of knowledge, is either a hindrance for academic positions or regarded as a limitation to one's competence, not as an extension of it.

In the UK, Women's Studies exists on all levels of university training. However, there has been a decline in undergraduate courses as well as in MAs and a development of reintegration of Women's Studies into traditional disciplines. The amount of specific Women's Studies jobs declined in the UK during the 1990s, implying that women who wish to establish an academic career have to turn to traditional disciplines. In the UK it used to be possible to obtain a teaching position at university without a PhD degree. This has changed in the last twenty years. This was clearly expressed by UK interviewees who stressed the importance of a PhD for them. The specific character of the French university system poses severe obstacles for Women's Studies scholars wishing to gain university positions. In Finland and Germany, too, the boundaries are high. In Southern Europe new mainstreaming policies have broadened the field of Women's Studies-related university positions in Italy and Spain. In Hungary and Slovenia positions are very scarce.

### Women's Studies offers professionalization of equal opportunities

The differences between the countries on the level, history and type of institutionalization of equal opportunities are quite big (see Chapter 2 in this volume). The countries with a high level of institutionalization also have a long history of equal-opportunities-related work. Hungary, Italy, France and Slovenia belong to countries with a recent development in equal opportunities. Particularly in the Italian and Dutch cases, the professionalization of equal opportunities depends on the political climate. Both countries had, at the time of the study, governments that were not very supportive of equal opportunities. An Italian past student also reflected on the importance of regional differences (important in Germany, Italy and Spain): 'Yes, there are many [job opportunities], but there are differences. For example, I know that Tuscany is much better than Lazio. In part, it also depends on the local traditions [...] In Florence there is a Women's Unit, while in Rome there isn't one [...] Unfortunately, the government plays a role. Until the last government, the Ministry for Equal Opportunities worked, now it's a real mess' (Barazzetti et al. 2003: 32).

In spite of the small numbers of positions, equal opportunities is a growing field, indicated by a French past student who was hired because of her feminist background:

> The [organization] [was] going through a time of change, the person who [had] taken over as Director at the national level [was] a feminist. She [was] trying to push for a more feminist approach at the local level, so there [was] quite a lot of movement going on. It just so happen[ed] that the new director of the branch in [Town] [was] in favour of the feminist orientation. When we first met, she told me that most of the members of her Board – the President, the General Secretary and the Treasurer – were not really in favour of recruiting someone with a feminist background, they would have preferred someone who had previous experience in an employment agency or something like that. But for the Director, it was clear that they needed someone with a Women's Studies background and so that's how I came to get the job. (Le Feuvre and Andriocci 2002b: 64)

In all nine countries, independent of the level of institutionalization, the number of positions in a strictly defined sector of equal opportunities is low. The level of institutionalization is, however, important with regard to the visibility of equal opportunities. The relationship between Women's Studies and the sector of equal opportunities also plays a role in how Women's Studies graduates perceive related job opportunities. In Italy the relationship between Women's Studies and equal opportunities is close (Barazzetti et al. 2002: 207) and there is an increasing interest in gender training for equal opportunities employees. There has also been a rise in equal opportunities measures, and the awareness of equal opportunities as a job possibility was high among Italian interviewees. This was lacking in the other countries. In the Netherlands there are many equal opportunities institutions, but the relationship between Women's Studies and equal opportunities is rather distanced and women are not likely to see equal opportunities as a career option. Two Finnish students had an employment history in equal opportunities, which was by no means representative considering the few positions in the field of equal opportunities. At present the relationship between Women's Studies and equal opportunities is rather distanced in Finland too. In France, several women were working in equal opportunities. This was due to the recent increase of equal opportunities positions, as well as to a bias in the selection of the interviewees. In Slovenia, gaining a position in any state institutions (including the Commission for Equal Opportunities) is difficult and there are very few positions.

In contrast to Italy, in countries with medium or high levels of institutionalization of equal opportunities the employers generally did not require or regard gender expertise as a qualification for jobs in this area. In Finland, Spain and the UK there are no requirements of gender training for equal opportunities employees, i.e. being a woman (or a man, for that matter) can sometimes be considered sufficient. Positions can also be closely linked to political power, which is exemplified by this Spanish past student: 'There's no real equal opportunities. Only on paper [...] Equal opportunities is being used as a political strategy [...] Also there are intrusions in this field because usually the jobs related to gender are political posts where no training is required. I think women's groups should demand that they require specific training for those jobs' (Carrera Suárez and Viñuela Suárez 2003a: 8).

In the UK as well as in Germany, however, training in gender issues was organized for equal opportunities employees. In Italy and Spain, equal opportunities was perceived as something to be enhanced in order to equalize with the more institutionalized countries of the EU. It is likely that this 'reaching the EU level' will also affect Hungary and Slovenia on joining the European Union in 2004. Finland, on the contrary, had a rather opposite stance by claiming to be one of the most 'equal' countries in Europe, even if the results of the EWSI background studies (Griffin, ed. 2002) do not quite support this view. In sum, it is possible that the employment sector in equal opportunities will increase in countries of low levels of institutionalization, while countries with a high level of institutionalization in the worst case scenario might feel that the sector is already fully developed.

In this section of the chapter, equal opportunities has been dealt with in a narrow sense, restricted to government, regional bodies, municipalities and organizational bodies (e.g. universities) that are explicitly working with equal opportunities. Other jobs linked to equal opportunities are, for instance, trade-union-sponsored on-the-job-training that plays an important role in the German case. It is also a field in which many of the politically motivated German graduates were already involved while studying. Equal opportunities can, however, also be regarded as a much wider field. This happened, for instance, in France where many spoke about being involved in equal opportunities, even if their work did not explicitly have to do with it, but the women were able to introduce women's or gender issues at work. Freelancing or self-employment by consulting, monitoring or evaluating equal opportunities measures might be new fields for Women's Studies graduates.

## Gender expertise is of use in civil society

Work in a non-governmental organization (NGO) often means working from a feminist perspective or with issues directly concerning women. It is innovative work where women can use their Women's Studies skills and knowledge. The downside of it is low income, insecure working conditions and often an overload of work. NGOs seem to play the most important role in the two countries with the lowest degree of institutionalization of Women's Studies: Hungary and Slovenia. In Slovenia, Women's Studies is not limited to academia. There were examples of women who first worked as volunteers in an NGO, then wrote an MA thesis on a relevant topic, and later found work in this field. This is, however, a somewhat marginal work trajectory in both countries.

In Hungary some women were associated with an NGO working on violence against women. One Women's Studies graduate working in this field said that she would not have been able to opt for this kind of work without financial support from her parents. On the other hand, it was an inspiring working environment and work that she enjoyed:

> Well, the financial side of it is rather bad. Obviously I needed to have a fam-
> ily who were forbearing enough when I didn't earn anything on this. Thank
> God they are really supportive. I can't say they pour money on me, but I
> could live there for a long time, practically without paying rent or costs [...]
> For years I didn't actually have to spend on bread, literally speaking. Right
> now the salaries are set [...] to reach the absolute minimum to survive [...]
> You usually find extremely creative people [in NGOs], pathfinders, pioneer
> type personalities, because these are new territories, and creative people are
> needed here. It is more or less true to all of us, that we would also be able to
> work in the traditional employment sector, but we wouldn't feel like it, or in
> those jobs we could only use fragments of our skills, talents, which is mostly
> creativity, non-hierarchical thinking [ ... ]. (Juhász 2003: 17–18)

There were examples of current students in Finland working as volunteers in a girls' project connected to a women's help-line, who spoke about
this as possible work in the future if they could get funding. France, too,

provided examples of associations working with action research projects and gender training for staff.

## Professionalization as mobility for specialists

Professionalization can also indicate mobility, i.e. climbing the career ladder or changing jobs. Conditions that influence mobility are country-specific. First of all, the amount of mature students, which in this chapter means women with a work history prior to Women's Studies training, varied greatly among the countries. In the UK, mature students formed a significant proportion of the interviewees. Their type of training was also significantly different. In the UK and in France, there were several women with specialist training (DESS in Gender and Social Policy in France and different MAs in the UK) which leads to a more specific profession. Women who entered Women's Studies training more or less directly after secondary education, obviously did not speak about 'changing career' or 'climbing the career ladder' as a result of the Women's Studies training, because they did not have a previous career. In the UK there were several women who completely changed jobs, were promoted, or entered the labour market after having been at home for many years. One British graduate who was contracted to do research on women and health after her degree said: 'I wouldn't have had access to that [research work] had I not done research [...] in a formal setting with Women's Studies. I think having a Women's Studies degree gives me a good skills mix' (Griffin 2003a: 47). Another past student was headhunted 'because I was the only one with a degree, there were only two of us in the country' (ibid., p. 44). These examples show a direct impact of Women's Studies training which was also part of a deliberate plan when these women decided to study. Furthermore, the British case provides many examples of career advancement (teacher to head of department) as well as movement from insecure to more secure jobs. Among them one can find housewives who returned to or entered the labour market. There are social workers, health workers and teachers who through postgraduate education moved into more qualified jobs such as teachers of health workers, lecturers, etc. Professional mobility also included complete changes of job (distribution manager to head of a college department), promotion within the same field (social work manager to senior social work manager) and acquisition of qualifications that were considered necessary to enter or sustain a career.

## Women's Studies students professionalize themselves in the labour market

A majority of the present students aimed for university positions as teachers or researchers in research institutions. It was obvious that research was the profession *par excellence* for Women's Studies students in this study. Although approximately a quarter of the past students ended up in the academic profession, it is impossible to conclude that this is common in the entire population of Women's Studies students. Both present and past students were, however, aware of the limitations of jobs in academia. They knew how scarce these are, how many are contract-based, insecure, in some cases with low pay and they also foresaw the difficulties of masculine workplace cultures and glass ceilings. Most past students, therefore, combined their idealism with a big portion of realism and pragmatism.

Gender expertise opens the fields of equal opportunities as well as voluntary organizations, NGOs and trade unions for Women's Studies graduates. This field is today quite small, but could in the future offer several new possibilities, for example for self-employment.

For women with a previous work history, postgraduate education in the form of an MA (DESS or equivalent) course or a PhD degree enabled upward mobility. As specialist programmes are likely to increase because of the Bologna process, a wider field of jobs will open in which expert knowledge in gender issues could be used. Finally, it is important to remember that there might be another majority of Women's Studies graduates that never make use of their expertise in their working lives or never finds jobs matching their specific expertise.

### The professionalism of Women's Studies graduates

In this section I shall explore the professionalism of Women's Studies graduates. I examine what women do in their jobs, what they strive for and what means they use to achieve this. The level of analysis is, on the one hand, at an individual level and, on the other hand, at a cross-national level, comparing results from the nine countries. The individual level includes questions such as occupational trajectories and internalized professionalism. Because occupational trajectories have not yet been traced among Women's Studies students (Le Feuvre and Andriocci 2002a), due to the relative novelty of the discipline, I shall deal with their internalized professionalism. The traditional paradigm of the sociology of the professions has been challenged since the 1990s by feminism, postmodernism, the cultural approach and the critique of the grand narratives of structural sociology (Davies 1996; Fourier 1999). The agent-focused approach which is used here is rather new in studies of professions. Because of the nature of the material, I cannot here deal in detail with the institutional or societal contexts in which the Women's Studies graduates operate.

Women's Studies students in all nine countries talked about certain competencies that they acquire through their training. Professionalism in this context refers to the ways in which Women's Studies students see their studies generate a certain knowledge and skills basis which further advances their work-related competencies. One example is how women work in a different manner as a result of their Women's Studies training. I distinguish professionalism from professionalization (Fourier 1999). This is, however, not a clear-cut division. Professionalism as certain knowledge, expertise and skill often results in the professionalization of the individual student. As a collective phenomenon it can also lead to professionalization, implying differentiation of the labour market into new professions, as seen above. Professionalism can also be used in any kind of work. It can refer, for example, to a librarian who works in a different manner as a result of her Women's Studies training.

Women's Studies professionalism denotes the competencies Women's Studies graduates acquire specifically through Women's Studies training, compared to what they might learn in other types of studies. Many competencies can also be acquired, and most certainly are, in other disciplines. However, women with Women's Studies training mention four specificities. First, they gain competencies which are transferable and include critical thinking, analytic abilities, innovative working methods, etc. Second, Women's Studies provides specific gender expertise and analytical tools to work with diversity, power and differences. This particular expertise is directly related to the content of Women's Studies training. Third, Women's Studies offers practical tools concerning working life and workplace cultures. This skill refers to how to act in a different manner in the workplace, for instance, working in solidarity with other women. Finally, women gain self-confidence through Women's Studies, which enhances their employability.

Highlighting professionalism gained through Women's Studies did not seem to be difficult for the students. Many talked about qualifications which are useful in any profession and at any workplace. However, there is also a competence which is specifically related to understanding gender, of use to varying degrees in different types of work. Here professionalism and professionalization overlap so that a certain competence adds to the professionalism of women in certain jobs. This, in turn, reflects the process of professionalization of both Women's Studies students and the field of Women's Studies. This can be seen, for instance, in Hungary where some of the interviewees saw 'gender' as a general perspective that can inform all disciplines and some viewed it as a profession that can be learned. However, in the Hungarian context (as well as the Slovenian), Women's Studies, or 'gender' does not exist as a discipline in its own right. Hence, there is no option other than to use gender knowledge in other disciplines and professions. Such Women's Studies students who actually have the chance (and will) to work in specific professions related to gender also create new professions.

## Transferable skills and the feminist lens

Gaining analytic abilities, being able to 'see things from another perspective' and learning critical thinking were frequently mentioned skills across countries. These are skills that Women's Studies cannot claim as its 'own'. All university education is supposed to, and most probably does, develop these skills. Women who undertake Women's Studies training, however, say that this is something that they have specifically learned through Women's Studies. Reasons for this could be found in the pedagogics used in Women's Studies, its transdisciplinary character as well as in the fact that Women's Studies is a rather new discipline in all countries open to new influences. There is something special about 'analytic abilities' or 'critical thinking' when linked to Women's Studies, that is often related to an enhanced understanding of power and differences (gendered, sexual, racial, etc.). One Finnish student said: 'I think the competence is that Women's Studies really supports one's academic and intellectual development, that one learns analytical–critical thinking and may write more than in many other subjects; yes, and produce and synthesise more. One is encouraged to do rather independent projects, draw conclusions of one's own and make one's own analyses' (Tuori 2003: 39).

One German graduate employed today in municipal politics described the ability to analyse through a feminist perspective as the most important result of her studies applied to her professional life. She said: 'Yes, simply to observe, also to analyse, how things work and then to reflect on the consequences to be drawn from it. Where can you expect change to start? And what will result from those changes, how will they affect the group, its goal or individual goals? So I would say that this skill in particular, to step back, to observe and to analyse, helps a great deal' (Schmidbaur et al. 2003: 54).

## Gender expertise

A unique Women's Studies competence, i.e. gender expertise, was expressed in slightly different ways in the nine countries. Gender expertise overlaps with both critical thinking and working life knowledge. It can be regarded as a synthesis of the knowledge of gender and of analytical abilities to interpret its meanings and ways of operating. Women reflected and acted in a different manner in the workplace, because they had learnt to critically analyse gender, power and differences. However, gender expertise could also address specific knowledge in one's field, for instance, violence against women.

According to our interviewees, gender expertise is needed everywhere, including in teaching at all levels. As one Italian student said:

Any job needs it [gender expertise], I think. Not only for women though, but for everybody. It should start from teaching at junior high school levels upwards. Gender knowledge means questioning roles. This means that you can't work in education, from kindergartens to university, without questioning roles, taking them for granted. The same is true for any other professional context. Be it the tertiary sector or – why not – a factory. Just consider, for example, the importance of a gender perspective when interpreting migration processes in relation to employment. (Barazzetti et al 2003: 31)

There were a significant number of teachers, both at universities and other levels of teaching, among the interviewees. Teachers spoke broadly about the ways in which they are able to use gender expertise in their work. This included both topics that they teach (for instance, studying women writers in literature) and how they related to the pupils/students, trying to deconstruct the gendered stereotypes that play a role in school.

The ability to deconstruct gendered stereotypes was also seen as something that generates competence to deconstruct other (gendered) stereotypes such as race/ethnicity or sexuality. This was particularly evident in the Dutch and Italian contexts, as exemplified by a Dutch past student:

Because of Women's Studies, but also because of my own research, it became very clear how gender is connected to ethnicity, sexuality, class, and age. Maybe this list sounds obligatory, but partly from my research and partly in daily life I found out that it is not possible to say that gender is the most important structuring principle [...] That knowledge gives you tools to position yourself [...] when you know something inside out, you also can make use of it for others [...] And being able to pass on such abstract information in an understandable way is a real merit. (van der Sanden 2003: 34)

## Innovative working life practices

Women's Studies training also develops skills in relation to how working life functions (or does not function) (Rantalaiho and Tuula 1997). There were several narratives on this topic. Women's Studies had taught students not to tolerate sexism or harassment either directed at themselves or at their colleagues. Many women also emphasized working in solidarity with other women, and taking part in anti-discrimination work.

There are, however, very different opportunities to influence workplace culture due to different working conditions. In most of the countries participating in the project, women tend to have temporary contracts which means occupying a rather weak position. Women civil servants in France, Italy and Spain have a better chance to change workplace practices due to their secure position. In Germany, the Netherlands and Finland, too, civil servants have a similar position, with the difference that access is available without separate examinations. For instance, in Finland, job security is currently rare among women civil servants. According to recent statistics, three-quarters of women under the age of thirty-four in the civil service have fixed-term contracts compared to around half of men (Acatiimi 2003: 28). However, some women do get permanent positions. One past student in Spain talked about the ways in which she works in order to have school documents rewritten in a non-sexist manner and to change sexist practices in school. She calls this 'sabotage', and was able to continue with it because she held a permanent position in the school.

Several past students insisted on their ability to raise their colleagues' (and bosses') awareness of gender issues at work. In France this was particularly important in a national context where the media coverage of equal opportunities legislation is poor: 'We had some problems with a Chief editor a few months back, I was working for this big company [...] the young women working there, under 30 years old, were being harassed – sexual and moral harassment – and they were in a real panic, not knowing what to do, too afraid to make a complaint for fear of losing their jobs, blaming themselves for what was happening. I had to wake them up to the reality of it all, to work on them not feeling guilty' (Le Feuvre and Andriocci 2002b: 60).

One important aspect of the workplace culture is teamwork, working in a collaborative manner and in solidarity with other women. One British past student said: 'I think a day doesn't go by when I don't think about some aspects that I learned on the Women's Studies course.' She thought that the training had changed the way she operated at work: '[P]eople can see that the way I work is perhaps a little different to how other practitioners work, it's a very open style, and I think that comes from Women's Studies' (Griffin 2003a: 36). A French current student wanted to be egalitarian in her future workplace: 'You have gender relations wherever you are. Professionally, I don't intend to work in an organisation that is specifically concerned with women's issues, that's not what I'm planning at the moment. But wherever I end up working, I'll always try to construct an egalitarian relationship with the people I work with or for' (Le Feuvre and Andriocci 2002b: 60). This was also the case for a Spanish current student who wanted to support women: 'Because of my personal experience and of the courses I took

I am now more conscious of [the situation of women]. And so I'm more sympathetic to women that go through the same things I do, that have the same problems. And in that sense, if I can help a woman, of course I do it, because it also means helping myself' (Carrera Suárez and Viñuela Suárez 2003a: 31).

In some of the countries women worked in highly feminized fields of employment such as teaching, healthcare (UK), or social work (France, Slovenia). For instance, in Finland, many of the interviewees were working in fields where highly educated women have low-paid jobs with few opportunities for advancement. The following quote is from a Finnish interviewee who works in a library in a teaching institution:

> I try to behave in a way that is in solidarity with women and also in solidarity with low salary employees [...] I see the kind of quite typical, stereotypical womanly picking on others. Personal relations are rather inflamed, as well, and one's own frustration is also taken out on one's colleagues and all that I try consciously to influence and I don't take part in it myself. There is constantly a miserable situation of everybody fighting for the same attention and the same salary, since everybody can't get a rise, and everybody can't get all the benefits but everybody tries to shine before the boss so that those benefits may come [...] I have really tried consciously to avoid underestimating others and instead try to praise others for what they do. And here Women's Studies has had a great impact. This kind of situation is probably more typical in female dominated workplaces, or where women are in positions where they can't climb or develop, where they do more or less typical routine work, which can of course be very frustrating. (Tuori 2003: 21)

*Gender sensitivity as the professionalism of Women's Studies students*
Women's Studies students in all nine countries talked about certain competencies, skills and qualifications that they acquired through Women's Studies training. Among them we identified critical thinking, analysing and synthesizing abilities, innovative working methods, teamwork skills, specific gender and diversity expertise, knowledge of working life and how to influence workplace cultures in a feminist way. The results look quite uniform. There are several reasons for this. First, as pointed out above, many of these skills are common among all university students. ICT and communication skills, organizational and managerial abilities also characterize Women's Studies. Second, Women's Studies is known for its innovative pedagogics, being supportive of criticism, analysis and teamwork. To criticize, analyse and engage in change could be defined as one of the main contributions of Women's Studies to university education. As a com-

paratively new field, teachers in Women's Studies also cooperate extensively internationally, which might streamline training in Women's Studies more than in other academic fields. This learning could be used in curriculum development under the Bologna process. Third, the composition of the interview samples underlines the positive side of Women's Studies training. Fourth, in addition there are students who see Women's Studies as one subject among others, and one which does not differ from the others. It should also be emphasized that not all occupations or workplaces have a demand for Women's Studies expertise. In fact, many interviewees said that they did not reveal their gender expertise in job interviews.

## Discourses of work and career

*The discourse of sheer luck and pure chance* A common feature among the interviewees in generalist programmes is that current students have rather vague ideas about future work and past students often talk about their present jobs as a coincidence, as something unplanned, unexpected, as sheer luck or pure chance. This discourse of sheer luck and pure chance was a dominant one which was found everywhere. For example, a Hungarian art historian said; 'It just happened to be the cool solution that I specialise in it, I mean in gender' (Juhász 2003: 18) and a Slovenian woman was just 'lucky' to find a job (Drglin et al. 2003: 30). A Spanish current student had not even considered the possibility of working in the field of equal opportunities. She was very surprised to get a job in a women's association: 'When I was doing my MA I thought "it'll be impossible to find a job related to this", but then it happened' (Carrera Suárez and Viñuela Suárez 2003a: 27). When asked what she did after completing her studies one German graduate working in a trade union said: 'this legal aid job in an attorney's office, this secretarial thing, it was simply a stop-gap for me. I just wanted to find any kind of job that allowed me to use my education. And it just so happened that this position was free and I applied.' When asked if she had planned to follow this career path, she responded: 'Well, it wasn't actually mapped out, but it was something I wanted, a dream I had [...] And then it just happened more like a coincidence that a job opened up. It was a coincidence that it happened like that.' Only when reminded that she had in fact taken steps that could lead to this result did she admit, 'Yes, OK. So it didn't just fall into my lap. I had to apply and take extra courses to qualify' (Schmidbaur et al. 2003: 47–8).

These examples make it evident that there is tension, if not contradiction, between what is generally thought of as active, self-directed 'career planning' and the 'lack of planning' and 'coincidence' which can be read in the interviews and the actual result of this 'lack of planning and coincidence'.

Many interviewees created the impression of having simply drifted, not knowing where they were going, and also of jumping at opportunities to work in those areas that interest them. Often they themselves were surprised to be in the right place at the right time. Thus, Women's Studies graduates were reluctant to use the word 'career', which they connect negatively with money-making. This also applied to career planning, which was seen as a conscious climbing of a specific career ladder, implying male work practices. On the other hand, all Women's Studies students – in contrast to their mothers in countries such as Italy and Spain, for instance – expected to work. In Finland, interviewees' mothers had been in full-time employment without any longer breaks, and the question of whether to work or not was considered odd, almost unthinkable. In Slovenia employment was also a self-evident and seldom questioned obligation. Some Slovenian interviewees explained this obligation via socialism: 'Look, we grew up during socialism. Even in the old days, my mum used to say: learn, study so you'll have your own money [...] When I came to Ljubljana and looked for a job I simply didn't have the option of not going to work, of someone supporting me' (Drglin et al. 2003: 27–8). All Spanish interviewees said that they always wanted to work in paid employment and took it for granted. They stressed the importance of being economically independent, which was seen as necessary for personal independence.

*The idealistic discourse* In addition to the general discourse of luck and chance, three other discourses operated around the concept of 'career'. Sometimes all three discourses were reflected in the response of one person. One of these was the idealistic discourse. Many students did not consider a career in its masculinist sense, that is involving money, power, climbing a career ladder and a modern, urban, yuppie lifestyle as important. Their own views of a career meant self-fulfilment, gaining space for oneself and political or social influence. This ideological stance seems to point to lifestyle and the way one conducts work. It includes 'important work' – a feminist kind of professionalism – and a new mixture of working life and private life. Sometimes these lifestyles included values such as sustainability, responsibility, solidarity and moderation. Nevertheless, many interviewees spoke in an individualistic manner. An Italian woman with an arts degree said:

> Career is a word that, as such, sounds unpleasant to me. In fact, I would tend to say a career? No way, how sickening. However, if we consider it as growth and development, it certainly becomes very important to me. Rather than a vertical career progression, I would be keener on doing something

that deeply gratifies me. I'm not interested in holding a powerful position. Obviously, I wouldn't like having a boss above me either [...] Yes, a career could be used as a means for other things. Holding a powerful position could be useful in order not to feel humiliated by somebody else, certainly not because in that way I could exercise my power [...] I think it is important to deal with people on an equal footing, in the spirit of working all together to do what there is to do in a cordial way. (Barazzetti et al. 2003: 33)

'If I only wanted to make money, I would have become a solicitor,' said a Dutch current student (van der Sanden 2003: 25). Spanish women who had Women's Studies PhD training were self-confident regarding the labour market and not afraid of the future. They were ready to travel, to try new jobs and to keep on learning. They wanted to do a job that they liked. Money was not a major goal, as long as the salary was enough to make them economically independent (that is, not only 'surviving', but also having money to travel, for leisure, etc.). In this sense, Women's Studies students were also ready to change location and life, they were not afraid of leaving things behind or breaking away from their backgrounds. They were sure that they would always find a chance to start again, and had self-esteem and self-confidence. Self-confidence and the wish to learn new things even if the salary is not too good were expressed by a Spanish past student: 'I want to find a job in which I can learn things [...] If I don't like it I won't stand still. I don't want to resign myself. And if the salary is going to be worse but the quality of the job is better, then that's fine' (Carrera Suárez and Viñuela Suárez 2003a: 25).

Most interviewees talked about career in terms of personal development or intellectual challenges, or of what is 'fun'. In this sense career was rather important for them. 'A career for me is a job in which I feel good, and where I have the idea that I am doing something important or that I approve of,' said a Dutch current student (van der Sanden 2003: 25). A Finnish PhD student explained: 'I probably wouldn't do this work if it was only work. I would probably try to find something much better paid, with more fringe benefits than now. So that this research [...] I don't necessarily always even consider it to be work, it is already becoming more of a life-style. So for me work and hobbies merge to quite a large extent' (Tuori 2003: 23–4).

The findings reflect a type of discourse which is idealistic in two ways. First, current students tend to be optimistic about their future and to view their future working life in idealistic ways. They wish to have important work, authority, influence and a pleasant life. Second, past students tend to be more pragmatic. They already know that they have or are likely to have jobs without specific career tracks and that their pay is not going to be very high. Nevertheless, they want to perform their work in a ideal, feminist way, to have a 'different' career, and to mix work with feminist engagement.

*The realistic discourse*  Another particular discourse on career that emerged was grounded in the interviewees' own knowledge and experiences: the realistic discourse. By choosing Women's Studies they opted for possibilities other than money-making and masculine careers. They were aware of the lack of career ladders in most female jobs (see also Nauta and Heesink 1992). Women's Studies graduates, who had already experienced the labour market, have identified its gendered patterns (Hakim 1994; Britton 2000). Some current students, too, were very aware of segregation, discrimination, low pay, bad working conditions, glass ceilings and non-women-friendly working life practices. The Slovenian case is an exception because few of the interviewees linked employment problems to segregation or discrimination. 'It is difficult to get a job, but this is not related to gender,' thought one Slovenian interviewee (Drglin et al. 2003: 31). 'Yes, [employment] worries me, but not because I'm a woman, because I'm a historian,' said another one (ibid.). In general, however, both current and past students were realistic.

Past students in Finland, and particularly those with children, were likely to reflect on working life critically. To invest in a career or work meant that one might have to give up other things in life. Women struggle with the realities of working life, combining work and children, and personal choices around these two. One Finnish past student worked for a long time in the public sector (social work, municipality administration), but then took care of her children for a couple of years:

> When one has children and a husband one notices that one can't just go out to get a job like men do. [...] I think this understanding includes knowing that I'm a woman [...] and in comparison with men [...] the fact that I know my salary at least statistically, that my chances on the labour market at least statistically are going to be worse and that statistically I'm going to work more at home than my husband, and all that. In that sense my view of women's life is perhaps a bit negative [...] It would be fun, of course, [to make a career] but in order to make a career I think one has to be quite ambitious and purposeful, and I have difficulties choosing this and leaving out that [...] I know, of course, at this time in my life that one has to pay quite a lot in order to acquire a good job. (Tuori 2003: 22)

*The career-oriented discourse*  A third specific discourse emerged of 'a career', meaning a conscious career or work orientation. This discourse im-

plies having ambitions for interesting, challenging, desirable work including self-fulfilment and influence, but in a more conscious and deliberate
way. The career-oriented discourse was found among women in specialist
education and among students who have used their social capital to find a
rewarding job (Bourdieu and Passeron 1977; Bourdieu 1984a, 1984b, 1989).
Such women were willing to invest time and energy in their work if it was
inspiring (research, media, caring, voluntary sector). Put in this way, most
of the interviewees could be said to have been quite career-oriented. One
of the women who was ambitious and ready to put a lot of effort into her
future career was an English current student: 'I am really, really determined.
I'm going to publish the PhD [...] I've got a book coming out in October
and I will continue to produce with this friend these sorts of textbooks and
I'm going to [be] a professor' (Griffin 2003a: 47).

Some interviewees considered having a career as an important political
tool to remove obstacles that women find at work, as this young Italian past
student pointed out: '[A career] is very important, for other people and for
myself. Not to become a model, for goodness' sake, no, I wouldn't dare.
However, it would be useful to open up a new avenue. To expose yourself.
To show that you can get to a certain point, break the glass ceiling, move
on' (Barazzetti et al. 2003: 33).

Some pointed to their social capital: the use of Women's Studies networks in connection to work (Kanter 1977). Often Women's Studies courses
produce results in this area. For Spanish academics or researchers, although
they do not seem aware of it, Women's Studies tended to be a channel for
obtaining research grants for funded projects and offering more opportunities to present papers at conferences or seminars or to publish books, as
well as stronger support from supervisors. Italian interviewees did not think
that an education in Women's Studies was much appreciated in the labour
market. However, at the same time, they used the networks of relationships
they had built up during their studies to create or strengthen their chances
to access an academic career. When they found jobs in associations or
other agencies outside the university, it was due to the contacts they had
made during their studies. In these instances, the interviewees seemed
to be unaware of the potentials of the Women's Studies course they had
attended (and which, in fact, helped them). Some interviewees did not think
that the knowledge acquired in Women's Studies could be applied in their
job, although they thought that these studies had bolstered their self-esteem
and enhanced their self-awareness.

In short, the findings document that a key factor connecting Women's
Studies with employment is the set of networks of relationships that these
studies facilitate. Italian respondents acknowledged the value of these net-

works only after having access to the labour market. In particular, according to a number of women, the ways of structuring courses in Women's Studies made it possible to build networks of relationships and exchange among students and trainers alike. Some interviewees, for example, created associations or cooperatives where they still work today thanks to these networks. An Italian past student explained how such contacts work:

> I work in training. All these courses gave me some useful ideas and more self-confidence. Through them, I met [important people], so it also worked at a relationship-building level. I ascribe my eagerness to be involved in a field like training to women's experience and especially to the experience of the collective. This resulted in collaboration with other fellow trainees [...] The last course we organised stemmed precisely from this experience. I was able to 'use' the network that was created during the NOISE[9] course. (Barazzetti et al. 2003: 29)

Feeling networked at a European level represented an important reference point for these women's identity and therefore strengthened their intellectual confidence. This was what happened, for example, to an Italian current student who was collaborating with a university department: 'I have a reference within the department and that is the Women's Studies centre. However, I see it within a wider perspective, I see the Women's Studies centre as part of a network comprising other situations, other Women's Studies in Italy and above all in Europe. I also see it as the opportunity to follow European research activities' (ibid.).

*Ambivalent discourses on career options of Women's Studies students* The foregoing section covered four discourses on work and career among Women's Studies students. Current and past students in programmes with a generalist orientation have ambitions but feel ambiguous about career patterns and working life practices associated with traditional masculinity: making money, climbing career ladders, or being boss does not interest them. Instead they envision a career characterized by self-fulfilment, pleasure and influence. The interviewees expressed their career ambitions in two ways: partly their present job was seen as the outcome of sheer luck or pure chance, and partly they expressed their work expectations in idealistic and realistic terms. The reasons for this might be found in their gendered socialization in school and at university, in the students' knowledge and experience of labour market structures and in working-life culture. Their own cultural values, such as economic independence, challenging work, an interesting life, partnership, friends, children and individualism, influenced the ways in which they spoke about their careers. Some interviewees were consciously career-oriented. They came mainly from specialist programmes and were among past students who worked in independent, interesting and influential jobs, which they got through female-based social networks. Women's Studies facilitates networking, of the importance of which many students remained unaware.

## Conclusion

In this chapter I have shown that Women's Studies significantly moulds its students' expectations and experiences concerning employment. Many students expect working life to be patriarchal and to meet greater difficulties than men. Thus, they play down the impact of Women's Studies on employment. Women's Studies is, however, a unique learning experience due to its content referring to the students' own experiences, and to its form, emphasizing innovative teaching methods, a woman/student-friendly atmosphere, and academic unorthodoxy. This experience does make the students different: they are better equipped for a changing and challenging labour market than many others. Women's Studies students, however, tend not to realize this general difference immediately. One reason for this may be the invisibility of Women's Studies in most countries. Only in Germany and the UK do universities offer named degrees in Women's Studies. In the Netherlands, one can have a degree with a specialization in Women's Studies, which is also written on the certificate. Universities remain unwilling to integrate Women's Studies fully in their provision and to market their own graduates for a labour market embracing new types of knowledge and training.

The specific mix of expectations and experiences Women's Studies students have leads to employment sectors like research and education; equal opportunities and gender mainstreaming; civil society; and the media. The health sector and social work are also important fields.

Women's Studies students gain professionalism through their training. They also learn how to professionalize their expertise. Some Women's Studies students work in jobs directly connected to gender expertise. These students participate in the professionalization of gender as a specific niche in the labour market. More frequently, however, Women's Studies students develop a wide range of jobs by introducing gender-sensitive ways of working. They use their Women's Studies skills, expertise and knowledge for new occupational choices and upward mobility. In the same way, and together with the other students, they exploit their professionalism for change and innovation. Women's Studies students work in the academic profession, in Women's Studies as well as in traditional disciplines. Equal opportunities jobs are an expanding field where gender expertise is necessary. This expertise is also asked for in many NGOs. Finally, MA programmes offering specialist training lead to career changes.

Women's Studies students use four different discourses when they talk about work and career. The most reported among these was the discourse of sheer luck and pure chance. Similar results have been found in studies on female jurists (Silius 1992: 152–64) and among male physicians specializing in pathology (Riska 2003). Few continental European universities offer professional career guidance that would make women aware of career options. According to the previous studies, the discourse of luck or chance seems to be connected to low-status jobs, invisibility or unawareness of gender, lack of peer networks and of mentor systems. Quite common was also the idealistic discourse. This is part of European university culture, which is reinforced by feminist ideals. The realistic discourse, for its part, can be understood as a mixture of feminist idealism and feminist knowledge. When utopia and reality collide, realism is an insightful and pragmatic choice. Not all Women's Studies students talk of a utopian future in terms of luck or chance. On the contrary, they express ambitions, are career-oriented and seek an important change in their life. The results show that students continuously negotiate between different discourses on how to relate to work, career and feminism.

In sum, Women's Studies training has a greater impact on employment than its students, the universities or the employers tend to realize. This finding needs to be disseminated much more effectively and much more widely by institutions, staff and students so that employers recognize the potential of the discipline for their employment sector.

## Notes

1 In this chapter, 'graduate' means a Women's Studies student with a university degree, usually at MA or PhD level. In most cases, Women's Studies cannot, or could not in the past, award its own degrees (see Chapter 3 in this volume). This implies that the amount of Women's Studies training that the graduates have received during their university education varies considerably.

2 This is not unusual for Humanities and Social Sciences students (see Griffin 2003b).

3 I am most indebted to Salla Tuori for her valuable help with this chapter.

4 See the Introduction of this volume for more details.

5 The interviews (of 60–100 minutes of length on average) were transcribed and analysed by each partner and were compiled together with survey data in national reports. The national qualitative reports were used as the basis for the thematic comparative reports. The quotations from the interviews are marked with country codes that refer to reports written by each partner. Thus, the codes are not identification numbers of the interviewees but refer to a page in the

qualitative data reports. The qualitative data reports contain the identification of the interviewees. The codes are the following: UK: Griffin 2003a; Finland: Tuori 2003; Netherlands: van der Sanden with Waaldijk 2003; Slovenia: Drglin et al. 2003; Hungary: Juhász 2003; France: Le Feuvre and Andriocci 2002b; Germany: Schmidbaur et al. 2003; Italy: Barazzetti et al. 2003; Spain: Carrera Suárez and Viñuela Suárez 2003a.

6  These will be published separately in autumn 2004 by the Ulrike Helmer Verlag, Frankfurt/Main.

7  It is commonly assumed that this is specific only to the British case (Bianchi et al. 2003: 16). Many Women's Studies graduates, however, have taken Women's Studies training as part of their degree in Social Sciences or Humanities. This means that they can be compared to graduates of Sociology, Literature, Philosophy, etc.

8  On the development of Women's Studies as an academic subject, its relation to the women's movement and to feminist research, see e.g. Griffin and Hanmer (2002: 16–43).

9  NOISE is an Advanced European Summer School in Women's Studies organized by the University of Utrecht together with sixteen partner universities.

# 5 | The impact of Women's Studies on its students' relationships and everyday practices

GABRIELE GRIFFIN AND JALNA HANMER

Women's Studies as a discipline has, since its inception, been viewed as a transformative project which imparts not only knowledge and learning but which, equally significantly, affects all areas of the lives of those who participate in it (see, for instance, Hull et al. 1982; Bowles and Klein 1983; Aaron and Walby, eds 1991; Griffin et al. 1994; Griffin, ed. 1994). This perception was borne out by the research we carried out between 2001 and 2003 among Women's Studies students.[1] As one Italian student put it: 'When you introduce gender in your studies, you tend to introduce it into all aspects of your life' (Barazzetti et al. 2003: 27). This chapter will explore the impact of Women's Studies training on women's relationships and everyday life practices as they emerged from the data we collected in that project. Our focus will be on the impact of Women's Studies on students' lives in the social and domestic realms of women's relationships with family, friends and partners.

## Accessing Women's Studies training

In order to understand the impact of Women's Studies training on women's relationships and everyday practices, we present our findings on why women take Women's Studies and how they access the subject. Students' motivation for taking Women's Studies relates to the impact the subject has on their lives. Women's choice of Women's Studies training in every country (see Chapter 3 in this volume for more details) is in part determined by two factors: (i) the visibility and prominence of the discipline within the country's education system; and (ii) the country's specific history of feminism and feminist activism. The visibility and prominence of the subject are influenced by its degree of institutionalization.[2] Women's Studies training is at different levels of institutionalization in the nine European partner countries that participated in the study (see Chapter 3 in this volume). For undergraduate and MA courses we can distinguish three different patterns which influence both the visibility of the discipline and the reasons why women enter Women's Studies courses.

1. Women's Studies located exclusively within traditional disciplines: Hungary (from 1990s); Finland (from 1970s); Slovenia (from 1990s)

2. Women's Studies located predominantly within traditional disciplines: Germany (from the 1970s); France (from the 1970s); Spain (from 1990s)

3. Women's Studies offered as free-standing, named degree routes (as well as within traditional disciplines): UK (from the 1980s); Italy (from the late 1990s); Netherlands (from the 1980s)

In addition, with the exception of Hungary, all project partner countries have Women's Studies research centres and the majority offer PhDs in the discipline, though not in every university.

One implication of the limited institutionalization of Women's Studies outside traditional disciplines is that – especially at undergraduate level where the vast majority of Women's Studies students in all European countries encounter Women's Studies in some form (see Table 3.4), and usually as a module in a traditional Social Sciences or Humanities discipline such as Sociology or Literature – students enter Women's Studies by *chance* rather than by design. Choice, based on knowledge of the availability of the subject, is limited primarily to postgraduates. Family and personal histories also influence the decision. The four main reasons why women took Women's Studies courses were:

1. chance (especially undergraduates)
2. choice (mostly postgraduates)
3. political/activist histories by parents and/or self
4. personal histories

These four reasons are not mutually exclusive, but they did shape the issue of the impact of Women's Studies training differentially, as discussed below.

*Accessing Women's Studies by chance* The implications of the patterns of institutionalization of Women's Studies are that undergraduates in particular, especially in Hungary, Slovenia, France and Spain, are likely to encounter Women's Studies by chance once they are at university rather than through proactively seeking out the discipline (see Table 3.5). One Italian student described the process of entering Women's Studies in a way that was fairly typical for students in countries where the subject has low visibility: 'At first my interest was limited to some readings, or to going to some meetings. Then ... I started attending some study groups. After that, I started thinking about doing a PhD course in Women's Studies. At that point, my own informal experience was joined by a recognized, more academic one: a PhD in women's history in Naples' (Barazzetti et al. 2003: 14).

Students who find Women's Studies by chance do not necessarily come to the subject with specific, fully conscious agendas. Instead, they are often on a journey of discovery and articulate it as such. As one British interviewee explained: 'A friend gave me a ring and said, "There is a course that is just made for you." I think she knew my feminist leanings, but I had no voice for them, I couldn't articulate feminism in any way at that time' (Griffin 2003a: 18). The impact of the subject on these 'unsuspecting' students' lives can thus be huge and, as will be shown below, students reported major impacts on their socio-emotional lifestyles and practices.

*Accessing Women's Studies by choice* Women's Studies as a discipline is more readily available and and named specifically at postgraduate rather than at undergraduate level. With greater visibility women are more likely to make a proactive choice for Women's Studies at postgraduate level and, in so doing, our interviewees tended to compare previous educational experiences with their experience of Women's Studies. A Finnish student said:

> At the time when [the Women's Studies department] didn't exist yet, it was absolutely horrible there in the [home] department. One was more or less labelled as being crazy or as a nutcase or otherwise a very strange person, so I remember what a wonderful feeling it was when I went to the [Women's Studies] department for postgraduate studies ... I remember that we talked – there was a whole bunch of students who went to that seminar – we talked about how wonderful it was that we didn't have to go to the [home] department. Somehow it just caused such a feeling of relief. (Tuori 2003: 17–18)

The choice of Women's Studies was frequently described in relation to two factors: the discrimination women felt they had experienced in other subjects because they were perceived to be feminists, and the desire to gain a better understanding of one's life: 'What concerned me above all was the desire to deepen my knowledge and attitudes in order to better answer my own questions' (Schmidbaur et al. 2003: 16).

*Accessing Women's Studies as a consequence of a history of activism* The commitment of PhD students to the subject and its concerns was the result of a variety of factors, in particular a prior history of activism, having encountered modules at undergraduate level, or particular personal or educational histories.

Involvement in feminist activism prior to Women's Studies training was particularly noticeable among the German and Italian interviewees and included parental activism: 'My mother used to attend feminist collectives, she was an activist. First of all, I'd like to say that I am a child of the 1968 movements. My parents were both activists. Politics have always been our

143

daily bread at home. When I was little, she [my mother] would take me with her to the feminist collective meetings. As for my father, anything political suited him, he thinks politics is essential in life' (Barazzetti et al. 2003: 41). Prior personal political experience could be a decisive factor. A Spanish interviewee recalled: 'I approached feminism from the groups, and through the street, and then I got into theory' (Carrera Suárez and Viñuela Suárez 2003a: 17). And a German student said: 'In the beginning I wanted to find out what was behind all the slogans, be it feminism or the development of the women's movement. I wanted to learn what it was, and of course to find out about the various concepts like quotas, gender mainstreaming, etc. And yes, simply to develop a theoretical background for my conviction that gender roles have to change' (Schmidbaur et al. 2003: 15). Some women had activist experiences in feminist or women's voluntary organizations prior to taking up Women's Studies. In Hungary the voluntary organization NANE, an NGO dealing with violence against women, provides Women's Studies training in return for help in the NGO.

In all of these instances, women looked to Women's Studies to provide them with a theoretical framework for their convictions and experiences, to cement their knowledge of women's issues, and to confirm their viewpoints and experiences. As one Hungarian woman said: 'you can't make feminism without activism ... activism is the central element of feminism. Throbbing life, putting theory into practice is its natural element. After all, it pushes the envelope of real social problems besides pushing the envelope of real scientific problems ... they have to be connected' (Juhász 2003: 32).

*Accessing Women's Studies as a response to particular life experiences* To explain why Women's Studies has such a major impact on the lives of many students includes, *inter alia*, examining cultural factors that restricted women before coming to Women's Studies. Some women came to the discipline because it resonated with their life experiences, usually negative ones of social exclusion. These went far back in the women's family, child-hood and educational histories. One British interviewee stated: 'My father was very much of the opinion that you married well ... you got access to marrying through your vocation which would be a secretary, air hostess or in the nursing profession where you would hopefully meet a doctor, settle down and he would take care of you. That was my father's attitude' (Griffin 2003a: 24). Such gender stereotyped views of girls' life trajectory were not at all uncommon. Secondary school education, too, frequently offered limited horizons for many girls (see also Acker and Piper, eds 1984; Skelton 1993). Another British interviewee, whose narratives were inflected by the racism that was interlaced with the sexism she experienced, said: 'As under-achievers when we left school – and we left without O levels and what have you ... of course ... girls went into secretarial or nursing or offices ... you weren't exactly fired up about it, but it was a choice of either nursing, secretarial, or in the office, so ... ' (Griffin 2003a: 24). Almost all the Women's Studies students interviewed experienced some kind of discrimination in the expectations that the education system expressed in relation to their future careers. From the accounts in the interviews, it would appear that the careers advice given to young women throughout the course of their secondary school education imposed even more limited horizons on their future than did their own parents (Le Feuvre and Andriocci 2002b: 22).

Social and family cultures could adversely affect both women from ethnic minorities and from the dominant population groups. One French Arab student said:

At primary school, I was really one of the better pupils, very bright, but by the time I went to secondary school, I was totally off balance. I was much younger than most of my classmates and my experiences at home were totally different from theirs. I come from a very traditional Arab, Muslim family. Here in France, you usually expect a girl to have more and more freedom as she gets older. In my family, it was the opposite, the older you got, the less freedom you had. So, from my first year at secondary school, from the time I had my first period, in fact, I took the full brunt of a culture that completely restrained, suffocated me and I had to deal with all that. (Le Feuvre and Andriocci 2002b: 20)

A woman from the Italian majority culture said:

In my life, I have always come across the fact that being a female was something less than being a male. I never wished to be a male though. However, I still have a series of memories: 'You can't do this, because you're a female'. 'No, not you, you're a female'. So, probably, I internalised these things and then, at some point, when I was able to do it, I got my own back. (Barazzetti et al. 2003: 41)

Taking Women's Studies could thus be a critical reaction – in every sense of that phrase – to one's family background. Inequalities in parental relationships, for instance, could lead to a consciousness and interest in Women's Studies. Interviewees described gender discrimination and behaviour in previous generations, both between parents and between grandparents, as well as in their own relationships.

My great grandma, the thing I remember most about her was great granddad coming in and whether he'd been in the garden or what, she knelt on

145

the floor and took his shoes off for him ... my granddad sat in the chair and
my grandma brought him a cup of tea and he shouted to her, 'Mavis come
and stir my tea' ... all I remember was her scuttling about, she was always in
a hurry, always doing. I can't ever remember seeing her sat down. (Griffin
2003a: 60)

The dialogic relation between personal experiences and Women's
Studies also meant that students would review previous experiences in
the light of their new learning. As one Finnish student put it:

I had a boyfriend, my family and my parents and so on – I started to see them
as if they had been living in another world. They were there and I analysed
them and saw that the more I studied, the farther I got from them, and I went
very far, or rather, I went as a rocket from where I had been. The place where
I was, and I saw at once, after about a month, I could look back and see that I
would never be able to go back. So this was a bit difficult, of course, and one
wasn't able to explain then why one was doing this, so that was a bit difficult
for others and for me, too. Things became very pre-emptory. So did I, I became very determined. And was called cold, I was cold then, oh Jesus, and
that was only a good thing, a positive thing. But then again, it caused a lot of
suffering. In spite of that, though, my own reaction was 'Yes!' (Tuori 2003: 48)

Where students' life experiences other than immediate relationships
were concerned, an interest in Women's Studies could be promoted by
issues such as a changing sense of sexual identity,[3] or personal histories
of violence and abuse. One Hungarian student, for example, said: 'There
is another thread in my life, a personal thread. It is not individual only,
but communal, but it started like a personal thing. Which made me more
susceptible to feminist thinking. I got close to lesbian organizations ... It
is quite evident, I think, that a critique of gender roles follows from this
type of identity' (Juhász 2003: 27). And a Spanish student explained her
experiences on a Women's Studies course in the Netherlands as follows:
'I was ill with anorexia and bulimia and I learnt a lot from [my lecturer]
... It helped me a lot. I started to talk, to get out of it and to understand
things ... my relationship with my father, with my mother ... It opened
my eyes ... thanks to [Women's Studies] I began to understand everything
... It saved me. So imagine the value it had for me!' (Carrera Suárez and
Viñuela Suárez 2003a: 37, 42). The same was true of a French interviewee
who described the following experience:

I think that I'll keep that image for the whole of my life. At the Library of the
Women's Studies Centre, it was huge, the Library, and when I saw that there
were seven long shelves of books on child abuse, on violence and sexual

abuse, it was like a revelation, at last there was recognition, those things exist, they were made public, it wasn't just about me as a person, because I was an unbearable little girl, and that's what happens to unbearable children, no. (Le Feuvre and Andriocci 2003a: 32)

Another woman from Britain who worked in housing talked about attending a course on domestic violence. An overhead was put on: 'it said what domestic violence was and as I'm reading it I could feel, "but that's me" and I never realised ... to think that you know I'd allowed that to happen for all those years' (Griffin 2003a: 61). This experience led her to higher education and to Women's Studies.

As the comments above indicate, many students (see also Griffin, ed. 1994) come to Women's Studies because its content reflects their personal concerns and experiences. Furthermore, they then find that Women's Studies enables them to develop a meta-discourse about their experiences which helps them to confront these experiences and, in time, to transcend and move beyond them.

### The impact of Women's Studies on its students' personal lives

One of the interesting findings of our project was that Women's Studies students systematically underestimated the impact Women's Studies would have on their personal lives. When we asked students about whether or not they had expected the subject to have an impact on their personal lives and if it actually had had an impact, we found a significant gap between their expectations and their assessment of the outcome (see Table 5.1).[4]

Expectations of an impact varied across countries from a low of 22 per cent for past and 33 per cent for current students in Hungary and a high of 73 per cent for German past students and 86 per cent for Netherlands current students. The actual impact was lowest for Hungary with 46 per cent for past and 48 per cent for current students, and highest in the Netherlands with 90 per cent for both past and current students. A possible explanation for these findings is that these two countries are marked by very different tolerance levels towards feminism and diversity. The greater intolerance in Hungary may have led many Hungarian interviewees to play down their feminist convictions, while the greater receptiveness towards feminism in the Netherlands allowed Dutch students to experience the impact of the subject much more openly.

Table 5.1 demonstrates how unexpected the subject's impact could be for both past and current students. The expectation that Women's Studies would have an impact on their personal lives was significantly less than actually occurred for both past and current students. This parallels the

147

TABLE 5.1 Expected and actual impact of Women's Studies training on the personal life of past and current students (%)

| Country | Past students | | | Current students | | |
|---|---|---|---|---|---|---|
| | Expected | Actual | Differ-ential | Expected | Actual | Differ-ential |
| Finland | 54 | 77 | 23 | 85 | 94 | 9 |
| France | 45 | 74 | 29 | 39 | 70 | 31 |
| Germany | 73 | 87 | 14 | 82 | 85 | 3 |
| Hungary | 22 | 46 | 24 | 33 | 48 | 15 |
| Italy | 66 | 78 | 12 | 66 | 74 | 8 |
| Netherlands | 66 | 90 | 24 | 86 | 90 | 4 |
| Slovenia | 48 | 76 | 28 | 66 | 77 | 11 |
| Spain | 44 | 76 | 32 | 54 | 59 | 5 |
| UK | 40 | 81 | 41 | 57 | 76 | 19 |

*Source*: Quantitative data reports, EWSI project, 2003

findings for Table 5.6 on family life where, as with Table 5.1, expectation was always lower than experienced change, particularly for past students. The expectation that Women's Studies would have an impact on their personal lives was greater for current than for past students in all countries. The differentials between expected and actual impact of Women's Studies on the personal lives of students was particularly marked for past students and reveals the extent to which students were unprepared for that change. Overall, these differentials varied between countries from a low of 3 per cent among current students in Germany to a high of 41 per cent among past students from the UK. In general, past students experienced a greater difference between expectations and actual impact than current students. Only in France did the difference between expectations and actual impact experienced by current students reach that of past students. The greater discrepancy between expected and actual impact among past students may be a function of the fact that many past students knew little about the subject before they entered it and could therefore not anticipate its potential impact to its full extent, while current students may be more aware of the subject's potential impact. Also, current students have had less time to experience any actual changes to their lives than past students. We shall discuss some of the specificities of these findings below.

## Women's Studies as an identity project

As the narratives under the sections of access indicate, the impact of Women's Studies could be deeply personal, and affect self-identity. As one interviewee said: '[Women's Studies] helped me to open my eyes and now I don't want to close them' (Carrera Suárez and Viñuela Suárez 2003a: 38). 'Of course it influenced me personally. Suddenly you see another world and you realise that I'd never stopped to think about this and it's there and it influences me everyday' (ibid.). Women's Studies was described as a 'turning point' in students' lives (Schmidbaur et al. 2003: 58), that 'led to greater thoughtfulness about a lot of things' and the opening up of other perspectives (ibid., p. 63). It did this by facilitating, systematizing and analysing experiences and values. The end result could be changes in subjectivity and identity. 'As far as I'm concerned, [Women's Studies] helped me with regard to my subjectivity and my identity' (Barazzetti et al. 2003: 26).

This change could be unexpected. 'I underwent something of an identity crisis' (Drglin et al. 2003: 56). Such crises often resulted in changed perceptions and behaviour.

> Thinking about female narcissism set a lot in motion ... So I don't shave my legs anymore despite the excessive hair that many people notice ... I learned in my studies that there are different types of women and that different kinds of women have emancipated themselves and that they looked very different from the majority ... It was all the same to them what men thought. And that changed me, simply the knowledge that, as they say, you really can escape the role. (Schmidbaur et al. 2003: 65)

Escaping the feminine role meant overcoming attitudes such as, 'My husband would say more and more often, "You wanted the kids too and it was clear that I'd be the one to go to work. You can go to work too once you've taken care of everything at home"' (ibid.).

One aspect of identity is sexual orientation. Among our questionnaire respondents the vast majority of women, indeed proportionately more than one would conventionally expect, declared themselves heterosexual (Table 5.2).[5]

Table 5.2 reflects both sample bias and cultural constraints on the free expression of sexual identity. Respondents were much more likely to declare themselves to be lesbian or bisexual in countries that are tolerant of sexual diversity, such as the Netherlands and Germany, than in countries where homophobia is more overt and lesbianism a taboo, such as in Hungary or Slovenia. Nevertheless, during the follow-up interviews a number of women commented on the ways in which, regardless of their own sexual orientation, Women's Studies could alter their understanding of sexual identity. For example, one woman learnt that she could move outside the categories of heterosexual and lesbian and this made it easier to engage in relationships with both men and women (van der Sanden with Waaldijk

TABLE 5.2 Sexual identity of past and current Women's Studies students (%)

| Country | Lesbian* | | Heterosexual | | Bisexual | |
|---|---|---|---|---|---|---|
| | Past | Current | Past | Current | Past | Current |
| Finland | 8 | 6 | 83 | 88 | 9 | 6 |
| France | 10 | 7 | 86 | 80 | 4 | 13 |
| Germany | 19 | 15 | 73 | 75 | 8 | 8 |
| Hungary | 2 | 0 | 94 | 98 | 4 | 2 |
| Italy | 7 | 4 | 84 | 86 | 9 | 6 |
| Netherlands | 16 | 4 | 74 | 75 | 10 | 21 |
| Slovenia | 0 | 0 | 96 | 92 | 4 | 8 |
| Spain | 2 | 0 | 93 | 98 | 5 | 1 |
| UK | 4 | 6 | 88 | 86 | 8 | 6 |

*Note*: * Figures do not add up to 100 per cent in all cases as a very small number of respondents chose other categories such as 'polymorphously perverse'.

*Source*: Quantitative data reports, EWSI project, 2003

2003: 34). During their Women's Studies course some women came out as lesbian or had their first lesbian experiences. One woman said she gained the 'insight that the categories of lesbian and heterosexual have trivial boundaries [which] opened up the possibility to be a bisexual woman', while understanding that the categories of men and women are not fixed identities made another woman feel more confident in her way of being a woman, which she felt was a bit 'masculine' (ibid., p. 35).

In the questionnaires we asked whether or not taking Women's Studies had impacted on the respondents' sexual identity (see Table 5.3). The impact figures were surprisingly high, with the percentage of women reporting a transformation of their sexual identity varying among current students from 14 per cent in Italy to 44 per cent in France and among past students between 12 per cent in Slovenia and 31 per cent in Finland. The precise meaning of these results is not clear since most current and past students described themselves as heterosexual.

TABLE 5.3 Transformation in sexual identity among current and past Women's Studies students

| | France | Finland | Spain | Hungary | UK | Germany | Slovenia | NL | Italy |
|---|---|---|---|---|---|---|---|---|---|
| Current | 44 | 41 | 26 | 24 | 22 | 19 | 18 | 15 | 14 |
| Past | 29 | 31 | 29 | 27 | 17 | 24 | 12 | 19 | 22 |

*Source*: Quantitative data reports, EWSI project, 2003

## How Women's Studies achieves its impact

In analysing the impact of Women's Studies training on the relationships and everyday practices of our informants, we relied on their perceptions as evidenced in their responses to our questionnaire and subsequent interviews. The questionnaire suggested that Women's Studies training fosters knowledge, skills and attitudes which then translate into the desire to effect changes in relationships and everyday practices. Chief among these were significant increases in gender awareness, self-confidence and critical thinking by both current and past students ( see Table 5.4).

The figures in Table 5.4 show that both gender awareness and critical thinking scored particularly highly in growth terms across all nine countries. Gender awareness was fostered by course contents. The growth in critical thinking was partly encouraged by Women's Studies' critical stance in relation to traditional forms of knowledge production and partly by its interrogative position which is the result of defending the subject and engaging persistently with critiques both within and outside the discipline. This fosters the ability to argue effectively. As one UK student described it: 'I think it was the confidence of actually doing well on that [writing her thesis] that made me think, I can string an argument together and if I can string an argument together ... I can say the toughest things in a coherent way' (Griffin 2003a: 48).

Table 5.4 shows that the growth in self-confidence tended to be more marked among students in countries where Women's Studies is well established (the UK, Netherlands, Germany) than in countries where Women's

TABLE 5.4 Growth in gender awareness, self-confidence and critical thinking of past and current Women's Studies students (%)

| Country | Gender awareness | | Self-confidence | | Critical thinking | |
|---|---|---|---|---|---|---|
| | Past | Current | Past | Current | Past | Current |
| Finland | 98 | 97 | 74 | 69 | 95 | 100 |
| France | 94 | 97 | 50 | 44 | 98 | 97 |
| Germany | 91 | 94 | 72 | 56 | 87 | 92 |
| Hungary | 81 | 89 | 53 | 48 | 82 | 87 |
| Italy | 91 | 94 | 63 | 67 | 87 | 94 |
| Netherlands | 96 | 98 | 73 | 63 | 95 | 96 |
| Slovenia | 81 | 82 | 69 | 59 | 91 | 91 |
| Spain | 88 | 84 | 53 | 49 | 90 | 84 |
| UK | 93 | 94 | 81 | 68 | 96 | 99 |

*Source*: Quantitative data, EWSI project, 2003

Studies lacks visibility and is less well established (France, Hungary, Spain). It was also more marked among past than among current students, possibly because past students have more experience of the impact of that growth in their post-training context. As self-confidence increased, so did demands on the self. 'I felt stronger within my self and mentally and I realised that I was going to have to make some very hard decisions and hard choices in my life in order to achieve the things we were talking about in theory [on the Women's Studies course]' (Griffin 2003a: 58). These impacts stand students in good stead in their personal lives and in the labour market. As one Spanish interviewee put it: '[Women's Studies] impacts on everything. And of course, it is very difficult to separate professional life from personal life, because the margins are not clear. Because [at] ... my workplace, I'm not an automaton, I'm still a person, with feelings. And, of course, my personal life is also here [at work], I have friends and relationships ... So the line is not clear ... [Women's Studies] impacts on everything' (Carrera Suárez and Viñuela Suárez 2003a: 4–5).

One important effect of students' growth in gender awareness, self-confidence and critical thinking was an increase in tolerance towards diversity coupled with a resistance towards intolerance as expressed through sexism and discrimination. Students professed themselves more likely to resist discrimination. A UK interviewee, for example, said: 'I suppose I was aware of gender discrimination ... in terms of helping me identify, articulate it and challenge it, yes, that's, that's been an evident benefit' (Griffin 2003a: 35). Another UK interviewee said: 'I am much more conscious of discrimination. There are times when I just, whereas I know before I would have just thought, oh well, that's not fair. Now I, I think well that's not fair and actually I could do something about it. And whilst I might only do things that are kind of small scale, it might just be going to the head teacher and explaining that there is a problem and saying that I'm concerned' (ibid., p. 36).

Students would also refuse to put up with sexism. A German interviewee, for example, stated: 'if I notice anything sexist in my private sphere I go jump on the barricades. Or I say to friends when I hear it's going on at work, I say, you don't have to stand for that. So I'm doing this kind of enlightenment work' (Schmidbaur et al. 2003: 66). The personal qualities developed through Women's Studies included a greater understanding of social life brought about through the broadening of horizons: 'It taught us to be more tolerant and more receptive to other people's situations' (Barazzetti et al. 2003: 42). Interviewees describe themselves as becoming 'less narrow-minded' or 'dogmatic' (Schmidbaur et al. 2003: 64), and also more sensitive and aware of one's limitations and capabilities (Barazzetti et al. 2003: 40).

Women's Studies empowered women through the destruction of illusion

(Schmidbaur et al. 2003: 63). 'Because you have a certain point of view, and everything in the world looks to be in its place – we have, in fact, specific roles – then suddenly, all this is shattered. And when you get rid of this androcentric point of view, a completely different world, a place of freedom, opens up to you ... so that we could compare this with a kind of enlightenment' (Drglin et al. 2003: 53–4). Women were able to assert themselves and became more 'belligerent', but also patient and persistent (Schmidbaur et al. 2003: 64). 'Women's Studies strengthened me in my beliefs concerning the position of women, that I was not alone in that and that it is an important issue to discuss' (van der Sanden with Waaldijk: 32). Women could feel supported in the choices they make and are more capable of substantiating their positions and choices (ibid.). Personal development could be seen as a professional quality. 'As Women's Studies does overall have a positive impact on women's lives, the well-being on a personal level is expected to be visible in other areas of life as well' (ibid., p. 35). A Slovenian interviewee found: 'I have become quite a lot more tolerant to different forms of womanhood, not just those that were near to me back when I was studying. I am more ready to accept something which I didn't accept before' (Drglin et al. 2003: 55). And an Italian interviewee stated: '[Women's Studies] taught us to become more tolerant and more receptive to other people's situations. More sensitive. All this – and being with other women in particular – has influenced me enormously. This experience taught me to have a different perspective and look for dialogue on some aspects I did not see before' (Barazzetti et al. 2003: 42).

## Cultural contexts and Women's Studies

Decisive influences of Women's Studies on daily life occur in relation to the interplay between cultural patterns of gender identity and greater sensitivity to discriminatory processes. As one German student put it: 'I always notice whenever some boundary is over-stepped' (Schmidbaur et al. 2003: 19). The vast majority of interviewees saw themselves as feminists and defined this in connection with the political aims of dismantling hierarchically gendered structures of inequality and discrimination. They saw Women's Studies and feminism as interrelated. 'You don't put up with gross comments, or malignity towards women. You don't let people question women's presence in the world ... At least, you can control your space and the space you share with others ... so there's respect' (Carrera Suárez and Viñuela Suárez 2003a: 39). Political feminism was confirmed as a lived philosophy, with fluid boundaries between politics, lifestyle and culture (Schmidbaur et al. 2003: 1).

We found that Women's Studies has a major impact on its students even though the socio-cultural context in which this occurs, including the academy, may create problems for them. The risk of being marginalized in academia was repeatedly articulated: 'One fellow student did not get any help because of her choosing this type of research path. It is something I acknowledge with a lot of bitterness' (Barazzetti et al. 2003: 17). Personal and social opposition to Women's Studies could be at its greatest when the discipline is first introduced, especially when it comes from abroad. Problems were particularly intense in Hungary where gender studies is regarded as a western import (Juhász 2003: 24). Hungarian society was described as macho and feminism is looked down upon, although one-half of the Women's Studies interviewees saw themselves as feminist:

> Feminism is a swearword in Hungary. Even women with strong feminist views and lifestyle refuse to be called a feminist because that would endanger their careers, as first and foremost feminism is interpreted as something anti-family, anti-child and anti-femininity. Hungarian women were described as priding themselves on being child-crazy and fashion-lovers (and strangely as anti-Central Europe – I don't know what you mean by this?). The kissing of hands was described as 'very fake now', while courtesies such as letting women go through doors first, helping women put on their coats, and opening the car door for women were signs of politeness in Central Europe rather than anachronisms. The lack of these behaviours by men in the West was interpreted as utter rudeness and ugly individualism. (Juhász 2003: 29–30)

The notion of the private sphere as untouched by politics remained a powerful illusion that created difficulties for young Hungarian women in moving beyond conventional gender stereotypes. Given this cultural understanding of appropriate gender relations, the impact of Women's Studies on the level of everyday practices was interpreted primarily as negative. Their new gender awareness created difficulties in their relations with men and sometimes even with other women.

Interviewees from other countries described similar effects. Their new sensibility made them vulnerable in debates with their male partners and friends of both sexes and even the butt of anti-feminist jokes (ibid., p. 27). 'Feminist glasses' could complicate their private lives (Tuori 2003: 49); in particular the impact on relations with their male partners could become more problematic.

> And you know that something is not quite right but you couldn't put your finger on it, but now you're in an environment [Women's Studies course] where you explore these things and it makes sense to you. And you then have

to go back out there in what I call the real world, and decide, 'Well, how I am going to use this?' You know, are you going to go home and be the little wifie and the little doormat still, are you going to be the one that does everything, or are you going to say well look, I would like some help here? And what is the reaction going to be and are you prepared for this reaction and what could be the final outcome of it? (Griffin 2003a: 65)

Perceiving Women's Studies as having a positive impact thus did not mean that it made life easier. Students' new knowledge and awareness could make life more complicated. As a Dutch student said: 'Women's Studies makes women think about everything and they cannot let go of the Women's Studies glasses' (van der Sanden with Waaldijk 2003: 33).

## Socio-domestic lifestyles

Many of the women we interviewed said that taking Women's and Gender Studies had changed their social relationships (see Table 5.5). Women's Studies 'has showed me life in a totally different way. This applied to my interpersonal, interfamily and work relationships and with my partner' (Barazzetti et al 2003: 39).

As Table 5.5 shows, although Women's Studies involved its students in renegotiating relationships and could engender conflict, very few past or current students regarded the impact as negative and few students reported a decline in their interpersonal relationships. Instead, in most countries Women's Studies was seen either as improving interpersonal relationships, or as not having harmed them. Improvements were attributed to

TABLE 5.5 Reported impact of Women's Studies on the interpersonal relationships of past and current students (%)

| Country | Improved | | Stayed the same | | Declined | |
|---|---|---|---|---|---|---|
| | Past | Current | Past | Current | Past | Current |
| Finland | 53 | 63 | 43 | 34 | 4 | 3 |
| France | 58 | 45 | 33 | 49 | 8 | 6 |
| Germany | 47 | 37 | 49 | 59 | 4 | 3 |
| Hungary | 40 | 26 | 58 | 71 | 2 | 2 |
| Italy | 64 | 65 | 34 | 32 | 2 | 2 |
| Netherlands | 57 | 44 | 36 | 52 | 7 | 4 |
| Slovenia | 70 | 50 | 28 | 39 | 2 | 11 |
| Spain | 53 | 53 | 45 | 46 | 2 | 2 |
| UK | 59 | 54 | 37 | 42 | 4 | 4 |

*Source*: Quantitative data reports, EWSI project, 2003

an enhanced ability to assert oneself in interpersonal relationships, to having a better understanding of why sexist attitudes arise, and to having greater tolerance towards diversity as a result of studying. Among past students Hungary and Germany were the only countries where the responses of 'staying the same' were greater than 'improved'. Among current students, 'staying the same' exceeded 'improved' for Hungary, Germany, the Netherlands and France. These results were particularly notable for Hungary.

The reasons for these differences are complex and country-specific. As previously indicated, Hungary was described by the Hungarian project partners as a particularly macho culture in which traditional forms of femininity were highly valued and feminism viewed as a despicable Western import (Juhász 2003). This meant that Hungarian feminists found it very difficult to negotiate changes in their lives in Hungary – hence the relatively low levels of improvement noted by Hungarian respondents – and in consequence many interviewees dreamt of going, or had actually gone, abroad. Alternatively, improvement might not be highly visible when significant proportions of interviewees already had strongly articulated and lived feminist positions before attending Women's Studies courses, as was the case in Germany (Schmidbaur et al. 2003).

Overall, the four types of relationships in which Women's Studies students described changes were

• within the family (meaning parents and siblings)
• with children
• with male partners
• in female friendship networks

We shall now discuss each in turn.

### Relationships within the family

The expected and actual impact Women's Studies had on family life for past and current students is presented in Table 5.6.

The expectations of impact were almost always lower than the experienced impact, particularly for past students. In all countries the expectation that Women's Studies would have an impact on their family life was significantly greater for current than past students. A possible explanation for these two findings is that as Women's Studies has become more established, knowledge of its impact has become more widespread. Additionally, current students are more likely to live at home with their parents, thus allowing for more opportunities to experience an impact on family life.

The number of students continuing to live with their parents both during and after their Women's Studies course reduced in all countries and most

TABLE 5.6 Expected and actual impact of Women's Studies on the family life of past and current students (%)

| Country | Past students | | Current students | |
|---|---|---|---|---|
| | Expected | Actual | Expected | Actual |
| Finland | 21 | 54 | 60 | 72 |
| France | 26 | 59 | 28 | 43 |
| Germany | 38 | 65 | 56 | 62 |
| Hungary | 20 | 33 | 33 | 41 |
| Italy | 18 | 33 | 36 | 40 |
| Netherlands | 26 | 49 | 67 | 60 |
| Slovenia | 28 | 52 | 40 | 54 |
| Spain | 28 | 54 | 41 | 38 |
| UK | 22 | 59 | 42 | 57 |

*Source*: Quantitative data reports, EWSI project, 2003

greatly for past students. The largest number of current students living with parents was in Spain (71 per cent), followed by Italy (44 per cent), Slovenia (44 per cent) and Hungary (40 per cent); countries where students are more likely to attend their local university. Far fewer did so in the UK (9 per cent), Finland (0.0 per cent), Netherlands (8 per cent), France (16 per cent) and Germany (10 per cent). Even fewer past students were living with their parents at the time of completing the questionnaire, although the largest number continued to be from Spain (38 per cent), followed by Slovenia (26 per cent) and Hungary (28 per cent). Very few past students compared to current students continued to live with parents in the other five countries. These results are related to students' age, to the economic contexts of their countries, and to the stage of family formation.

When comparing past and current students, the impact on family life remained approximately the same for respondents from the UK, Slovenia and Germany, while it was greater for Finland, the Netherlands, Italy, Hungary, and less for France and Spain. The increasing institutionalization of Women's Studies is likely to have had a positive impact on student experiences of Women's Studies and may account, at least in part, for some of the variation between past and current students. In countries where the actual experience of change has decreased among current students, it may be that greater knowledge of Women's Studies has led not only to a more realistic assessment of expectations, but of change itself.

The direction of change in family relationships was either positive or it stayed the same, with few past or current students reporting a decline (see Table 5.7).

TABLE 5.7 Direction of change in the family relationships of past and current Women's Studies students (%)

| Country | Improved | | Stayed the same | | Declined | |
|---|---|---|---|---|---|---|
| | Past | Current | Past | Current | Past | Current |
| Finland | 45 | 53 | 51 | 47 | 4 | 0 |
| France | 38 | 45 | 49 | 49 | 13 | 6 |
| Germany | 20 | 37 | 70 | 59 | 11 | 3 |
| Hungary | 27 | 26 | 73 | 71 | 0 | 2 |
| Italy | 27 | 65 | 69 | 33 | 4 | 2 |
| Netherlands | 28 | 44 | 69 | 52 | 3 | 4 |
| Slovenia | 44 | 50 | 54 | 39 | 2 | 11 |
| Spain | 33 | 53 | 65 | 46 | 2 | 2 |
| UK | 32 | 54 | 58 | 42 | 10 | 4 |

Source: Quantitative data reports, EWSI project, 2003

Overall, the numbers of students who reported that their family relations stayed the same was higher than those who reported an improvement. Family relations tended to improve more among current students than among past students. Sometimes, as our interviews showed, improvements could be a function of the students' greater degree of tolerance and improved interpersonal negotiating skills which might lead them to avoid conflict. One German student said: 'I'll probably always avoid talking to my mother about feminism ... I think it's as much a generational problem. My mother is 70 ... There aren't really many changes in the content of what we talk about although I think, really, both sides have begun to take more moderate positions' (Schmidbaur et al. 2003: 64). The greater tolerance towards diversity fostered by Women's Studies could thus result in an enhanced ability to negotiate effectively between different positions without feeling compromised in their own views. Women's Studies could have a positive influence on relations with parents, especially mothers (Le Feuvre and Andriocci 2002b: 76).

Parental backgrounds were important in determining the acceptability of the content of Women's Studies. Fathers often did not take an interest in the specific content of their daughters' studies but some at least recognized the value of their educational attainment: 'My father is very happy. He doesn't really know what I'm doing but he hears "doctorate" and it's like, wow!' (Carrera Suárez and Viñuela Suárez 2003a: 17). Mothers were more likely to take a closer interest in their daughters' pursuits. Parents did not always understand why their daughters kept on studying, especially when the parents had not been to university themselves (van der Sanden with Waaldijk 2003: 34). OECD findings confirm that children of parents who have gone to university are more likely to go to university themselves. However, a significant number of interviewees were also the first in their family to go to university. 'My family is very traditional ... they know that I like to study and to be on my own ... I'm the crazy one in the family, the one that never fits anywhere' (Carrera Suárez and Viñuela Suárez 2003a: 41). Students with feminist mothers/fathers encouraged their interest in Women's Studies and, when mothers were feminists, they had a new subject to talk about.

Table 5.8 shows that the perceived transformation of relationships with parents as a function of taking Women's Studies varied between 34 per cent in Hungary and 61 per cent in Spain for current students and between 24 per cent in the UK and 55 per cent in Germany and Spain for past students. Although not a perfect association, this variable appears to be more salient for those living with their parents than those who were not.

TABLE 5.8 Transformation in relationships with parents of current and past Women's Studies students (%)

| | Fin-land | France | Ger-many | Hun-gary | Italy | NL | Slov-enia | Spain | UK |
|---|---|---|---|---|---|---|---|---|---|
| Current | 49 | 57 | 36 | 34 | 39 | 36 | 44 | 61 | 41 |
| Past | 49 | 47 | 55 | 48 | 31 | 38 | 40 | 55 | 24 |

*Source*: Quantitative data reports, EWSI project, 2003

Taking Women's Studies also could have a positive impact on siblings, especially sisters (Griffin 2003a: 68). Students found that younger sisters might follow in their footsteps in terms of going into higher education, or in terms of changing their attitudes towards sexism. 'It's a theme in relationships and friendships ... discussion with your parents and in your circle of friends and acquaintances' (Schmidbaur et al. 2003: 63).

### Relationships with children

The numbers of Women's Studies students who had children at the time of their training varied greatly across the project partner countries. Table 5.9 indicates that the number of students with children ranged from a high of 76 per cent among past Women's Studies students in the UK to a low of 2 per cent for past Hungarian students, and a high of 32 per cent for current UK students and a low of zero for current Hungarian and Spanish students.

TABLE 5.9 Past and current Women's Studies students with children at the time of the study (%)

| Country | Past students | Current students |
|---|---|---|
| UK | 76 | 32 |
| Netherlands | 43 | 12 |
| Slovenia | 32 | 2 |
| Finland | 27 | 0 |
| France | 25 | 3 |
| Spain | 24 | 4 |
| Germany | 23 | 16 |
| Italy | 14 | 16 |
| Hungary | 2 | 0 |

*Source*: Quantitative data reports, EWSI project, 2003

The proportion of students with children related to the number of mature students; more numerous in the UK for both past and current students than in any other country. The other factor of relevance is the increasing average age of motherhood in Europe which is at its highest for university-educated women. For example, in France, the average age of motherhood for university-educated women was above thirty years in 2003, while the average age of current students in 2002 was twenty-four years and that of past students thirty-three years (Le Feuvre and Andriocci 2003a: 74). In Spain only one interviewee had older children at the time she was taking Women's Studies. She said: 'My children (now adult) loved it ... it meant seeing me at their level. At home my mother and my husband knew it was a hobby, so they thought it was fine for me to entertain myself. But my children did like it a lot' (Carrera Suárez and Viñuela Suárez 2003a: 42).

The perceived transformation of Women's Studies' students' relationships with children for current students varied between zero in Finland and 18 per cent in Hungary, and for past students between 3 per cent in

TABLE 5.10 Transformation in relationships with children of past and current Women's Studies students

| | Fin- land | France | Ger- many | Hun- gary | Italy | NL | Slov enia | Spain | UK |
|---|---|---|---|---|---|---|---|---|---|
| Current | 0 | 4 | 13 | 18 | 17 | 2 | 13 | 20 | 20 |
| Past | 20 | 20 | 10 | 3 | 21 | 9 | 20 | 18 | 26 |

*Source*: Quantitative data reports, EWSI project, 2003

Hungary and 26 per cent in the UK (see Table 5.10). There is no correlation between that transformation and living with children. Few current students lived with male partners and children during their Women's Studies course (between zero in Hungary and the Netherlands, and 14 per cent in Italy), while between 2 per cent of past students in Hungary and 31 per cent in the UK did so after completing their Women's Studies course. Even fewer were living alone with children before, during and after their Women's Studies course.

In the UK, which had by far the highest number of Women's Studies students with children, four types of impacts on children were noted. These were:

- educational role-modelling of mothers, effected through children seeing their mothers studying
- trying to raise children in a non-sexist manner
- having a greater degree of exchange with children
- gaining respect from children

One overseas student who went to the UK to study consulted her son and waited until he was prepared to let her go abroad to study (Griffin 2003a: 66). Another talked to her daughter about her work: 'I remember my daughter asking me about my teacher and what did my teacher think. So in the same ways that we would discuss her parents' evening, we'd have this kind of discussion about how my course was going ... and that was interesting' (ibid., p. 67). Mothers were role models for their children, and Women's Studies could equalize their relations with their children. One major concern was to avoid raising their own children, especially their sons, in a sexist manner. Women described themselves as close to their children and often closer to them than their male partners/husbands. Respect could be gained from older children by gaining a postgraduate qualification.

### Relationships with partners and domestic arrangements

Women's Studies could lead to challenges to, and even a rewriting of, the heterosexual marital domestic contract. This was because the impact on personal relationships on the part of the women students involved a recognition of unequal treatment through awareness-raising, an identification with that recognition, and, when followed by action, a rewriting of the heterosexual marital domestic contract. That contract was described as 'unspoken and certainly unwritten ... he assumed ... and I've changed, I've really changed' (ibid., p. 63). Developing new bases for heterosexual partnerships was a major challenge that could involve conflict. Changes could mean challenging interruptions by a male partner, challenging unequal involvement with childcare, and unequal participation in household tasks. Rewriting the domestic marital contract could result in heated exchanges as men were often a major source of resistance. One woman reported that when her husband said, 'I don't understand the washing machine', she responded, 'No, you are an intelligent professor and you're actually far more technological than I am, that's garbage. And if you don't understand I will keep telling you about it until you do understand' (ibid.).

Personal change could be un-anticipated by the student herself as well as by her partner. One woman explained that there were 'powerful fights and heavy conflict initially, but readiness to communicate and less rigid positions later on. Because I already knew my partner before I started studying, it must have been a hard time for him because I changed dramatically as a result of my education' (Schmidbaur et al. 2003: 64). The adjustment of the unwritten marital contract included adjustments of fundamental emotional needs and past interactions. Thus, one student described herself as having been a 'typical housewifely kind of person even though I wasn't married'. She was living with her boyfriend and, 'I just stopped being that woman overnight, and I still question all the time if it is really my turn with the washing up' (Griffin 2003a: 58).

There could be substantial emotional losses for the male partner as women withdrew unqualified support or refused to respond to childhood-based need. One woman said: 'he has lost really, he's got a friend, he's got a lover, he's got a wife, but he hasn't got somebody whose job is to support his career at any cost, no more' (ibid., p. 64), and another said, 'this had a huge impact on my partner because he was used to me being his little mummy' (ibid., p. 65).

One woman explained, 'It is not my private life that has changed but me, myself, and private life is only one aspect of this. How did it change? Well, my needs were verbalised, things that earlier were wreathing like fog' (Juhász 2003: 27). Many women said their problems had been given a name.[6] As the distance between naming the difference and understanding it became shorter,

> I understood my previous problems with the world, in my relationships, my expectations in my relationships. I think it really changed in the sense that now I am able to put into words what I want and what I can do, and I know what my duties and my rights are, things I didn't really know until then. Now I cannot find myself in a situation that would confuse me, that I wouldn't know what to think of it, that it would make me uncertain. I cannot be subdued, suppressed, humiliated, and other things cannot be done to me that are graver than these. Many things found their places – what you can do in

a relationship, what you can't. I think that's how it changed. The changes happened mostly in my head, and that shows later. It shows in your relationships too. (Juhász 2003: 27)

Gaining knowledge about the mechanisms of gender inequalities could also help students negotiate changes in their relationships in a relatively non-conflictual manner (Le Feuvre and Andriocci 2003a: 77). Relationships could improve because 'you understand things better', and have 'more insights in (role) patterns', and experience 'equality and respect within relationships with men' (van der Sanden with Waaldijk 2003: 33). Women were trying to live non-traditional lives as they valued economic independence and a balanced vision of work and household/care tasks. They would both reject a 'male breadwinner' model for themselves and also be wary of falling into a 'female carer' role. Some women gave considerable thought to whether or not to have children. Less frequently, partners were sympathetic to feminism or saw themselves as feminist, so that they shared childcare responsibilities, for example. 'Fortunately my partner shares, he is not the type who helps, he shares' (Carrera Suárez and Viñuela Suárez 2003a: 41).[7] Women's choice of partners was relevant here. One Slovenian woman said: 'I have chosen partners in such a way that they have supported me absolutely, whatever I have done, so that here there was no problem. I have had absolute support' (Drglin et al. 2003: 52).

Rewriting the domestic contact also can have implications for partners outside the immediate relationship. Once a woman has recognized gender inequalities she is clearer in their identification and less likely to let them pass. 'We were at a party and in conversation with a man ... a professor here, in his 50s. And he was giving the usual clap trap about how this university doesn't discriminate ... I just laid into this guy with facts and figures ... my husband was not pleased, I mean he really felt I had overstepped the social boundary' (Griffin 2003a: 61–2).

Dissatisfaction with present marital or long-term relationships was higher among interviewed current than past students. Where issues around the (heterosexual) domestic contract could not be satisfactorily resolved, women tended to leave the relationship, sometimes after many years of cohabitation. One woman who left her husband of thirty-two years said, 'Well, I just feel liberated' (ibid., p. 62). Another said: 'A lot of my friends and other women see me now, they think I lead a charmed life ... here is this woman who left, she's got her own house, she's got her own car and men actually are frightened of me and some of them are not happy for their wives to be friends with me because they think, because of the way I am, I will lead them astray' (ibid.). Dissatisfaction with present marital or long-term relationships was higher among interviewed current than past students. But however dissatisfied, not all women left unsuccessful relationships, or initiated leaving. One woman expressed a sense of failure at not having left: 'I still have this nagging feeling at times, you should have left, you should have left, you should have left' (ibid., p. 63). It was, however, also possible for a boyfriend to use Women's Studies as an excuse for breaking up a relationship (van der Sanden with Waaldijk 2003: 34). There was a general feeling that a better understanding of macro-level gender relationships improved the quality of those partnerships that survived Women's Studies training. More realistic expectations of male partners could develop (Le Feuvre and Andriocci 2002b: 75).

Women's Studies students thus emerge as compromisers, pragmatists and innovators. As a Dutch interviewee said: '[Women's Studies] gives you ammunition that other people don't have, because I have engaged myself pretty thoroughly during my studies. Yes, it is knowledge; self-knowledge and security that helped me hold my own in male surroundings, because you see through certain patterns' (van der Sanden with Waaldijk 2003: 21).

### Female friendship networks

One of the most important positive impacts of taking Women's Studies reported by the students was the transformation of their female friendship networks (Table 5.11).

This transformation took the form of gaining new friends, especially like-minded ones who could offer support both within and beyond the course. Women's Studies students were very active, organizing discussion meetings and study groups (van der Sanden with Waaldijk 2003: 34). 'I met many friends through feminism and all my friends are feminists. I don't have many male friends, but the ones I have are very, very good friends ... and they are very respectful' (Carrera Suárez and Viñuela Suárez 2003a: 40). 'You know I met lots of people that I still have relationships with now' (Griffin 2003a: 68). Students found very good women friends and made up a network that enriched their lives. These friendship networks were based on shared feminist views and activities as 'you can't make feminism without activism' (Juhász 2003: 31). Occasionally, men too could be re-educated and come to accept some feminist views (ibid., p. 27).

The acquisition of knowledge of social relations, gender relations, ethnicity and power structures assisted students' awareness of their own positions. They described this as empowerment and the ability to discuss and exchange ideas and experiences with kindred spirits as a factor in its attainment (van der Sanden with Waaldijk 2003: 32). 'Being with other women

TABLE 5.11 Transformation in female friendship networks reported by past and current Women's Studies students (%)

| | Spain | NL | Germany | Italy | UK | France | Finland | Slovenia | Hungary |
|---|---|---|---|---|---|---|---|---|---|
| Current | 70 | 67 | 66 | 65 | 64 | 60 | 55 | 41 | 21 |
| Past | 62 | 66 | 78 | 77 | 58 | 71 | 52 | 51 | 31 |

*Source*: Quantitative data reports, EWSI project, 2003

in particular – has influenced me enormously' '(Barazzetti et al. 2003: 42). Women's Studies was seen as favouring and encouraging relationships with other women and both enabling and urging a redefinition of goals.

The transformation of friendship networks was of greatest importance to all past students but those from Hungary, where transforming relationships with parents was more important. Among current students, too, the transformation of friendship networks was of greatest importance for all but students from Slovenia and Hungary, where transforming relationships with parents was more important. These two types of change were the most frequently mentioned by past and current students from all countries. On average six out of every ten past and current students experienced transformations in their friendship networks and four out of every ten in relationships with parents.

### Overall quality of life

In general, students felt that their Women's Studies training had improved the overall quality of their lives (see Table 5.12). Quality of life was defined as having control over one's life: 'you can decide everything, where you want to live, who you want to live with ... what you are going to do' (Drglin et al. 2003: 52).

Improvement in quality of life was particularly high for past students in the UK, Finland, the Netherlands, Italy, Spain and Slovenia, varying from almost seven to over eight out of ten students, and less so for past students from France, Hungary and Germany where the variation was almost six out of ten for France, almost five out of ten for Hungary and 3.5 out of ten for Germany. The number experiencing improved quality of life was less for current students, but still substantial for the UK, Finland, the Netherlands, Italy and Slovenia, and less for France, Germany and Hungary. Very few past or current students experienced a decline in their quality of life as a result of taking Women's Studies.

While there were country variations, improvements in quality of life exceeded those achieved in interpersonal relationships (see also Table 5.5). This suggests the importance of personal change and development to quality of life, irrespective of its impact on personal relationships, and is a conclusion in keeping with interviewee comments. On the whole, women were of the opinion that their quality of life had improved as a result of their Women's Studies training, even if the results could sometimes be painful. On the one hand, women faced questioning from their friends, families and acquaintances, and, on the other hand, most women created networks of friends through Women's Studies and feminist activism. Thus their social worlds changed as a function of their changed knowledge and perceptions. As one woman said of her Women's Studies experience: 'I had a great time, finally in a feminist country. At last, women who aren't afraid of being seen as feminists ... it was so wonderful to be part of what seemed to be the norm ... we understood each other' (Le Feuvre and Andriocci 2002b: 70).

The research findings detailed above demonstrate that Women's Studies facilitates personal, social and intellectual development in past and current students. Women with children reported improved relations with their children through gaining respect from the children, acting as role models for them, and attempting to be non-sexist. Relations with mothers sometimes underwent very positive changes as women found new shared topics and as mothers were more likely to take an active interest in their daughters' education than fathers were. Most particularly, however, Women's Studies has an impact on students' relationships with female peers and male partners. Women taking Women's Studies find new female friends who become very

TABLE 5.12 Effect of Women's Studies on overall quality of life by past and current students (%)

| Country | Improved | | Stayed the same | | Declined | |
|---|---|---|---|---|---|---|
| | Past | Current | Past | Current | Past | Current |
| Netherlands | 86 | 76 | 13 | 22 | 1 | 0 |
| Italy | 83 | 71 | 15 | 29 | 2 | 0 |
| UK | 79 | 71 | 18 | 26 | 2 | 3 |
| Spain | 76 | 38 | 24 | 62 | 0 | 0 |
| Slovenia | 70 | 62 | 30 | 38 | 0 | 0 |
| Finland | 67 | 63 | 33 | 37 | 0 | 0 |
| France | 59 | 33 | 39 | 64 | 2 | 3 |
| Hungary | 47 | 50 | 53 | 50 | 0 | 0 |
| Germany | 35 | 47 | 65 | 50 | 0 | 3 |

*Source*: Quantitative data reports, EWSI project, 2003

important sources of support and mentoring. At the same time, Women's Studies enables its students to review their relationships and to articulate the inequalities they experience within these. In particular, many women begin to review the domestic contract, often unspoken, they have with their partners. They themselves change and are empowered by their studies but also recognize that their partners have to cope with these changes and adjust to them. This means that previous patterns and practices of interaction in the home, such as the assumption that women will do all or most of the housework, are called into question, with women refusing to accept such inequalities unquestioningly. This can lead to conflict and, if unresolved, to the dissolution of unequal partnerships. Students reported that their overall quality of life had improved, even if they had experienced conflicts as a result of their changed perspectives, and that they did not want to be without the gender awareness that Women's Studies had provided them with.

## Notes

1 For more information about that research see the introduction to this chapter and the project website <www.hull.ac.uk/ewsi>.

2 See background data reports on Women's Studies for this project, available at <www.hull.ac.uk/ewsi>

3 It has to be said that this was a surprisingly infrequent occurrence in our sample, surprising especially in the light of the commonly held prejudice that Women's Studies fosters lesbianism.

4 For actual numbers on which the samples in this and subsequent tables were based, please see Table in the 'Introduction' to this volume.

5 Bryan Magee (1966) thought, as his monograph's title indicates, that *One in Twenty* women and men were likely to be homosexual.

6 This resonates with Betty Friedan's early, deeply influential study of women's experiences of family life, described as 'the problem that had no name' (1963). Her research among home-bound women was a key text leading to the women's liberation movement.

7 Such perceptions would, of course, need to be corroborated since many women assume that their male partner does much more in the household than he actually does, a function of the over-valuing of men's participation in domestic tasks in a context where they tend to do little work.

# 6 | Educational migration and gender: Women's Studies students' educational mobility in Europe

BORBÁLA JUHÁSZ, ANDREA PETÖ, JEANNETTE
VAN DER SANDEN AND BERTEKE WAALDIJK

Travelling to learn has a long tradition in Europe. From the thirteenth century onwards universities in France, England and Italy attracted students from all over Europe to study liberal arts and philosophy, law, medicine and theology, thus creating a European cultural space. For students in the European past, travelling was a constitutive element of training and education. The psychological and intellectual gains were considerable: those travelling were confronted with new values and cultures, could satisfy their curiosity and widen their mental horizons. They became more assured and empowered. The modern counterpart of this tradition is called 'student mobility' and it helps to create what the Bologna Declaration of 1999 calls a 'Europe of Knowledge', described as 'an irreplaceable factor for social and human growth and as an indispensable component to consolidate and enrich the European citizenship, capable of giving its citizens the necessary competences to face the challenges of the new millennium, together with an awareness of shared values and belonging to a common social and cultural space'.[1]

Within the context of the project Employment and Women's Studies, in which the authors of this chapter were partners and researchers, this chapter explores the issue of Women's Studies students' educational mobility. It provides information and analyses of data about the following:

1. The number of Women's Studies students who travelled to other universities.
2. The countries from which and to which they travelled.
3. Comparative data from Erasmus about student mobility in general and gender equality.
4. The courses students took and the credits they earned.
5. The availability of information and funding.
6. The motives for and impediments to going abroad.
7. The experience of studying abroad.
8. The impact of educational migration on women's employment and on their lives more generally.

9. The ways in which empowering experiences contribute to European citizenship.

A closer look at the place of women, gender and Women's Studies in the process of educational migration is imperative for two reasons. Historically, women have not participated to the fullest in migration for educational purposes. Their movements have been restricted by real and imagined dangers for their safety, and by social and religious expectations that they stay at home and take care of children. In addition, women were often formally excluded from the professions for which the university prepared. When Elena Lucrezia Cornaro Piscopia travelled from Venice to the University of Padua in 1678 to receive her doctorate in philosophy, she was probably the first woman in Europe to receive a university degree. For a long time educational migration for women took the form of attending expensive boarding schools and monasteries far away from home for aristocratic girls, and it was only in the late nineteenth and early twentieth centuries that women began to enjoy the advantages of academic training. Then women began to travel for their education in larger numbers, as is exemplified by women from Scandinavia and Finland, and by the number of Russian women who studied in Switzerland before 1917.

Since European citizenship will to a large extent be based on competences acquired in a European system of higher education, it is crucial that the advantages of educational mobility be shared democratically by men and women alike – not only in terms of numerical equality of exchange students, but also in the lasting effects for those answering the challenge of international educational experience. Is the experience of travelling abroad indeed an empowering experience for Women's Studies students?

In this context we need to take into account that Women's Studies as a discipline developed only recently and is unequally integrated into academic programmes in different European countries (see Barazzetti and Leone 2003; Chapter 3 in this volume). This raises important questions about the role of student mobility in the process of international compatibility of qualifications in an innovative academic field. Will international cooperation and student exchange between advanced and new programmes contribute to the creation of European standards of education in general and of Women's Studies in particular? For Women's Studies, the question we must answer is whether educational migration contributes to the empowering of programmes and knowledge about gender.

The part played by gender both as an academic subject and as a lived experience of female exchange students allows us to draw conclusions about the gendered implications of a European area of higher education as the key way to promote European citizens' mobility and employability.

This chapter is based on questionnaire returns and interviews with Women's Studies students from nine different European countries.[2] The interviews provide us with an unprecedented insight into the motives and experiences of women travelling for education. However, a note of theoretical and methodological caution should be sounded. We have collected very few failure stories. Even the failures and difficulties are narrated later on as success stories. This is partly due to the empowering impact of Women's Studies' educational migration, but the character of the genre of interviews about life experiences also plays a role. The retroactive character of explaining motivations of action in relation to present career choices, for example, is likely to produce stories of empowerment. In this sense, the stories that recall the experience of studying abroad also belong to the folklore of future national elites. Consequently, the stories in the interviews are and should be success stories: 'Eventually I got more self-confidence by [going abroad]. I felt very welcome and taken seriously. It was a real booster, and its effect works on. Professionally and personally it broadened my horizon. I must say it really is one of the best things in my life, absolutely' (van der Sanden with Waaldijk 2003: 30).

## Student mobility in Women's Studies – the numbers

In every country participating in the project, Women's Studies students studied abroad or intended to do so. As Table 6.1 shows, the number of women studying abroad differed across countries. For current students,[3] Germany and the Netherlands had the highest proportion of travelling students; for past students, the numbers for Germany and Italy were the highest. Looking at both current and past students, Germany had the highest percentage of students studying abroad (43 per cent) and Slovenia the lowest (7 per cent).

In all but two countries (Spain and Italy), current students studied abroad (or planned to do so) more often than past students. Since the figure for current students includes those planning to study abroad, it may be higher than the actual level of educational mobility ultimately achieved. However, the fact that many present students had plans for studying abroad is interesting in itself, not least because there was an overall increase in the actual and planned mobility from past to present students. A possible explanation for this is that more exchange programmes/opportunities have been established. In Finland, for instance, the possibilities for educational migration grew significantly in 1995 when Finland joined the EU and became part of the Erasmus/Socrates agreements. The lower, and actually decreasing numbers for Spain may be explained by the fact that although the vast majority of students have not been abroad to do Women's Studies courses, a much higher percentage of these Women's Studies students have taken part in Erasmus programmes in other disciplines (Carrera Suárez and Viñuela Suárez 2003a: 34).

TABLE 6.1 Proportion of questionnaire respondents who studied abroad (%)

|  | Current students who studied abroad or intended to do so (n) | Current students who studied abroad (n) | Total of students who studied abroad (n) |
| --- | --- | --- | --- |
| Germany | 46 (31) | 39 (22) | 43 (53) |
| Italy | 30 (15) | 36 (18) | 33 (33) |
| Netherlands | 33 (17) | 21 (17) | 26 (34) |
| Finland | 31 (11) | 21 (12) | 25 (23) |
| France | 31 (22) | 10 (5) | 22 (27) |
| Hungary | 18 (9) | 14 (7) | 16 (16) |
| Spain | 7 (6) | 21 (9) | 12 (15) |
| UK | 16 (16) | 7 (8) | 11 (24) |
| Slovenia | 8 (4) | 6 (3) | 7 (7) |

Source: EWSI questionnaires, 2002

## 'Receiving' and 'sending': divisions by country

Similar to the general typology of migration, we can distinguish between 'receiving' countries and 'sending' countries. Table 6.2 details patterns of educational migration by country. The countries where students go to take Women's Studies courses are mainly located in north-western Europe (as in the political West). All countries participating in the EWSI project received students. However, in the questionnaires, additional European countries (Ireland, Denmark, Sweden, Portugal, Greece, Norway, Austria and Belgium) were mentioned. By far the most popular, though, were destinations outside Europe (the USA and Canada). Apart from these, respondents reported educational trips to Peru, Brazil, Indonesia, Ecuador, Zimbabwe, Swaziland, India and the Dominican Republic (each country mentioned once). Some students also studied abroad in more than one country. Additional information from the interviews shows that women took Women's Studies courses, did work placements or research in countries such as the Czech Republic (Drglin et al. 2003: 45), Cyprus, Wales and Egypt (Schmidbaur et al. 2003: 58), and Thailand and Suriname (van der Sanden with Waaldijk 2003: 28). For all but a few students, going abroad meant studying in other European countries. The exception was the UK where students were at least as likely to go to non-European countries, predominantly the USA.

Looking at the countries to which Women's Studies students travelled

TABLE 6.2 Patterns of educational migration of Women's Studies students: countries of destiny for Women's Studies courses taken abroad by current and past students

| From: To: | Finland | France | Germany | Hungary | Italy | Netherlands | Slovenia | Spain | UK | Total |
|---|---|---|---|---|---|---|---|---|---|---|
| Finland | x | | | | 1 | | | 2 | 1 | 4 |
| France | | x | 6 | | 1 | 4 | | | 1 | 12 |
| Germany | 2 | | 4* | | 2 | 2 | 3 | | | 13 |
| Hungary[2] | | | | x | | | 1 | | | 1 |
| Italy | | 1 | 1 | | 1* | 1 | 1 | 1 | 1 | 6 |
| Netherlands | 8 | 1 | | 2 | 17 | 18* | | 1 | 3 | 50 |
| Slovenia | | | | 1 | | | x | | | 1 |
| Spain | | | 5 | | 6 | 2 | | 1* | 1 | 14 |
| UK[1] | 4 | 3 | 4 | 4 | | 5 | | 2 | 2* | 26 |
| USA | 4 | | 7 | | | 2 | | 3 | 8 | 24 |
| Canada | 4 | 3 | 2 | | | 1 | | | | 10 |
| Ireland | | 1 | 3 | | | 3 | | | | 7 |
| Denmark | 3 | | | | | 1 | | | | 4 |
| Portugal | 1 | | 1 | | | 1 | | | | 3 |
| Greece[3] | 1 | 1 | | | | 1 | | | | 3 |
| Sweden | 2 | 1 | | | | | | | | 3 |
| Norway | 2 | | | | | | | | | 2 |
| Austria | | | 1 | | 1 | | | | | 2 |
| Belgium | | | 1 | | | | | | | 1 |
| Yugoslavia | | | | | | | 1 | | | 1 |

| | | | | | | | | | | Total |
|---|---|---|---|---|---|---|---|---|---|---|
| Brazil | | | | | | 1 | | | | 1 |
| India | | | | | | | | | 1 | 1 |
| Indonesia | | | | | | 1 | | | | 1 |
| Dominican Republic | | | | | | | | 1 | | 1 |
| Ecuador | | | | | | | | 1 | | 1 |
| Peru | | 1 | | | | | | | | 1 |
| Swaziland | | | | | | | | | 1 | 1 |
| Zimbabwe | | | | | | | | | 1 | 1 |
| Total | 27 | 12 | 35 | 10 | 33 | 42 | 8 | 12 | 20 | 199 |

*Notes:* 1. UK = England; in one German case Scotland 2. Hungary = Hungary and Bosnia 3. Greece = Greece and Yugoslavia * These are students from another country so they are actually in a foreign country. For instance, a Polish student in Germany or students visiting the Netherlands from Poland, Switzerland and Belgium.

*Source:* EWSI questionnaires, 2002

most to take courses (Table 6.2), one can see that the Netherlands and the UK were the leading countries hosting foreign students, followed by Spain, Germany and France. The East European countries (as in the political East) Slovenia and Hungary received the least students. Countries outside the project that attracted many students were the USA and Canada, followed by Ireland. It may be possible to explain the popularity of a country as a goal for educational migration by the degree of institutionalization of Women's Studies programmes. The countries with a high degree of institutionalization of Women's Studies training include Finland, Germany, the Netherlands and the UK (Silius 2002; Chapter 3 in this volume), and are all countries that receive many Women's Studies students. The 'core countries' where students can seek out Women's Studies courses also include the USA.

However, apart from Women's Studies institutionalization, other factors play a role as well. In the UK case, the higher number of current students interviewed who had come to Britain to study (in comparison to past students interviewed), was in part a function of the specific sample since many of the past interviewees were not only mature students (and therefore less likely to migrate) but also came from a college of higher education with no history – at that stage – of student exchanges abroad (Griffin 2003a: 51).

Language plays an important role in the choice of a country. Countries with a widely spoken language, the UK and USA, are obviously attractive. However, countries where courses are taught in English also attract students. Women's Studies courses in the Netherlands and Finland are to a large extent available in English (van der Sanden with Waaldijk 2002: 144, Tuori and Silius 2002: 95). But whereas Dutch Women's Studies courses attract educationally mobile students, this was not the case for Finland, possibly because students from abroad are simply not aware that Finnish Women's Studies courses are available in English. Over the past few years, however, Finland has attracted an increasing number of students thanks to courses offered in English (Commission of the European Communities 2002). The courses offered by Dutch and Finnish universities, often in combination with summer schools, intensive PhDs or individual tutoring, offer foreign students ample options to choose from. Looking at OECD countries, countries whose language of instruction is French and German also dominate in hosting foreign students (OECD 2002a). Indeed, many students do go to countries where languages other than English are spoken, such as Denmark, Greece, Italy and Portugal, and hope to learn the language.

Language skills also play an important part in the considerations that precede a decision to go abroad. Consequently, countries where language skills are fostered send out more students (the Netherlands, Finland). The UK students study abroad mainly in Anglophone countries (i.e. the USA). Although many women travel to English-speaking countries, another language may also function as an enticement. Language skills are in some cases essential to acquiring knowledge about Gender Studies. For instance, before 1990 very few feminist texts were translated into Hungarian so in Hungary knowledge of other languages was essential for gaining access to feminist thought (Gaszi et al. 2002: 366). Language skills can be a requirement and an impediment for studying abroad, but learning a language or improving one's language skills can also be a motivation for going abroad. This tendency has been supported by grants for language students. In the Hungarian case, students went abroad because they received a grant to study English, Dutch or Swedish (Juhász 2003: 24).

## Erasmus student mobility in general and gender equality

Data from the EU-sponsored Erasmus programme in the partner countries overall show that in most of the nine project partner countries there is more outward mobility than inward mobility (see Table 6.3). The UK and the Netherlands, and to a lesser extent France, are the only countries that have more educational immigration than emigration through Erasmus (in absolute numbers). For the UK this means that there are only a few mobile students. For the UK and the Netherlands these data resemble the project data that indicate that those countries do attract many Women's Studies students.

The UK has a long history of far fewer students migrating abroad than coming into the country to study. The high number of educational

TABLE 6.3 General student mobility through the Erasmus programme in Europe, 1999–2000

|  | Incoming students | Outgoing students |
| --- | --- | --- |
| UK | 20,705 | 10,056 |
| France | 17,890 | 16,824 |
| Spain | 15,197 | 16,297 |
| Germany | 14,691 | 15,751 |
| Italy | 8,029 | 12,421 |
| Netherlands | 5,896 | 4,418 |
| Finland | 3,030 | 3,486 |
| Hungary | 457 | 1,627 |
| Slovenia | 9 | 170 |

*Source*: <http://www.europa.eu.int/comm/education/Erasmus/stat.html>

Educational migration and gender

175

immigrants, especially from former Commonwealth countries rather than from Europe, must be viewed in the light of the underfunding of British universities as well as the country's history as a colonial empire. This implies that on the one hand so-called 'overseas', as opposed to European students, are considered particularly desirable since they generate significantly more income than either home or EU students. On the other hand, Britain attracts overseas students from its former colonies because many of them were brought up in an education system not dissimilar to that of the UK and because they are likely to speak English. The three current students who had travelled to the UK to study Women's Studies were non-EU students; in the interview sample women from Taiwan, Indonesia and Madagascar were represented.

The attraction of the UK as a host country is also partly a function of the fact that English has increasingly become the lingua franca of the globalized world. The discrepancy of the numbers of students entering the UK compared to those going abroad is so large that some British universities will no longer allow Erasmus student exchanges if tutors cannot guarantee an equal exchange of numbers coming in and going out. In late 2002, the Higher Education Council of England (HEFCE) put out a tender to investigate the implications of this lack of mobility among students from Britain. The low number of UK citizens migrating to study elsewhere is due both to the lack of knowledge of other languages and to financial considerations among students (Griffin 2003a).

In France there is in general as much outgoing as incoming migration, and French Women's Studies students seem to be more mobile than other French students. Regarding inward mobility, the French EWSI-questionnaire responses (compared with OECD data) seem to suggest that Women's Studies in France attracts fewer foreign students than other disciplines (Le Feuvre and Andriocci 2002b: 68). This may support the tentative conclusion that the degree of institutionalization of Women's Studies programmes – relatively low in France – plays a role in attracting incoming exchange students. In France, students from the North and West African countries, the countries that constituted most of the foreign students in France until the mid-1990s, are less likely to apply to Women's Studies courses than to other disciplines. Educational migration policy is one of the factors that may have an impact on this. Each year, at least two African students are admitted to the DESS postgraduate course in Gender and Social Policy at Toulouse-Le Mirail University (Ibid., pp. 70–1).

Information about the overall participation of students in Erasmus programmes shows equality between the sexes (see Table 6.4). Of all Erasmus participants in 2000–01, 59 per cent were female. This corresponds to the fact that women are the majority of students within higher education (European Commission 2000).

TABLE 6.4 Outgoing Erasmus students by gender, 2000–01

| | Female (%) | Male (%) | Total |
|---|---|---|---|
| UK | 66 | 34 | 9,021 |
| Hungary | 63 | 37 | 1,624 |
| Spain | 60 | 40 | 17,158 |
| France (figures relate to 1999–2000) | 59 | 41 | 17,093 |
| Slovenia | 59 | 41 | 232 |

*Source*: SCRE, Pirrie et al. 2002

However, when all foreign students are taken into account in a certain country (not only Erasmus students), men represent a larger part of foreign students in the OECD countries: 52.2 per cent of foreign students were male (see Table 6.5). In the partner countries, a male over-representation was the case in Finland, Germany, the Netherlands and the UK. There were no data on France and Slovenia (OECD 2002a).

TABLE 6.5 Foreign enrolment by gender, 2000

| | Female (%) | Male (%) |
|---|---|---|
| Hungary | 53.3 | 46.7 |
| Italy | 51.2 | 48.8 |
| Spain | 50.7 | 49.3 |
| UK | 47.2 | 52.8 |
| Netherlands | 47.1 | 52.9 |
| Germany | 46.9 | 53.1 |
| Finland | 42.5 | 57.5 |
| Country mean of all OECD countries | 47.7 | 52.2 |

*Source*: OECD 2002a

Opportunities for student mobility are very important for women. After their studies, especially when women have families and care responsibilities, it is more difficult for them to travel abroad. Indications that more men than women participate in staff and faculty mobility also suggest a decrease in the mobility of women after their studies. A recent study showed that in the UK over 73 per cent of those who took part in teacher mobility in 2000–01 were men, and in Hungary more men than women appear to participate in outgoing staff mobility (Pirrie et al. 2002).

## Courses and credits

The experiences of past mobile students reported in the EWSI project cover the period from 1980 to 2002. Current students reported studying abroad from 1990 onwards. The length of their stays varied, and varies, widely. Students received education abroad for periods that ranged from one-day seminars to six years. Of the different types of Women's Studies courses abroad that Women's Studies students participated in, the option most frequently taken (by 137 students) was staying a semester or for an entire year abroad (see Table 6.6). Forty-seven students reported attending a summer school, and only a few (seventeen) women reported having decided to take a whole course or programme abroad. The average length of all (not only Women's Studies) Erasmus student mobility is just under seven months (Commission of the European Communities 2002). Finally, thirty-one women told us they went abroad for purposes that were related to education, such as conducting research and performing fieldwork and/or internships, rather than to attend specific courses.

A summer school that was often mentioned was the NOISE Women's Studies summer school, organized yearly with support from the Erasmus programme. For many students this was their first experience of studying abroad and was often followed by other forms of educational migration.[4]

The existence or otherwise of a similar degree in the home country is an issue when it comes to having courses taken abroad accredited in the home country/institution. In many countries where Women's Studies institution-alization has not yet reached the level of a separate degree, students, unless they are willing to lose a year, have to take up a semester in a department which has its home equivalent, such as Sociology, Literature etc., rather than do Women's Studies. The European Credit Transfer System (ECTS) has contributed to solving this problem but, as the results of our research show, there still remains much to be done.

Women studying abroad do gain certain qualifications. Data from the questionnaires showed that some women, though not all, received credits, certificates, diplomas or degrees for their study time abroad. Sometimes these women knew that the credits earned would also count at their home university (ECTS credits), though more often there was no information on this. Certificates in some cases were only certificates of attendance. The degrees that women gained varied from BA to MA and PhD. The qualitative data reports of the partner countries suggest that only a few current and

TABLE 6.6 Type of course taken abroad by current and past students

| | Semester / Year | | Summer school | | Whole course | | Other | |
|---|---|---|---|---|---|---|---|---|
| | Current | Past | Current | Past | Current | Past | Current | Past |
| Finland | 9 | 9 | 1 | 3 | | 1 | | |
| France | 14 | 3 | 4 | | 3 | | 1 | 2 |
| Germany | 24 | 17 | 2 | 2 | | | 5 | 3 |
| Hungary | 6 | 3 | 3 | 2 | | | | 2 |
| Italy | 4 | 7 | 7 | 6 | 2 | 2 | 2 | 3 |
| NL | 9 | 7 | 5 | 2 | 1 | 1 | 2 | 7 |
| Slovenia | 2 | 1 | 2 | 1 | | 1 | | |
| Spain | 4 | 2 | 1 | 4 | | 3 | 1 | |
| UK | 12 | 4 | 1 | 1 | 2 | 2 | 1 | 1 |
| Total | 137 | | 47 | | 17 | | 31 | |

*Source*: EWSI questionnaires, 2002

past students earned degrees. In most cases, it was not clear whether or not their achievements were recognized by their own universities.

The narratives of the overseas students studying in the UK show that degrees from the UK were held in high regard in their country and were essential to achieving high status positions (Griffin 2003a: 46). Some overseas students needed the qualification to get promotion in their work either as academics or, for instance, as social workers in their home country, and they went to the UK with the intention of getting a degree there. A PhD from Britain was viewed as a symbol of ability and authority, bestowing professional status on the degree holder: 'If you got a PhD people will trust you, what you have done and what you say' (ibid.).

Although one would want recognition of credits earned abroad in the home country, a stay abroad could also be positive if that was not the case. A German interviewee, who was not sure whether any credits would actually be recognized at her home university, said: 'I've come to see that year abroad as a true watershed, in every way. Regarding my studies ... it gave me a kind of freedom because it wasn't at all clear if anything I did during that time would count' (Schmidbaur et al. 2003: 58).

### Information and funding

The desire for mobility mobilizes. From the interviews it was clear that students who want to travel will search for ways to make it possible. Here, the information about opportunities for studying abroad and the possibilities of funding educational migration play a role in the number of students who study abroad.

Educational migration and gender

Women received information about possibilities of educational migration in different ways. Gender studies networks and exchange programmes between Women's Studies, such as NOISE and WINGS,[5] stimulate student mobility (both are part of the Socrates programme). Some institutions are much more active regarding student exchanges than others. Where institutions are well networked and project the expectation that students will study abroad, it is much more likely that students do so than in cases where the institution is not supportive, does not advertise schemes well, and has little expectation of student mobility. In several cases, personal recommendations from teachers played a role. In Germany, the Netherlands, Slovenia and the UK, people were asked whether they were interested in going abroad by their professor, and such interventions frequently resulted in students' mobility.

The European schemes such as the earlier TEMPUS, then Erasmus and Socrates, are significant sources of funding for studying abroad. Some regional funding possibilities play important roles in the respective regions,

TABLE 6.7 Past and current Women's Studies students' funding sources for educational mobility (%)

| | | Self-funding | Socrates/ Erasmus | Other (including government) | Total |
|---|---|---|---|---|---|
| Spain | Past | 70 | 0 | 30 | 100 |
| | Current | 40 | 0 | 60 | 100 |
| France | Past | 60 | 20 | 20 | 100 |
| | Current | 57 | 14 | 29 | 100 |
| Germany | Past | 57 | 0 | 43 | 100 |
| | Current | 78 | 6 | 16 | 100 |
| UK | Past | 50 | 50 | 0 | 100 |
| | Current | 40 | 27 | 33 | 100 |
| Italy | Past | 47 | 21 | 32 | 100 |
| | Current | 50 | 0 | 50 | 100 |
| Netherlands | Past | 39 | 46 | 15 | 100 |
| | Current | 42 | 42 | 16 | 100 |
| Slovenia | Past | 25 | 25 | 50 | 100 |
| | Current | 25 | 25 | 50 | 100 |
| Finland | Past | 9 | 58 | 33 | 100 |
| | Current | 25 | 50 | 25 | 100 |
| Hungary | Past | 0 | 11 | 89 | 100 |
| | Current | 0 | 67 | 33 | 100 |

*Source*: EWSI questionnaires, 2002

such as NORDPLUS in Scandinavia and Soros networks (OSI, CEU, CEP) in East-Central Europe. The thematic Women's Studies networks NOISE and ATHENA also promote educational migration, as do national organizations such as the German DAAD, and other national scholarship schemes. Sporadically, especially mature students with a definite goal find that private foundations offer grants to carry out research abroad. Grants may cover a semester or year abroad (typical for Erasmus exchange students), a few weeks or a month's research trip, or a summer school. Work placements and internships (especially in the case of Germany) and in-service training (e.g. visits to NGOs with a similar profile) also offer opportunities for educational migration. But overall, public funding of student mobility remains low and difficult for students to access. As Table 6.7 shows, self-funding played a major role in study abroad among the project's questionnaire respondents. In Spain, France, Germany, the UK and Italy, 50 per cent or more of past or present students were self-financing.

## Motives for and impediments to studying abroad

Both current and past Women's Studies students decided to study abroad for a variety of reasons and a combination of factors (see Table 6.8). Information from the questionnaires shows that the most common reasons involved having greater access to academic resources (libraries and faculty), the wish to learn a language, and a specific interest in a Women's Studies course. Also mentioned was the desire to improve career opportunities. To a lesser extent, study abroad was motivated by the desire to take a course not available in the student's home country, or the need to gain a specific qualification. Some indicated that they wanted to go abroad for 'comparative study and contacts'. Other reasons that women mentioned for going abroad were more personal and less explicitly educational, indicating that they wanted to expand their horizons, find new contacts, and have the experience of going abroad.

Access to libraries and other academic sources was a reason for going abroad mentioned in all countries. Especially in France, Slovenia and Spain, this seemed to be very important. In France, a very important motivation, particularly for students who studied in the UK, the USA or Canada, were the relatively comfortable conditions of students in foreign universities, which offered a stark contrast to the rather impoverished conditions they had experienced in their home universities. A past French student who was interviewed remarked: 'Once I was in the [European University Institute], with only my PhD to prepare, I really benefited from excellent working conditions: computers everywhere, access to my own E-mail, an enormous library, where you could order books from wherever you wanted, I really

TABLE 6.8 Reasons for studying abroad (multiple response possible)

| | Access to libraries and other academic resources | Learn the language | Interest in a specific Women's Studies course | Improve career opportunities | Take a course not available in home country | Gain a specific qualification | Other reasons |
|---|---|---|---|---|---|---|---|
| Finland | 8 | 9 | 6 | 10 | 8 | 2 | 7 |
| France | 13 | 10 | 7 | 3 | 9 | 0 | 10 |
| Germany | 18 | 39 | 12 | 25 | 3 | 8 | 15 |
| Hungary | 11 | 3 | 9 | 5 | 4 | 3 | 2 |
| Italy | 18 | 8 | 15 | 3 | 14 | 6 | 1 |
| NL | 11 | 11 | 18 | 11 | 8 | 4 | 8 |
| Slovenia | 5 | 1 | 4 | 1 | 1 | 0 | 0 |
| Spain | 8 | 7 | 6 | 6 | 0 | 1 | 2 |
| UK | 3 | 3 | 8 | 10 | 5 | 0 | 6 |
| Total | 95 | 91 | 85 | 75 | 52 | 24 | 52 |

*Source*: EWSI questionnaires, 2002

couldn't complain, it was like being in a dream' (Le Feuvre and Andriocci 2002b: 70).

Women's Studies students from some countries went abroad because there was a lack of courses in Women's Studies in their own country. This was clearly the case in Hungary, Italy and France. For Hungarian students, educational migration was crucial because of the lack of institutionalized, independent Gender Studies; many studied abroad because they wanted to study gender while others had exhausted all existing possibilities in Hungary. Due to the lack of institutional gender training in Hungary, the most committed and single students (women rarely travel with families) could not but choose the option of educational migration. In Hungary all students went abroad because they won a grant, mostly as language students (English, Dutch and Swedish), and some secured research grants.

For many Italian students, studying abroad was an occasion to attend more institutionalized Women's Studies courses, or their choice resulted from their desire, or need, to study in more detail a given Women's Studies subject or specific theories that are not available in Italian universities. Many Italian interviewees started attending Women's Studies in the late 1980s/early 1990s when there was no consolidated course offer available in Italy (Barazzetti et al. 2003: 14; see also Chapter 3 in this volume). In France, the interest in specific Women's Studies courses offered at foreign universities was related to the low levels of Women's Studies institutionalization (Le Feuvre and Andriocci 2002b: 69).

There were also several examples of students who first discovered the existence of Women's Studies while on an international mobility programme. In Hungary, students who had no idea about gender but happened to spend a year abroad studying were introduced to the discipline and came back with an awareness and created the need for further gender courses (Juhász 2003). One past French student applied to do a Women's Studies course in France after having followed a course on Women and the Law as part of an MA in the Netherlands. She had never received any training on the legal aspects of equality during the three undergraduate years she had studied in France (Le Feuvre and Andriocci 2002b: 70). Some Italian students 'discovered' Women's Studies abroad (the Netherlands, USA) and came back with a whole set of information and materials that were still unknown in Italy (Barazzetti et al. 2003: 36).

Numerous young women considered travelling abroad as an opportunity to get to know new countries and people rather than a specific training opportunity in the field of Women's Studies. Their desire to study abroad was, for instance, linked to the desire to live abroad for a certain amount of time, understand how universities somewhere else work, have new experiences, or a chance of becoming more fluent in a foreign language. Some German students specifically chose to study English, French, Greek and Portuguese. Perfecting English was a privileged aim, justified by the hope of improving one's university achievement by greater ease in reading original English texts (Schmidbaur et al. 2003: 58). For nearly all women, it made sense to refresh languages abroad.

Academic reasons were important, too, particularly for current overseas students who travelled to the UK to obtain a British degree. For them, getting a British degree was desirable, and for two of them it was a necessity employment-wise (Griffin 2003a).

The personal reasons for going abroad were very diverse. They could be 'general' as displayed by many cases in the Netherlands where personal growth was an important motivation to study abroad. To be on one's own, for example, or to enrich one's life were often combined with other reasons.

Women's Studies students revealed a considerable interest in studying abroad. However, there was a discrepancy between their mobility aspirations and their actual mobility. Students mentioned three key reasons for not going abroad: lack of funding, family and/or work-related responsibilities, and lack of language skills. A high number of Women's Studies students said that they did not go abroad because they would have to rely on self-funding, or the grant they had been offered was too little and they could not accept it. The following comment of a current Spanish student is illustrative:

I went to England when I was in secondary school with a grant from the Ministry of Education, but it was for an English course. Later, during University, I went back there but to work, during the summer. I would have liked to go on an Erasmus exchange, but I didn't have the money. And what they give you is not enough. But I would like to go abroad, maybe as a (language) assistant. I'd like to go to a place where I can continue my research. (Carrera Suárez and Viñuela Suárez 2003: 34)

Lack of financial resources was reported in France, the Netherlands, Slovenia, Spain and the UK. In Spain, however, most women who went abroad did have good (research) grants that paid for their trip (Carrera Suárez and Viñuela Suárez 2003: 35). This is not the case in Slovenia, where the excessive costs are an obstacle in many cases. But thanks to the Soros programmes and scholarships, attending the Central European University in Budapest is easier. In France the most important source of funding came from personal resources. Because large numbers of students combine their studies with some form of employment, this is problematic for the realization of mobility (Le Feuvre and Andriocci 2002b: 69). In the Netherlands, students often work alongside their studies. Financial difficulties may also play a role in other countries, but interviewees did not mention them. For instance, in most cases in Germany, a number of different financial sources had to be combined to make foreign study possible. Apart from a grant, parental support, for instance, was necessary (Schmidbaur et al. 2003: 57).

Having a family and/or children was mentioned as a reason not to study abroad by women in Finland, Germany, Hungary, Slovenia and the UK. Career commitments and other personal responsibilities, such as union educational work, also played a role. Student mobility was a greater issue for mature students who make up a significant proportion of Women's Studies students in the UK than for younger students, since many of the mature students have family and career commitments that do not allow them to spend significant periods of time abroad (Griffin 2003a: 49). In Hungary, the women who travel are often single students. There are women, however, who, despite having a partner and/or child, do go abroad. For instance, a past Finnish student went on an exchange with her one-year-old child. She enjoyed the course very much, despite not being able to participate fully because of the presence of the small child:

It was a splendid course, yes. I took only one, it was twice a week and that, too, became a bit difficult to arrange [...] However, the lectures went quite smoothly, but I had difficulties asking for more help with child care, so exercises and other such things tended to be badly taken care of. It meant a lot of effort, even though I didn't go through the course with flying colours. But the teaching itself was so very good so that just to be there was very rewarding. [...] What was left out completely, of course, and which would have been nice to be part of were the student activities. But I just had to go straight to the lectures and straight back again afterwards; there were very interesting people so it would have been quite nice to be able to socialize with them. (Tuori and Silius 2002: 44)

A lack of knowledge of other languages prevented women from the UK and from France from going abroad. For the UK this is one of the explanations for the low number of UK citizens migrating to study elsewhere.

## The experience of studying abroad

Students who migrated for educational purposes commented mainly on three factors:[6]

- the educational methodological schism they perceived in European higher education articulated as a key difference between the Anglo-American and the continental European tradition
- differences in resourcing
- the liberation of experiencing less repressive environments for women

The latter was especially strongly articulated by women migrating from the eastern and southern countries of Europe to north-western ones.

A learning experience the students emphasized in the interviews was the discovery of the 'great educational methodological schism' in European higher education. This is closely connected to the structure and financial background of universities. Students explained at great length the differences between the ways of teaching in different countries. Interviewees reported that at universities in Britain, Ireland, the Netherlands and Finland, classes are smaller, tutoring and individual counselling make these universities more personal and effective. In the smaller-size seminars there was space for more discussion, active participation and questions. Creative analytical thinking was encouraged instead of simply memorizing data. The professor–student relationship was perceived as more democratic and less hierarchical than at Spanish, French or German universities. Professors seem to feel more responsible, and take grading papers more seriously. All in all, students claimed that learning was more fun in this system and encouraged more intellectual growth. A French student talked about her study experience in the UK as follows:

There were only four of us in the feminist epistemology class and 8 or 9 in the Women's History class. That completely liberated me, it was a totally new experience for me and I thought it was great; people were actually interested in what you thought. You really had to take part in the discussions; you were really encouraged to speak up. I was really surprised, because the other women there didn't have any problem with speaking in class [...] They used examples from their own experiences, which they used to illustrate the texts they had read. It was really interesting, because they didn't have a distant relationship to the academic knowledge, they really applied it to their own experiences and there was no idea of a hierarchy between what they already knew and what they were learning in class, both kinds of knowledge were recognised. (Le Feuvre and Andriocci 2002b: 70)

Such experiences of differences in the way of teaching cannot be separated from the fact that facilities and resources are described as far better in some countries than in the continental universities. Libraries are very good, and interlibrary loan works very efficiently (the USA was first and foremost praised for this). Easy access to computers, e-mail accounts provided to students, and free photocopying facilities for students were the norm.

The position of feminism in a country, the development of a feminist community and the relationship between academia and activism also made an impression on students. A Hungarian student said of her experience in Germany:

[In Berlin] I saw that this feminism has such a great literature, and then I jumped at the feminist books in the library. It was so supporting to see that a whole bookcase is full of feminist books. Then I started Xeroxing like mad. This really reinforced in me the notion that we are not totally alone then over here, because it is such a commonplace thing in the West [...] It was interesting to me that S. [her husband and colleague] also read these books with me then, and accepted these thoughts. So you don't have to explain this *gender* aspect and things to him. From this point of view abroad is a fieldwork, it reinforces you that it is worth doing it. Maybe I say this because I just recently got back, but I think without it you wouldn't bear it in Hungary, you would be pulled back. (Juhász 2003: 27)

## The impact of study abroad on educational migrants

Women's Studies' students reported the following key impacts of studying abroad: the development of greater tolerance towards others; an enhanced understanding of other cultures and how things could be done differently; the inauguration of change (for instance, in education) in their home countries; and a positive impact on their employment (opportunities). Educational migration increases openness and flexibility. Countries that are strong in Women's Studies can 'enlighten' the students. A relevant comparative survey, however, clearly showed the impact of national differences in implementing gender equality. The Scottish Council for Research in Education (SCRE) published a study on gender equality in the Socrates programme, comparing data from Spain, France, Norway, Hungary, Slovenia and the UK, thus including almost all the project partner countries (Pirrie et al. 2002). They found great differences in the way principles and practices of equal opportunities and gender mainstreaming were integrated into Socrates projects. In the case of Hungary, for instance, the National Agency that provided the research team with data on the projects administered by them could not identify any projects that had a strong gender equality component, and no monitoring or evaluating of gender-related aspects was practised. In a context where gender mainstreaming and equal opportunities between men and women exist only on the level of international agreements but do not form part of everyday thinking or practice in education, students find other contexts where gender relations differed from those 'at home' liberating and revolutionary. Here, revolutionary in its etymological sense implies that their intellectual outlook 'turned around' and 'revolted' in a new direction.

Along these lines we identified different types of 'revolutions' or discoveries in our sample. One such discovery came from two different sets of students from Hungary, an East-Central European EU enlargement country where Women's Studies institutionalization is of a low level (Gaszi et al. 2002); and students from former colonies arriving in France and the UK. In both cases, the gender roles and expectations in the societies they came from are so different from those of the host countries that the students had to make major adjustments in their perceptions. They thus became pioneering social agents in relation to women's situation in their home countries, reaching educational levels not commonly available to women in their countries and challenging the gender contracts of their home countries. Two students in the UK who came from Taiwan and Madagascar spoke about the difficulties they faced at home because they wanted a successful academic career. One of them said: 'Madagascan men are quite eh, frightened of em, women who are more educated than them [...] because [...] they are afraid this woman might overshadow them, overshadow them [...] most of them like to have greater control over women. I mean, in a relationship for example [...] they would want somebody who is less educated than them, who is more pliant [...] who is quite conciliatory as to their own eh, opinions or needs' (Griffin 2003a: 56).

A Hungarian student who studied both in France and the USA returned with a changed view of gender roles:

[My opinion] changed a lot [...] Not really at the university. Rather in everyday life, on the level of the social distribution of work roles. There are breathtaking differences between Western Europe and Hungary, not to speak of America. In '97 when I came home from France, there were many surprising things, small things [ ... In France], for instance, it was completely normal that a boy started doing the washing-up during or after a party, or getting the place ready before. So, he just took the dish mop out of my hand, it was so natural. At home then, even in my circles, so among the people I meet, this is not like this. Or these terrible sexist jokes in Hungary, so, my own group mates, whom I thought to be enlightened and intelligent people, were abundant. So things like that in France, I emphasize now that from the mouths of people like me, I didn't hear. (Juhász 2003: 26)

On the personal level many students mentioned gains connected to self-growth. Women's Studies students referred to personal and cultural growth. A Slovene student formulated this clearly: 'It is very healthy for a person to disconnect from their domestic environment [...] to begin to think in a different way, to function differently' (Drglin et al. 2003: 46).

The perceived relation between education and employability differed from country to country. In countries where the connection between Women's Studies and employment was not strong, students did not see a relation between having studied abroad and employment. This was for instance the case in Spain (Carrera Suárez and Viñuela Suárez 2003: 35). However, most women were able to apply what they had learned abroad to their further studies or their (academic) jobs. On the whole, Women's Studies students perceived the impact of studying abroad on employment as positive. Sometimes it was viewed as something that enlarges employment possibilities; at other times the impact described was more general. It was reported to be beneficial for the interviewees in a professional or academic sense. In no country were negative effects reported.

Self-growth is obviously beneficial for the development of different skills that enhance one's value on the employment market. One Dutch student referred to the fact that employers value a stay abroad because it proves that the applicant is daring, flexible, autonomous, demonstrates diverse language skills and has had broad experiences. In short, 'it looks good on the curriculum vitae' (van der Sanden with Waaldijk 2003: 30). Gaining knowledge of a foreign language and having stayed abroad was seen as a means of improving one's chances of getting a job after graduation in several countries. Sometimes women even planned to perfect their foreign language skills in the light of future employment. This was, for instance, the case in Germany. There especially, work experience abroad was viewed as desirable (Schmidbaur et al. 2003: 57). Several Dutch women thought that employers value a stay abroad because it shows that they are ambitious, competent and flexible. The Dutch women also talked about personal growth in terms of employability. They mentioned, for instance, knowing your own capabilities and being curious and open towards things that are different (van der Sanden with Waaldijk 2003: 30).

An impact of educational migration on the choice of a job or the jobs women acquired was mostly, but not solely, reported by PhD students or women who (wish to) stay within the academy. They especially considered their educational migration experience as extremely important. It provided them, for instance, with theoretical and practical tools they did not have before. Four women from Germany chose to pursue academic careers immediately after having completed their study abroad. Two other German graduates with foreign experiences were promoted to upper management. One of them thought that her work placement in Egypt was crucial because she found out that way that she no longer wanted a career in the field of development (Schmidbaur et al. 2003: 59). A Finnish past student spoke about gaining self-confidence in Women's Studies so that she thought PhD studies felt like a natural alternative. In the Netherlands two women said that the courses they took abroad helped them in getting a certain job.

Professional focusing was also one of the results of getting to know new Women's Studies courses and theories: women became aware of the direction in which they wanted to develop or specialize.

For migrant students coming into the UK, the acquisition of a degree was the key to getting high-status employment after returning to their home country. In contrast, the relationship between going abroad to study from Britain and employment was less clear. However, having a British degree was considered very useful for working abroad.

Viewed from an academic career point of view, studying abroad is often the first time that Women's Studies students feel they are being taken seriously and treated more like colleagues and equal partners than students. It is also an important time for students to establish contacts and become part of the international network of Women's Studies. Many exchange students reported that they felt their study abroad experience was the first time they could really concentrate on academic work since other daily routines and activist work did not take up their time. For several students, the chance to develop this 'professional identity' was a first step towards an academic career in Women's Studies.

The experience of mobility makes students more mobile and influences subsequent employment mobility. Some German respondents worked abroad for a period. One woman from Spain moved on to work in the USA

189

as a primary schoolteacher. And in general, in Spain, as a result of the self-confidence that students gained from their Women's Studies training, they were ready to move to different cities or countries to work as well as to change jobs, thus broadening their employment opportunities. In the Netherlands, for some mobile students working abroad was an option. One woman taught summer courses abroad. One woman had lined up a job in Singapore; she said that she might not have done that if she had not studied abroad. Yet another woman had her first job in Moscow. Many mobile students said how much they enjoyed working together with people from different countries.

In Hungary, the lack of real job opportunities for gender experts means that some students see their future abroad and all of them hope for the best with the enlargement of the European Union. For the young women interviewed in Hungary, continuing their university studies with an MPhil or PhD abroad was itself an employment option, as the grant they get might be higher than any salary they could possibly earn in academia as a beginner. With high foreign grants, staying abroad was thus an option, especially for those who have already spent some time abroad during their studies: 'Or, which is another chance, EU enlargement, and you know, I have spent so much time abroad, that it doesn't seem totally absurd to live maybe not in Hungary, but abroad' (Juhász 2003: 19). Although foreign grants are attractive, Hungarian women who consider this option are often discouraged by their visions of remaining unmarried and childless, or their parents remaining without help in old age. If they have a partner, husband or children, it is most probable that they will never take foreign grants, because their spouses would not give up their jobs and follow them. The males of the same generation are not impeded by such considerations and often stay abroad beyond their thirties. Working abroad could also mean that people would lose touch with Hungarian academia and miss opportunities of integration into the local system.

The overseas students in the UK did not expect to have any difficulties in finding a job in their home countries. A past student from the UK had been to the Netherlands and got a taste for travel and work abroad; instead of pursuing postgraduate work as she had originally intended, she went to teach English in Japan. The British degree she had was important for getting this job. After having married a Japanese man, she continued to work, which is not the norm in Japan. In her teaching this woman then introduced gender issues:

I find that in a lot of my advanced classes they often want to talk about gender. When they ask me what university degree did you study and I always say

Gender Studies, and they get their dictionaries out and look it up, men and women (*whispered*) and they always ask me can you give us a presentation on it, so I have done this quite a lot of times. [ ...] They love it, they are so interested. (Griffin 2003a: 52)

In France there are increasing employment opportunities for graduates with equal opportunities training from a French university, because of the progressive integration of gender equality issues in the development programmes of international NGOs in North and West African countries. Indeed, almost all the men who apply for admission to do the Gender and Social Policy course in Toulouse are from Africa. Most foreign students who apply to this course already have some work experience in 'Gender and Development' programmes in their home country. This would seem to suggest that there are already significant employment opportunities in this field in some African countries. Obtaining a degree from a French university was more important for improving the career prospects of men and women already working on development programmes than it was for helping them gain access to jobs in this field in the first place (Le Feuvre and Andriocci 2002b: 71).

The most important factor that emerged from the interviews was the experience of women's own power as an active agent in their lives. Most of the women considered their time abroad as a transformative period. One German graduate summarized her experience in the USA: 'I've come to see that year abroad as a true watershed, in every way' (Schmidbaur et al. 2003: 58).

To conclude, Women's Studies students reported a positive impact of educational migration on their employment possibilities. They made international contacts, improved their language skills and widened their horizons workwise. They acquired new theoretical and conceptual tools and skills which they could import into their home countries, became more mobile and open to different and new experiences. In short, educational mobility enhanced employment opportunities.

## Educational migration and European citizenship – some conclusions

At the beginning of this chapter we raised the question of whether the experience of studying abroad in Europe is shared democratically by men and women. We argue that gender equality should not only pertain to the numbers of exchange students, but also to the lasting effects of empowerment brought about by international education. In the past, education abroad has provided many generations of male students in Europe with an empowering experience. It stimulated self-confidence, international orientation and employability. This phenomenon is so pervasive that stories about temporary stays abroad have long since become part of the folklore of national elites in many European countries. As such, they have become part of the male *Bildungsroman*. The question we tried to answer in this chapter was whether the experience of travelling abroad is an equally empowering experience for women who travelled between 1990 and 2002 as part of their academic training in the field of Women's Studies. Women's Studies as a discipline has developed only recently and is unequally integrated into academic programmes in different European countries. This raises important questions about the role of student mobility in the process of achieving international compatibility of qualifications in an innovative academic field. The question we want to answer is whether this educational migration contributes to the empowering of programmes and knowledge about gender. Studying gender both as an academic subject and as a lived experience of female exchange students allows us to draw conclusions about the gendered implications of a European area of higher education as the key way to promote European citizens' mobility and employability.

A few conclusions can be drawn. The language skills that are required for studying abroad can be seen as an impediment, but are often perceived as an additional advantage of study abroad, and after educational migrants have returned to their countries, language skills are a major factor in their increased employability. In the non-anglophone countries, Women's Studies programmes that use English in their curriculum or in part of it, attract more students from abroad than programmes that offer courses only in their national language. This does not mean that exchange students only take courses in English; on the contrary, they often learn the language of the country they visit, and perfect their command of the language during or even after their stay. But a few courses in English induce inward mobility.

The different degrees of institutionalization of Women's Studies programmes play a role in attracting incoming exchange students. The European cooperation in this field, in Erasmus, the NOISE summer school and the Thematic Socrates Network Athena 1 and Athena 2, prepares students for their stay abroad: their professors can tell them what to expect and where to go and the topics taught in the participating programmes reach beyond the national scope of gender relations. Almost all students felt they had acquired useful knowledge and competencies in the field of Gender Studies; they broadened their national knowledge, and felt confident to use the new competencies in their own country.

The question whether or not educational migration contributes to employability is crucial to the issue of gender equality in employment. In all countries it was strongly felt that international experience is extremely important for employers and that it will contribute to career chances. In particular, academic careers (research, doctoral degrees) are nearly impossible in many countries without international experience. In view of women's lagging labour participation in Europe, and the low numbers of women in higher positions, it is crucial that women participate in educational migration. For many students the first experience of studying abroad was often followed by other forms of educational migration. This is an important finding since it has implications for women and their careers. For many women in Europe, the time when they attend university is one of the rare periods in their lives when they are without caring responsibilities. They use this opportunity to the fullest. After graduation, however, the number of women travelling for educational purposes drops, and more men than women participate in staff and faculty mobility programmes. If travelling abroad as a student increases educational migration after graduation, it is crucial that women continue to travel as students, and that solutions are found for childcare whenever necessary.

A further conclusion addresses the perceived educational methodological schism between the different educational traditions. Smaller classes, more tutoring and individual counselling, as well as less hierarchical relations between students and professors, encouraged more intellectual growth. From this it may be concluded that educational cooperation across Europe would profit from more explicit discussions about educational formats. The experiments in open and distance learning as elaborated in several European Women's Studies projects, as well as the first European textbooks and readers in Women's Studies[7] will certainly contribute to these debates.

The most important factor that emerged from the interviews was female students' experience of their own power to be an active agent in their lives. Most of the women considered their time abroad as a transformative period. On the eve of the acquisition of full gender equality in the European Union in the twenty-first century, this will prove to be the most important lasting effect of educational migration. Without women who feel empowered to partake in public space, European citizenship will remain an ideal limited to men.

## Notes

1 Bologna Declaration, see <http://europa.eu.int/comm/education/socrates/Erasmus/bologna.pdf>

2 These interviews were part of the research project EWSI, see Introduction to this volume.

3 'Current' students refers to students who were taking Women's Studies courses in 2002.

4 The NOISE European summer school, a two-week intensive course, has been organized annually since 1994 and is hosted by different NOISE partner universities with the participation of a broad range of students and teachers from all over Europe and beyond. Each year, the NOISE summer school hosts around fifty participating students. The students range from advanced final-year undergraduate students to postgraduates and PhD students. The partner universities (2003) in NOISE are Universitaire Instelling Antwerpen (Belgium), Syddansk Universitet (Denmark), Universidad Complutense de Madrid (Spain), Aristoteleio Panepistimio Thessaloniki (Greece), Universita degli studi di Bologna, Universita di Firenze, Universita della Calabria, Universita degli studi di Milano (Italy), Universiteit Utrecht (Netherlands), Åbo Akademi University (Finland), University of York, University of Lancaster (UK), University of Lund, Linkoeping University (Sweden), Lodz University (Poland) and University of Ljubljana (ISH) (Slovenia). <http://www.let.uu.nl/womens_studies/>

5 In WINGS (the Women's Studies Interdisciplinary Network on Gender and Society in European Higher Education), the universities of Antwerp, Aarhus, Nijmegen, Potsdam, Torino and Lancaster participate. <http://www.kun.nl/cvv/>

6 The cultural and educational background of the interviewees strongly influenced the way they experienced their stay abroad. Supporting our findings on this issue is a report of the European Commission Directorate General for Education and Culture on the socio-economic background of Erasmus students (European Commission 2000). Its findings show that family economic background or the occupational status of parents is not a significant factor in the selection of Erasmus students, but family educational background is. There is also a bias in the selection process towards students from the advantaged socio-cultural groups.

7 The first of these was Griffin and Braidotti, eds (2002a).

# 7 | Gender, race, ethnicity and nationality in Europe: findings from a survey of Women's Studies students

GABRIELE GRIFFIN

## Race, ethnicity, migration and Europe

In May 2004 ten additional countries joined the European Union. These countries, mostly Eastern European, constitute an other of 'Europe', partly feared and partly welcomed, and as such representing *'das Unheimliche'*,[1] the both familiar and strange, which Julia Kristeva has so richly analysed in *Strangers to Ourselves*. Drawing on Freud, she writes: 'Strangely, the foreigner lives within us: he is the hidden face of our identity, the space that wrecks our abode, the time in which understanding and affinity founder. By recognizing him within ourselves, we are spared detesting him in himself' (Kristeva 1991: 1). That step towards recognition which Kristeva maps and which she views as a mechanism for holding at bay xenophobia is one not yet taken within the European countries where foreigners are just that, foreigners, intruders whose presence is constantly challenged and contested, as continuous battles about asylum seeking, racially motivated attacks and other such occurrences amply demonstrate.[2]

In the debates about European enlargement, this problematic of the non-recognition of the foreigner experiences a refinement, at once specific and universal, namely the issue of an anticipated 'invasion' of migrants from Eastern EU countries seeking employment and benefits in the north-west European countries. That refinement, the simultaneous fear of the foreigner who takes your job and draws on your benefit system is not new, nor is the introduction of regulations to prevent such migration. It is augmented by fears of the illegal worker who is part of the same phenomenon of economic migrancy. As Michael White reported in the *Guardian* (12 February 2004): 'All current 15 EU member states, including the majority who have imposed transitional controls up to 2011, are vulnerable to il-legal workers in the black economy once the 74 million citizens of the 10 accession states join the Union on May 1.' The uncanny here visits the heart of capitalism into which the foreigner imports his or her labour, 'the only property that can be exported duty free, a universally tried and tested stock for the wanderer's use' (Kristeva 1991: 19). The possibility of its illegal and/or unregulated activity, graphically illustrated in the UK in February

2004 by the death of at least twenty Chinese workers digging for cockles in the dangerous sands of Morecambe Bay (Meek and Watts 2004), creates anxiety not because of an assumed concern for the workers (Morris 2004)[3] but because of the discovery of the seemingly hitherto undetected presence of such workers – possibly illegal, potentially endangered, significantly alien – in 'our' midst.[4] As Meek and Watts (2004: 3) wrote about one such worker: 'in the rich world he was invisible. He only became visible by dying.' The very fact that asylum seekers may and can melt away into their environment, that illegal immigrants can blend into their environment especially in urban contexts but not only there,[5] only serves to augment that fear, raising questions, sometimes unanswerable, of who are these strangers, where are they, what do they do?

Kristeva's description of the foreigner, and European reactions to that figure in the guise of people from the accession countries, raise the questions of who that foreigner is, and who the 'us' are whom Kristeva gestures towards and who resurface in the legal provisions by those European countries who seek to debar people from other member countries from entering their terrain without work permits. For, and here Kristeva (1991: 17) has pointed to a crucial issue, 'The foreigner is the one who works.' But where does that person come from and how is s/he defined? In a telling poem entitled 'Crown and Country' in which the mixed-race Scottish poet Jackie Kay (1997) uses the metaphor of teeth and dentistry and health migration to analyse questions of inter-national identity and identification, she talks of 'our people' and 'just across the border', indicating the intimacy of separateness and the proximity of difference, both of which haunt Europe as a geopolitical space. Kristeva (1991: 18) describes the following incident: 'I have [ ... ] come across, in a French village, ambitious farmers who had come from a different region [ ... ] wanting to "make a niche" for themselves by the sweat of their brows, hated as much for being intruders as for being relentless, and who (the worst of insults during demonstrations) heard themselves called Portuguese and Spaniard.'

Kristeva here relates the ever-widening circles of xenophobia that begin with an assertion of regional specificity, thus rejecting as 'foreign' all those who do not come from that region or, indeed, even more precisely, that village, to an assertion of national specificity, rejecting those from (certain) other nations as unfit and unfitting outsiders, here the Portuguese and Spanish. A similar hierarchization of diverse European nations manifested itself in the summit in February 2004 of France, Germany and the United Kingdom in the face of the imminent enlargement of the European Union. This hierarchization, which takes the shape of an inner circle of the three countries delivering 54 per cent of the EU's income, and declaring their alliance as based in this reality, and an outer circle of all those excluded from that alliance, reproduces through its nation-based specificities the problem of nationalism that has haunted Europe's history over the past three centuries. Here the European idea/l breaks down as visions of economic strife translate into nationalist sentiments and the articulation of hierarchized difference and exclusion.

The articulation of fear of the foreigner, within recent EU debates conceived as people from Eastern Europe, raises an issue that has inflected European racism throughout the twentieth century, namely that of othering those who are phenotypically similar to ourselves (see Griffin with Braidotti 2002a); indeed, othering 'other' Europeans. This stands in stark contrast to the USA where race politics have traditionally been drawn along the black and white binary. This binarist notion of race assumes, *inter alia*, the visibility of race, its bodily materialization at the surface of the skin through visible differences that allow seemingly easy categorizations into white and black. Although that presupposition of visible difference has been variously contested, most poignantly perhaps in the work of the American philosopher and artist Adrian Piper (1988, 1996), it is one that has dominated thinking about race in post-Second World War Europe, not least because the Holocaust was also inflected by a race politics based on an assumption of biological and morphologically visible differences. However, as the Holocaust also showed, such assumptions were spurious and were part of a process of visibilizing difference that included the demand that Jewish people wear a yellow star to make them visible and other from their 'Aryan' neighbours. Similarly, the ethnic wars of the 1990s in the former Yugoslavia were concerned with the process of visibilizing a difference that had not been present before and justifying it through appeals to nationalist sentiment (see Papic 2002; Slapsak 2002). As Lisa Price (2002: 254) put it: 'If nationality is a belief in both commonality and distinctiveness, nationalism is a political ideology which both encourages such belief and pursues a programme of national self-determination.'

That kind of programme of national self-determination, appealed to for instance in Britain as part of an anti-European stance that views national self-determination as threatened by too close an allegiance with the European Union, cuts right across the European idea/l of harmonization and integration since it resists the subsumption of national identities under a European superstructure. Here one of the fundamental tensions within Europe and one of its key differences from the USA emerges, for one of the ways in which Europe is fundamentally different from the USA is that Europe, unlike the United States, suffers from indeterminacy. Made up of nation-states that assert their nationhood in different and distinct ways, manifesting high degrees of internal diversity, polylingualism and multiculturalism, Europe is politically, culturally, geographically unstable, economically diverse, the quintessential subject-in-process, always becoming, never being. The European Union, as ideal and as geopolitical entity, is emblematic of the unstable nature of Europe, as indeed debates about whether Turkey is more western or more eastern, and how to treat the countries that became member-states of the EU on 1 May 2004 demonstrate. That unstable nature which is counteracted by the recourse to national identity whenever it makes itself manifest, accounts for the tensions that persist in Europe between the European Union's aspirations for integration and harmonization, and the realities of the nation-states that constitute the European Union's member-states.

Thus the desire for harmonization which underlies the policies of the European Union is instantly called into question, for example, when one conducts research on the ground, so to speak. In *Three Guineas* (1938: 125), Virginia Woolf famously proclaimed: 'As a woman I have no country. As a woman I want no country. As a woman my country is the whole world' – a statement that might have opened her up to the post-national possibilities of Europe. But actual gender research in Europe instantly demonstrates that 'as a woman I live the realities of my country', even as or maybe despite being a migrant, diasporized, displaced. This is evident, for instance, in the poetry of the Irish woman poet Eavan Boland (1987: 50) who describes her childhood experiences in post-war Britain, weaving together the personal and the political in 'An Irish Childhood in England: 1951'. Migration from Ireland to England leaves the child of that poem lost between two worlds, striving towards an accent and a language she finds hard to emulate, and leaving her open to the reprimand, 'you're not in Ireland now' as she struggles to pronounce words the English way. That intimate binding-up of personal identity with national identity and political history which resists the desire of harmonization so deeply embedded in European Union politics and policies becomes immediately manifest when one does research in a cross-European context. In the project on Employment and Women's Studies (see the 'Introduction' in this volume), we found that what haunted the daily tasks of conducting the research was not 'our common European heritage' or future but the specific circumstances of the individual partner countries. Various chapters in this volume, in particular possibly Chapters 1 and 2, make this amply clear. As Le Feuvre and Andriocci in Chapter 1 demonstrate, there are clear differences regarding women's employment expectations and prospects between European countries that are mainly agrarian and ones that are highly industrialized. Carrera Suárez and Viñuela Suárez in Chapter 2 show that equal opportunities infrastructures in European countries are highly dependent on the good-will of local parties, and are set up or closed down depending on which political party happens to be in power. Locality matters. And since it is locality or where you happen to be that determines your experiences, since the imbrication of the local in the global is fairly specific as evidenced in the ways in which the USA as a superpower decides to intervene or not in various locales around the world,[6] it is not surprising that people's identities are embedded in the local, not least in the case of women who tend to figure as bearers of regional and national identity (Papic 2002; Bosch 2004).

Women's embeddedness in their locale is a strategy of social integration that ensures women's place and participation in the community, even if within historically and socio-culturally conditioned constraints. Such embeddedness extends to an understanding of how race, ethnicity, gender and their intersectionality are understood in a given context. When the female project partners from the EWSI project (2001–03; see the Introduction to this volume) came together to discuss the questionnaire content in preparation for collecting survey data, various partners proposed different questions that they wanted to have added, and which they considered vital to the research on what happens to women who undertake Women's Studies training in the employment market (see also Chapter 8 in this volume). The British partners suggested that a question on respondents' ethnic background be included on the basis that it would be important to find out the ethnicity of those who study Women's Studies. Including that question was without doubt, from the British perspective, also a matter of intellectual habituation and cultural conditioning; after all, it is common practice in the UK to ask about ethnic origin in the context of collecting equal opportunities data, as part of job applications, for instance, and in national surveys such as the census. However, if we look at the categories of ethnic origin asked about both in equal opportunities forms and in the census, we not only see a reproduction of the former British empire and its associated history of migration; we also see a pattern inflected by an assumption of visible difference. Thus the main categories of differentiation of question 8 of the 2001 census, 'What is your ethnic group?', were: 'A) white, B) mixed, C) Asian or Asian British, D) Black or Black British, E) Chinese or other ethnic group'. These categories articulate phenotypical distinctions, replicated in the sub-divisions under category B) 'mixed' which differentiated further between 'White and Black Caribbean', 'White and Black African', 'White and Asian', 'Any other mixed background: please write in'. We might therefore argue that the British model of race and ethnicity is closely aligned to the American binarization of black and white. However one thinks about this representation of ethnic or racial groupings in Britain, being asked about one's ethnic background is standard practice in the UK. However, in countries that have less entrenched equal opportunities data collection (see Chapter 3 in this volume) and, perhaps more poignantly, in countries with fascist histories such as Germany where race and ethnicity were exploited as part of the strategic elimination of whole sections of the population, such questions are not common and, indeed, are resisted since they are associated with that problematic history.

## Answering the question about ethnic background

In the project questionnaire the question about ethnicity was framed in an open-ended manner, simply asking 'Your ethnic background?' This was intended to give respondents the opportunity to identify their ethnic background in their own words rather than have to select from a pre-existing range. It should be noted that when we agreed to have this question in the questionnaire, none of the partners thought this in any way problematic. When the questionnaires came back, however, we found that many interesting issues were raised by that question. The first of these was the actual response rate to the question itself which showed distinctive patterns (see Table 7.1).

Thus, whereas in four countries (Finland, the Netherlands, Slovenia and the UK) the response rate was very high, in four other countries (Spain, Italy, France and Hungary) only about half or less than half of all the respondents answered the question. Germany occupied an interesting in-between ground in that well over half of the respondents actually answered the question. Thus while the vast majority of female respondents in about half the countries felt able to answer the question, half the

TABLE 7.1 Percentage of questionnaire respondents who answered the question about ethnic identity (%)

| | Past students | Current students |
| --- | --- | --- |
| Slovenia | 94 | 94 |
| Netherlands | 94 | 92 |
| Finland | 88 | 71 |
| UK | 87 | 92 |
| Germany | 62 | 52 |
| Spain | 49 | 52 |
| Italy | 48 | 42 |
| France | 8 | 45 |
| Hungary | 3 | 3 |

*Source*: Quantitative data reports, EWSI project, 2003

women in four other countries did not. Phoenix (1995: 40), referring to a British sample, reports that 'Young women were more likely not to rank nationality as important than were young men.' This may account for some of those who did not answer the question; though, as the findings below show, 'ethnicity' was differentially interpreted by women both within and across European countries, and it may be differentiated from nationality in a variety of ways.

Importantly, as will also be indicated below, in the British sample in particular 'ethnicity' was more likely to be interpreted as referring to skin colour, a function possibly of the ways in which questions about ethnic identity are conventionally framed in British equal opportunities and census data collections.

Significantly, as I shall indicate shortly, the countries with the greatest homogeneity of response – Slovenia and Hungary – topped and tailed the table; that is, Women's Studies students from Slovenia were most likely and Women's Studies students from Hungary least likely to answer the question, in both instances possibly because they thought the answer (i.e. 'Slovenian' or 'Hungarian') would be self-evident. Overall, respondents in countries where fascist movements had turned into regimes – Germany, Spain, Italy and France – were less likely to answer this question than those from countries without such histories. One reason for this, as indicated above, is clearly the association of specific ethnic identities with persecution, and the concomitant resistance, in such countries, to the use of ethnicity as an identifying category.

TABLE 7.2 Category of response used to describe ethnic identity by questionnaire respondents, past and current students (%)

| | Colour: white/black | | Nationality | | Region/ geography | | Religion | |
|---|---|---|---|---|---|---|---|---|
| | Past | Current | Past | Current | Past | Current | Past | Current |
| UK | 85 | 84 | 1 | 4 | 12 | 7 | – | 1 |
| Spain | 76 | 93 | – | 2 | 25 | – | – | 2 |
| NL | 21 | 19 | 61 | 40 | 8 | 25 | – | 4 |
| Finland | 20 | 7 | 79 | 93 | – | – | – | – |
| Italy | 16 | 43 | 62 | 57 | 12 | – | 8 | – |
| Germany | 11 | 1 | 71 | 70 | 12 | 10 | 6 | 3 |
| France | – | 3 | 100 | 87 | – | 9 | – | – |
| Hungary | – | – | 100 | 100 | – | – | – | – |
| Slovenia | – | – | 100 | 100 | – | – | – | – |

*Note*: Figures may not amount to 100% since multiple responses were possible.
*Source*: Quantitative data reports, EWSI project, 2003

Gender, race, ethnicity and nationality

In analysing the ways in which the women who responded to the question about ethnic background articulated that ethnicity we found that four identifiers dominated, though in differing orders for the diverse countries. They were colour, nationality, geographical region and religion (see Table 7.2).

## Colour matters

Interestingly, the UK and Spain here emerge as the countries in which colour as a marker of ethnicity dominated whereas nationality dominated in the other European countries. The greatest degree of diversity of responses, as Table 7.2 shows, could be found in the Netherlands, Germany, Italy and to some extent the UK. The relative dominance of colour as the marker of ethnicity in the UK, Spain, the Netherlands and Finland is not matched by a significantly greater degree of range of skin colours prevalent in these countries or referred to in the answers of the respondents. Indeed, only in the UK was the colour black as well as white named (see Table 7.3). In all other countries where colour was named it was only as 'white'. This might point to the colour blindness of dominant groups (i.e. white people not identifying themselves as 'white') as has repeatedly been raised in whiteness studies (Hill 1997; Frankenberg 1993; Ware 1992).

TABLE 7.3 Colour-based responses (words used) to the question of ethnic background by country

| Country | Responses |
| --- | --- |
| Finland | white, Finnish white |
| France | white (only one woman used this) |
| Germany | white |
| Hungary | – |
| Italy | white, white European, western white |
| Netherlands | white |
| Slovenia | – |
| Spain | white |
| UK | white, mixed race, black |

*Source*: Quantitative data, EWSI project, 2003

We may also attribute such a monochrome response to bias in our samples that were, after all, non-random (see Introduction to this volume). But it also indexes the contexts where colour matters and is routinely associated with ethnicity, where phenotype plays an overt role in local race politics.

The absence of people from divergent ethnic backgrounds who might identify themselves in terms of colour in all project partner countries except for the UK indicates partly the small actual numbers in the local population of such people, but also the issue of access to higher education of so-called minority groups right across Europe. It is as rare to find Turkish students in German universities as it is to find Arab or North African students in French universities, or (still) Asian and Black students in British universities. This is as true of Women's or Gender Studies cohorts as it is of other disciplines.[7] Most of the respondents in the British sample who identified themselves as black were in fact overseas students who had undertaken educational migrations to the UK (see Chapter 6 in this volume), not least because they responded to the gender agendas of international organizations and of their own countries (see Griffin 2002a). They were thus less likely to be indigenous black women, of whom the sample in fact included only a very small proportion. Overall, in the UK one needs to distinguish between different ethnic groups when considering their educational attainments. Thus data analyses in Britain of the 1991 census showed that while Indian and black African people had significantly higher percentages of higher education qualifications than their white counterparts, these percentages were significantly lower for black Caribbean, black Other, Pakistani and Bangladeshi people (Owen 1994a: 19–21; Owen 1994b: 20–3). Overall, the number of women and men participating in higher education from so-called ethnic minority backgrounds remains a concern.

## Nationality

The range of identifiers of ethnicity articulated in the responses (Table 7.2) reveals our understanding of difference, and indicates that there was little common understanding across Europe of what 'ethnicity' means. As Table 7.2 shows, nationality emerged as by far the most common response to the question of ethnic background, accounting for almost all the responses of past and current Women's Studies students in France, Hungary and Slovenia, and for almost all the responses of current students in Finland. German, Italian and Dutch respondents, too, used nationality as their signifier of ethnicity. Only in Spain and in the UK was ethnicity not understood to mean nationality.

The responses detailed in Table 7.4 reveal that the category 'nationality' hid some diversity among the respondents with the greatest range of answers being displayed by respondents from the Netherlands, France and Germany, and the least degree of diversity being indicated in answers by Italian, Spanish, Hungarian and Slovene respondents. As Chapter 6 in this volume shows, this range maps on to countries of educational immigration and emigration respectively: France, Germany and the Netherlands were likely to have greater numbers of educational immigrants than Italy,

TABLE 7.4 Nationality-based responses (words used) to the question of ethnic background by country[8]

| Country | Responses |
| --- | --- |
| Finland | Finland, Sweden |
| France | American, French, Moroccan, Polish |
| Germany | German, Swiss, Indian/British, Taiwan |
| Hungary | Hungarian, German (only N = 4 respondents in total) |
| Italy | Italian |
| Netherlands | Netherlands, Belgian, German, Italian |
| Slovenia | Slovene, Croatian |
| Spain | Spanish |
| UK | British, Irish |

*Source*: Quantitative data, EWSI project, 2003

Spain, Slovenia and Hungary from where students tended to emigrate. The Finnish, Slovene and UK responses also index intra-national tensions between groups that view themselves as aligned to one identity that might be viewed as national while living in a country that has a different national identity. This is as true for the Swedish-speaking minority living in Finland as it is for the Irish in Britain and for the Croats in Slovenia. It bespeaks the fact that geographic location constitutes only one element in one's ethnic identity, and the tenacity of national sentiments even at times of displacement.

## The matter of regions

A number of respondents used words describing regional affinities as a way of defining their ethnic background (see Table 7.5), with 'regional affinities' here being defined severally to mean supranational regions such as Europe or Scandinavia, continents such as Africa, regions within countries such as Asturias in Spain, towns and self-descriptions that do not strictly fall into categories of national, religious or colour identity. Imprecise as this might seem, it shows that there is a small but not insignificant group of women who identify either as European or in other non-national ways that privilege region at either supra- or sub-national level as more significant than national identity. In our project we did not follow up questions of ethnic identification but, especially within the European context, it would be useful to understand further those respondents who identified themselves as European, not least because they might provide significant clues regarding the factors that shape a European as opposed to a more nationally oriented self-identity. This is also interesting in view of the fact

TABLE 7.5  Region-based responses (words used) to the question of ethnic background by country

| Country | Responses |
| --- | --- |
| Finland | European, Hame region, Finnish Swedish |
| France | European, Mali, North Africa, Sao Tome, Scandinavian |
| Germany | European |
| Hungary | – |
| Italy | European, Italian/German, western, Naples, Fiulian |
| Netherlands | Dutch region, Flemish, Haarlem, Indo-European, Limburg, Dutch East Indies, Surinamese |
| Slovenia | – |
| Spain | Asturian, European, Indo-European, Slavic |
| UK | African, Afro-Caribbean, Asian, Cypriot, Latin American, European, half Ukrainian, Celtic |

*Source*: Quantitative data, EWSI project, 2003

that in Ann Phoenix's study (1995: 39), 'None [of the British interviewees] expressed any desire to live in European countries other than Britain.' If, as Phoenix suggests, we are dealing with 'imagined communities' at the European level, then we need to understand more about what fuels that imagination.

The responses in Table 7.5 indicate that region is not an important marker of ethnic identity in either Hungary or Slovenia. Indeed, as Table 7.3 shows, the same was true of Finland and France. In countries where region played a role, it was more important for past than for current students, thus possibly marking a shift away from region towards other indicators of identity. Significantly, region played a role in the countries where the greatest range of responses to the question of ethnic identity was found, that is in the Netherlands, Germany, the UK and Spain. This suggests countries with complex histories of unity and division (e.g. the Netherlands and Germany), of migration (the UK), of systems of regionally-based governance (Spain). Here identification at the ethnic level becomes a matter of choice and multiplicity, of diverse possibilities defying the notion of some over-arching unity.

## Religion and ethnic background

The least used category to signal ethnic background was religion, a fact that highlights the increasingly secular nature of Western states, the suppression of religion under the former communist regimes, women's non-alignment with religious institutions, particularly where the women have a background in Women's Studies that will lead them to interrogate the role of religion in the oppression of women. The responses that articulated religious affiliation as ethnic background showed particular patterns (see Table 7.6).

TABLE 7.6 Religion-based responses (words used) to the question of ethnic background by country

| Country | Responses |
| --- | --- |
| Finland | – |
| France | – |
| Germany | Protestant, Jewish, Roman Catholic |
| Hungary | – |
| Italy | white Catholic, Somalia/Muslim |
| Netherlands | Jewish, German Jewish |
| Slovenia | – |
| Spain | Catholic |
| UK | Jewish |

*Source*: Quantitative data, EWSI project, 2003

In four countries (Finland, France, Hungary and Slovenia) religion did not figure at all, signalling the severance between religion and ethnicity as a function of secularized state formations as well as histories of the suppression of religions. Catholicism was mentioned, predictably, in both Italy and Spain where the Catholic Church has a very active role in everyday life, and secularization is less pronounced than in countries with Protestant majorities. Germany occupies a particular place in that context in that, for historical reasons, it has areas with majority Protestant populations (mainly in the north of the country) and areas with predominantly Catholic populations (mainly in the south). The state and church are still significantly imbricated, with civil service jobs in many *Länder*, for example, conventionally going to applicants who have the religious affiliation (indicated by the church to which you pay taxes) of that *Land*. Thus it is very difficult in some *Länder*, for instance, to attain a university position if you profess yourself non-affiliated to a church (through opting out of the church tax) or do not belong to the dominant church in that *Land*. The political impasse concerning the European constitution conditioned in part by the demand from the Catholic-dominated countries – Poland, Italy and Spain – that Christianity be explicitly mentioned in that constitution indicates the role that, within the Christian spectrum, the Catholic Church especially continues to play in the imaginary and indeed legal framework of some European nation-states. That Protestantism has fared rather differently is evident in the fact that it was raised as the definition of one's ethnic background in only one country, Germany, where, as I indicated above, institutionalized religion still plays a significant part in the day-to-day governance of the people.

In three countries (Germany, the Netherlands, Britain) respondents identified 'Jewish' as their ethnic background. Both the Netherlands and Britain were, of course, recipient countries of Jewish refugees during the Second World War, and still have significant Jewish communities, especially the UK. Although anti-Semitic attacks, however they may be defined (i.e. whether as anti-Jewish or anti-Israel), are on the rise in Britain (Bennetto 2004), they are not, of course, linked to the Holocaust history that defines Germany's relation to Jewishness. The presence of a Jewish respondent in the Germany sample is more interesting since many Jewish people would still refuse to live in the country responsible for the Holocaust. It may thus be that the articulation of Jewishness in the German context is about a new confidence in the very possibility of being Jewish in Germany. It may also be an act of defiance, an assertion of an identity that is always under threat and therefore asks for articulation to defy that threat.

We do not have access to the sub-texts of the definitions offered here and it also has to be pointed out that Jewishness has been variously viewed as a religion and as an ethnicity. The fact of a woman declaring her ethnic background as Jewish does not tell us anything about the degree of her religious observance, a fact that is equally true of all the other respondents who cited a religion as their ethnic background. It means that we cannot know to what extent the Somali/Muslim woman was describing religious observance or life practices when she asserted her Muslim ethnic background. Since we asked neither about religious affiliation per se nor about nationality, respondents did not have the choice to offer more differentiated responses to the question we asked by being provided with other spaces in which to articulate those other potential dimensions of their identity.

### Other ways of seeing ethnic background

Two other responses deserve mention. One French respondent declared herself a 'citizen' and one Spanish respondent defined herself as a 'person'. Since the concept of citizenship, articulated during the French Revolution, has such a powerful tradition in France, it is perhaps not surprising that one respondent asserted her citizenship. Again, we have no access to the subtext and cannot determine whether this response was ironic, assertive of a particular relation to the state, a misunderstanding of the question, or the representation of a specific sense of self.

Similarly, in the case of the one Spanish respondent who chose to identity herself as a 'person', we are confronted with an indeterminancy of meaning – this woman might not have understood the question, might be deliberately refusing to engage with 'ethnicity' as a category of identity that might be marked through national or religious background, might be asserting the primacy of 'personhood' over other potential identity categories, etc. Both responses, 'citizen' and 'person', if not simply the result of a misunderstanding, signal traces of resistance to the question of 'ethnic background' which are useful when one considers the role ethnicity has played in intra-European wars and civil unrest. The refusal of categories that have been mobilized to legitimate acts of atrocity and persecution is one way in which it is possible to work towards the European idea/l.

## Conclusions

Ethnicity as a category of identity has not served Europe well as it attempts to move towards harmonization. More importantly, it has not served nation-states well for, as the intra-European wars of the twentieth century have shown, the issue of ethnicity, mobilized to elaborate hierarchized differences and legitimate atrocities, has, in fact, been an intra-national, rather than a cross-national one. Ethnicity as articulated in Nazi Germany, the former Yugoslavia and in Northern Ireland, has always been part of intra-national tensions, manifesting themselves across Europe but of course not only there, as the wars in Rwanda and other African countries of the same century indicate.

Women have been both the bearers and the victims of the ascription and assumption of ethnic identities (Djuric 1995). It is therefore perhaps not surprising that a significant proportion of female Women's Studies students whose learning, after all, focuses on gender relations and women's situation chose not to answer the question on ethnic background, particularly from countries with fascist histories, and from countries where equal opportunities monitoring, including for ethnic background, is not well entrenched.

The findings from the EWSI project detailed above show that 'ethnicity' as a category is differently interpreted in different European countries. The majority of respondents who answered the relevant question understood it to be about national identity, a fact that may have been fostered by the absence of a question about national identity. It is clear from the evidence discussed in the other chapters in this volume that women – and, indeed, presumably men, though they were not the focus of this study – are and experience themselves as both most effecting and most affected by the locale in which they find themselves. Some who find that locale unbearable or deeply problematic choose to migrate if they can (see Chapter 6 in this volume). For the vast majority, however, to move is neither an option nor something they particularly desire. Among those who answered the question about ethnic background, nationality figured as their primary identifier, thus demonstrating the importance of nationality in that identity formation. One of the key challenges for the European Union therefore remains the integration of those identities into a European one. This might entail the fostering of multiple affiliations rather than of mutually exclusive categories, the elaboration of political and socio-cultural strategies that enable such multiple affiliations (see also Phoenix 1995). Such a possibility is undermined by legislations in diverse European member-states that cut across the idea/ls of the European Union of freedom of movement for its citizens, for example, since such legislation generates nation-based differences among the member countries, simultaneously reinforcing national/ist sentiment and weakening the idea/l of Europe as a cohesive entity.

In only two countries, the UK and Spain, was skin colour used as a marker of ethnic background. But, as Ann Phoenix (ibid., p. 42) wrote à propos of the identifications professed of young black people in Britain: 'Defining oneself as African Caribbean is sometimes useful in the British context where it speaks to a shared history and (mythic) shared cultural origin. However, it provides no clear point of political mobilization or political clout in the rest of Europe where the relationship of European states to Caribbean former colonies is different or non-existent.' The point here is not only one of the historical specificities that prompt certain identifications, and the latter's ability to travel effectively as part of a nation-transcending political project, but also, much more simply and in line with the EWSI project findings, that colour plays much less of a role in the ethnic imaginary of many other European countries than it does in the UK and, seemingly, in Spain. This is a function of many factors including, without doubt, colour blindness towards 'white' as a colour category, the dissociation of that colour from the notion of ethnic background by most of those who are 'white', histories of fascism that have exploited phenotypical diversity as a source of oppression, but it also suggests habituation in Britain and possibly in Spain to answering ethnicity questions through the colour lens. Finally, though, it also reveals that colour is not the primary marker of ethnic background for most of the questionnaire respondents. This has important, as yet not fully acknowledged, implications for how issues of race are addressed in Europe since it goes back to the point made earlier that the history of 'racing' Europe is one of seeking to visibilize invisible differences, to attribute phenotypical specificity (where it does not exist) and, failing that, to mark those constructed as bearers of difference by forcing them wear signs signifying that difference.

A significant minority in our sample in several countries including Italy, Spain, France, Germany, the UK and the Netherlands understood ethnicity to be about a regional or geographic identity such as Asturias in Spain, Slavic or Scandinavian. That regionalism, too, has a powerful history in certain European countries and has been – albeit somewhat inadvertently – fostered by the European Union in its attempts at economic harmonization through the creation of objective one and two regions, in other words regions that qualify for extra financial support because they suffer from significant economic underdevelopment, recession or deprivation. The shift in ascription of objective one or two status that will occur as a consequence of a series of poorer countries joining the EU in May 2004 is already much discussed, fuelling renewed regional and national sentiments, as regions that have come to expect additional financial support from the EU will be catapulted out of their deprived status by those even more economically depressed than they are. Regionalism has long histories in some countries such as Spain and Germany but less in other countries. Again, it is worth noting that the regionalisms most mentioned in the questionnaire responses operate at sub-national level. The gulf between a sense of European identity and other, more localized identities remains wide.

While the vast majority of respondents identified their ethnic background either in national or in regional terms, a very small group used religion as their marker of ethnicity. Despite rising tensions across Europe in the wake of the bombing of the World Trade Center, and inter-ethnic tensions, specifically between Muslims and non-Muslims, few women in our sample saw religion as the primary marker of their ethnic background. Since the identification of oneself as Catholic, Muslim or Jewish does not indicate degrees of religious observance or observance of other religiously prescribed life practices such as eating fish (rather than meat) on Fridays, observing prayer cycles, wearing particular clothes etc., it is not entirely clear what the naming of that identifier signifies. However, it is clear that few women saw religion as a key aspect of their ethnic background. This is understandable both in the context of predominantly secular, north-west European countries, in post-communist countries, and in countries which adhere to a strict separation of state and church. It is also explainable in terms of the fact that Women's Studies as a discipline fosters the critical engagement of its students with ideologies, beliefs, institutions and practices that oppress women in a variety of ways. Hence it would have been surprising to find many respondents who saw religion as key to their ethnic background. Finally, this attests to the fact that Women's Studies in many European countries remains resolutely 'white', a function of the lack of access of women from diverse ethnic backgrounds to higher education.

Across Europe, then, women's identities are tied up with the national and the local rather than with the supranational. As the European Union negotiates its enlargement we need to be mindful of the fact that the enlargement of spring 2004 potentially fosters rather than weakens national sentiment. However, if one of the European Union's objectives is to harmonize the various member-states into European unity, it needs to address the question of how identification with such a unified body can be promoted. The intra-national strife that characterized the Balkan wars of the 1990s and the British presence in Northern Ireland remains – active and dormant to different degrees in the different member countries. National identity is strong in the Eastern European countries as the responses in our project attest, but also in Finland, France and Germany. If the expected migration of Eastern European workers to Western European countries occurs, we can anticipate more such strife, and greater intra-national tensions as well as intra-European tensions as questions of who is supposed to police which borders and how may well increase. This means that we can anticipate the renewal of the 'othering' of those whom we still fail to recognize as ourselves, new antagonisms born out of the visibilizing of a difference not visible, and fresh anti-European sentiment derived from a sense that it was the broadening of that Union that brought about the economic migrations anticipated at the moment.

We can take heart from the fact that many women respondents chose not to answer the question on ethnic background. This may not have been merely a function of unfamiliarity with such a question, or historically induced reluctance to respond to it, but also recognition of the pernicious nature of that category in many contexts. It parallels the qualitative findings of the EWSI project discussed in Chapters 4 and 5 of this volume that Women's Studies students reported a greater tolerance of diversity in their professional and personal lives as a result of their training, an ability to connect their own experiences of disadvantage and disempowerment, and their theorizations with those of others, as well as demonstrating an understanding of the intersectionality of gender, race and class, which recognized the problematic of ethnicity as a political dimension in individual and social identity formations.

## Notes

1 Freud (1919: 340) describes *'das Unheimliche'* or the uncanny as 'that class of the frightening which leads back to what is known of old and long familiar'.

2 On 19 February 2004 the European Union together with the World Jewish Congress organized a seminar to discuss anti-Semitism in Europe (Black 2004; Castle 2004). This is just one indicator of the abiding issue of racism and ethnicism that Europe faces.

3 The lack of concern for foreign workers was made clear in relation to the Chinese women and men who drowned at Morecambe Bay by the fact that the UK government had dismissed earlier representations by the local MP about the dangerous working conditions with reference to the lack of immigration staff to deal with such problems (Morris 2004; White 2004).

4 The paradox of the Chinese cockle pickers' situation is that their existence was known about; indeed, the local MP Geraldine Smith had written to the Home Office one year before the tragedy occurred seeking intervention (Wintour and Ward 2004). In the tension between allowing gaps in the labour market to be filled and keeping control of migrational flows, the Home Secretary David Blunkett proposed electronic tagging in 2003, a device that reproduces the drive to make invisible presences visible that haunts European race relations.

5 The film *Dirty Pretty Things* (dir. Stephen Frears), released in 2002, addresses these issues.

6 In the spring of 2004, one obvious comparison is the war in Iraq compared to the civil unrest in Haiti; the USA decided to intervene in the local politics of the former while leaving the latter to sort out its own problems (Agencies in Gonaives 2004).

7 In Britain students from ethnic minority backgrounds tend to congregate in certain subject areas where they can be overrepresented. For instance, many students from Asian backgrounds go into accountancy, pharmacy and the sciences or medicine rather than into arts, humanities or social sciences subjects to which Gender Studies belongs.

8 For actual numbers of questionnaire respondents, see Table in note 6 of the 'Introduction' to this volume.

# 8 | Comparative research in Europe

JALNA HANMER

This chapter analyses selected issues in undertaking cross-national research in Europe. The issues arose during the conduct of a two-year Framework 5, European Union-funded research project.[1] The aim of this chapter is to contribute to the understanding of common problems in conducting European research by examining the research process for when and how issues surfaced, attempts to overcome problems, unresolved issues and suggestions for their resolution. The research project itself set out to identify the specificity of social forms and institutional structures in nine European Union and accession countries by examining a wide range of factors in three major areas: education through Women's Studies, equality policy and implementation, and women's employment. By examining the connections between Women's Studies, equal opportunity policies and employment, it was hoped to address key concerns in Europe that would lead to an improved understanding, greater knowledge and, ultimately, policy recommendations on employment and education. The research proposal was exceptionally well received by its European evaluators, obtaining a rarely achieved score of 100 per cent in the four categories of assessment.

In this chapter, after a general introduction to the project, selected issues are examined in some detail, beginning with the strengths and weaknesses of multidisciplinarity teams of researchers and communication frameworks for different stages of the research process. As the research project progressed, a series of issues arose regarding the comparability of data between countries. Concepts and intellectual mapping began a process of raising issues of difference and diversity. These surfaced through language and translation concerns, and through divergent views on the value of quantitative and qualitative research methods. Comparability became an issue in the collection, analysis and synthesis of data produced by each method: document analysis, survey research and semi-structured interviews. Attempts to obtain comparability were shaped through consistent efforts to standardize the research processes.

Over the two years, the multi-method research study both focused on different aspects of the issues to be studied and gradually built up knowledge for cross-national comparisons. The research process both avoided and encountered issues and problems with attempts at resolution and mediation.

Insufficient initial understanding of socio-cultural settings and differences in disciplinary and national research traditions were particularly relevant for raising unanticipated issues between partners and their research assistants. Careful planning based on prior knowledge succeeded in avoiding some of the negative research issues identified in other studies that cross national boundaries, but not all could be (Hantrais and Mangen 1996). The issues discussed in this chapter are inherent aspects of cross-national research at the present time.

The project brought together an all-female multidisciplinary research team from Finland, France, Germany, Hungary, Italy, the Netherlands, Slovenia, Spain and the UK. As is common in European research projects, countries with different stages of economic and social development were included and the nine countries have distinct historical, political and cultural systems. Within the European Framework 5 funding programme, these diversities became assets. The team and the research topic neatly fitted into the European Commission strategy to 'mainstream equal opportunities' and 'promote the participation of women in all fields of research'. The all-female research team with senior academic partners and research assistants in itself promoted career opportunities, training, employability and mobility while studying their impact on other women.

**Research questions and design**

While planning for the project began with incomplete knowledge of the area to be researched within and between the participating countries, the partners in this project knew anecdotally that Women's Studies has a significant impact on women's employability, on the promotion of equal opportunities, on their innovatory potential in the labour market, and on individual lifestyles and choices. Although the information was limited, partners also knew that across European countries Women's Studies training differed in its extent, type and institutionalization (see the SIGMA Report, 1995). Employment opportunities also varied and were affected by work–life balance, especially family responsibilities, as did equal opportunities policies and women's specific employment goals. But no scientific data had been collected, either by region or comparatively, which would provide information on the precise nature of these differences, their impacts, inter-relationships and policy implications.

The studied area is rooted in the personal, i.e. lifestyles, beliefs and value systems; in the structure and functioning of social institutions, i.e. Women's Studies in higher education and in equal opportunities; and in social and economic processes, i.e. women's employment. The interpretive approach adopted was an inductive method, with loosely defined hypotheses. The aim was to gather information from past and present Women's Studies students on Women's Studies, equal opportunities and women's employment; areas that are moulded by national institutional, social and economic processes. Thus, the study incorporated both cross-national and cross-cultural issues, although the ways in which these were interrelated and differentiated were not clearly specified or fully discussed between partners at the planning stage or later on (Oyen 1990). This was partly because planning has to occur without funding and therefore virtually, and partners thus have limited resources to invest in a project prior to its commencement. Once the project has started, the focus is on its successful execution. Process issues can be relegated in favour of an outcome focus when timetables are tight.

The fundamental research question for the EWSI study was: How does Women's Studies affect women's opportunities and interventions in the labour market? To develop a research design to explore this basic question required taking into account the complexities of Women's Studies education and training, of employment opportunities for women, and of other factors that influence women's employment. Accepting these complexities and identifying other personal and institutional factors that needed to be considered led to a series of sub-questions. How does Women's Studies affect individual women's subsequent employment achievements? Given the structuring of employment opportunities, what did women do, once trained? What is the relationship between equal opportunities policies, Women's Studies and women's employment? What impact do Women's Studies have on the changes women seek to generate in the workplace? How do Women's Studies impact on professional and other duties undertaken in the workplace? How do Women's Studies affect the relationship between family and work, and changing and managing relationships within the family?

These are questions on consequences, or effects, and raise relational questions about Women's Studies, women's employment and equal opportunity policies (Ember and Ember 2001). To achieve the research aims required teasing out connections between employment, education, equal opportunities and the institutionalization of Women's Studies. The relationships of specific interest were between equal opportunities policies and the institutionalization of Women's Studies training; differences in Women's Studies in institutionalized and non-institutionalized settings; and women's expectations and their actual experiences of Women's Studies in relation to the labour market. The impacts to be examined on women's employability were the institutionalization of Women's Studies through the professionalization of women; educational mobility; women's choices and interventions in the labour market; and Women's Studies training on women's lifestyles and choices (see Chapter 5 in this volume).

Three possible relationships were identified. First, that the degree of institutionalization of Women's Studies training is significantly related to the impact of Women's Studies on women's achievements in the labour market. That is, as institutionalization of Women's Studies increases so do women's achievements in the labour market. Second, that the degree of institutionalization of Women's Studies in individual countries is related to the equal opportunities policies in that country. That is, the implementation of equal opportunities policies increases the institutionalization of Women's Studies. Third, that the degree of institutionalization of Women's Studies and the presence and implementation of equal opportunities policies impact on women's professionalization. That is, women's professional employment increases with the institutionalization of Women's Studies and the implementation of equal opportunities policies.

As with other comparative studies, the partners set out to examine specific issues in more than one country with the intention of comparing their manifestations in different national settings. The aim at the planning stage was to develop a coherent proposal that would both recognize and be responsive to differences between national settings while producing a research design capable of providing comparable datasets. A multi-method research design was developed to identify, analyse and explain similarities and differences in order to gain a better understanding of the impact of Women's Studies on social life and social institutions. Initially the research design had four phases of six months each.

Phase 1 focused on the collection of national background data through document research on employment, equal opportunities and Women's Studies and the preparation of instruments for use in phase 2. Phase 2 consisted of the collection, analysis and reports on empirical data, both quantitative and qualitative. Phase 2 methods were to conduct a nine-country descriptive statistical survey, followed by semi-structured interviews with a sub-sample of the survey.[2] Phase 3 then utilized Phase 1 and 2 findings for cross-country comparative analyses on selected topics. Partners were to draw on the country reports in phase 1 and the quantitative and qualitative data reports in phase 2 to analyse, from a cross-European perspective, one key dimension relevant to the impact of Women's Studies on women's employment. Phase 4, the dissemination of findings, became integrated throughout the life of the project as reports were either published in paper format or placed on the project website as phases were completed and dissemination continued after its conclusion.

Each phase not only increased cross-country knowledge of Women's

Studies, employment and equal opportunities, but led to a more intensive cross-national and cross-cultural analysis. The primary data, both quantitative and qualitative, were based on non-random samples as the total Women's Studies population and its distribution within each country could not be identified for a variety of reasons associated with sample size relative to population, and national data collection practices. Thus, countries varied greatly in the number of their higher education institutions and the Women's Studies courses on offer and not all national higher education institutions maintained information on past students. Questionnaire samples of fifty current and fifty past students, including students who studied in other countries, were to be selected by type and length of course and routes into Women's Studies in different universities and other institutions of higher education within each country. Ten current and twenty past students who took their courses at different times were to be selected for interview from the returned questionnaires. The type and length of courses varied greatly between countries, with the full range including pre-university modules, and undergraduate and graduate modules and degrees. The meaning of the descriptive statistics derived from questionnaire data were to be amplified and clarified through qualitative interviews that explored the cultural context. Table 8.1 presents the research methods and outcomes.

TABLE 8.1 Research methods and outcomes

| Method | Type of data for analysis | National data reports | Nine country overview |
|---|---|---|---|
| Document searches | Secondary, non-harmonized | Yes | Yes |
| Quantitative survey, non-random | Primary, harmonized | Yes | Yes |
| Semi-structured interviews, non-random | Primary, loosely harmonized (standardized categories) | Yes | No |

On completion of the outcomes in Table 8.1, partners undertook one of eight cross-national comparative report topics. The topic allocation was based on the expertise of each partner and the degree of differences/contrasting cases in each key dimension. The purpose of the comparative reports was to provide a comprehensive analysis drawing on the quantitative and qualitative data, earlier document research on Women's Studies, equal opportunities and employment, and any additional material that was appropriate. The eight comparative report topics were: the organizational forms and degrees of institutionalization of equal opportunities in Europe; the institutionalization and focus of Women's Studies training across Europe; employment opportunities for women in Europe; the relationship between Women's Studies training and women's employment expectations; women's expectations concerning the labour market and employment outcomes following Women's Studies training; professionalization of Women's Studies graduates in Europe; relationship between educational migration and Women's Studies students' employment; and the impact of Women's Studies training on women's lifestyles. The comparative reports were to contain examples of best practice and policy recommendations.

## Multidisciplinarity

The design of the study was based on differences between, and the strengths of, the eleven partners from the nine countries. The disciplinary backgrounds of the partners and their research assistants were in the Humanities and Social Sciences, specifically philosophy, literature, applied social sciences, sociology, cultural studies and history. Taken together the partners had specific expertise in the areas of quantitative and qualitative data analyses, women in the professions, women's educational migration, Women's Studies, women's non-governmental organizations, women, work and employment, feminist and women's history, feminist theory and the representation of women. Individually, their prior knowledge of the institutionalization of Women's Studies, women's employment, equal opportunities and women's professionalization, and specific experience of individual research methods, ranged from high through medium to low. These differences reflected both the development of Women's Studies within the nine countries and in disciplinary areas. Collectively, the multidisciplinary research team had specific expertise and knowledge in the institutionalization of Women's Studies training, women's employment, equal opportunities, women's professionalization, and the various research methods utilized in the study.

The project was based on the assumption of shared research traditions, common to Women's Studies. As underlying disciplinary traditions surfaced and, when combined with a gendered ideological representation of research methods (Oakley 2000), this assumption proved problematic. Women's Studies is variously understood as being a discipline in its own right or as an inter- or multidisciplinary field of study. Women's Studies can be understood as the same as, or varying from, Gender Studies. A feminist perspective can be seen as the epistemological bedrock or an add-on to both Women's and Gender Studies. Although Women's Studies curricula may reflect these differences, this nine-country study demonstrates the centrality of gender or women's consciousness to its findings, while the issue of the relative merit of the research methods used in this project lay at a deeper sub-stratum to be exposed as the research gained momentum.

While multidisciplinarity in European research is usually understood to be positive, there is a downside to differences in academic backgrounds that should be acknowledged. Multidisciplinarity meant that there were similarities and differences in the methods and backgrounds of partners and their research assistants as well as content specialization. Looking back on this project, while partners and research assistants had different strengths, all were expected to contribute equally to the collection, analysis and writing up of data. This represents a democratic ideal of research which may be inappropriate in some research contexts. In the case of this project, for instance, prior knowledge of Women's Studies, equal opportunities and women's employment and of the differing research methods used in the study of these fields varied considerably. Beginning with the background country reports, not all partners and research assistants were equally equipped to undertake document and literature research. Unevenness in the national background reports reflected these differences as well as that of translation. While partner and research assistant contributions to quantitative data were limited to questionnaire planning and data collection, there were substantial variations in prior basic knowledge of quantitative methods, data analysis and even of SPSS. All had some research experience with qualitative methods, particularly interviewing, but there was no time for more than a brief discussion of the type of interviews that was expected (Fontana and Frey 2000), while ways to undertake systematic comparable analyses were under-developed. This project suggests multidisciplinarity may be most successfully utilized and its strengths developed when methods are limited to shared research method knowledge among partners.

## Frameworks for communication

As team-working is the predominant method for European Commission-funded cross-national research, creating frameworks for communication between researchers is necessary in order 'to broaden their perceptions of the research agenda and to prepare to negotiate with their colleagues' (Rainbird 1996: 118). Working in cross-national teams brings to the fore diversity in perceptions of research issues, theoretical perspectives and methods of conducting research, which makes ongoing negotiations essential. The potential for new knowledge and insights are advantages that draw participants into cross-national and multidisciplinary team-based research, but in practice communication and negotiation are restricted when coupled with a rigid time-bound, legally-based research contract. The EWSI project expands on the issue of communication and negotiation in several ways; illustrating the impact of truncated time and restricted communication during early and later stages of the research process.

The prior networking of senior Women's Studies partners in the study facilitated this European collaboration. Negotiations began with establishing the research agenda. As with many other projects, the communication framework for the EWSI study was to circulate the proposal to partners for comment and, when suggestions were received, to discuss them and make changes. No comment, either in general or on specific aspects of the proposal, was interpreted as agreement. The proposal was written by researchers from one country and, while in the strict sense research questions and methods were not imposed by one national source (Rainbird 1996), the proposal incorporated a national view of research that, as the research process unfolded, was not always fully implementable by other national partners and/or their research assistants.

Although there was no other practical way that the eleven partners from nine countries could have developed the research questions, the research design and its implementation, it emerged later that agreeing to participate in the project did not preclude differences in understanding and interpretation of the proposal. An expanded communication framework involving more time and joint meetings to prepare the proposal was not feasible. Although the partners had not undertaken cross-national research together before and not all were known to each other, there was no opportunity for the proposed partners to meet in advance to ensure that all aspects of the research proposal, its research questions, aims, methods, the work plan and project management were understood fully and regarded as appropriate for each country. The time pressures on senior academics combined with the low success rate of proposals for European Commission funding meant it was not a viable option to use academic time or institutional finances in this way.

Experience suggests the need for clarity at the proposal stage on the subsequent role of partners in undertaking the study, should funding be received. In the EWSI project, in practice, senior researchers could be closely involved or more distantly positioned. Research assistants could be the only representative from their country at research meetings or always, or almost always, accompanied by the senior partner. The degree of personal involvement by senior partners was not always directly related to the degree of research experience of their research assistants who could be highly experienced or PhD students, involved throughout the project or subject to change. Research assistants varied in the degree of responsibility carried for understanding and completing the work. This seemed to be partly the result of national research traditions that do not value empirical research to the same degree as more abstract, definitional and idealist theoretical expressions as well as the demands of other commitments on senior researchers. More importantly, it raised questions of research process and researcher management, and in particular the question of whether the appointment of a researcher was in itself sufficient to guarantee the appropriate conduct of the research itself or not. It certainly was the case that senior project partners understood the management of their junior researchers in very different ways, with some taking a close interest in the actual work and directing and managing the junior researcher accordingly, and others expecting the junior researcher to take full and virtually sole responsibility for the research. The latter was not always appropriate, especially where junior researchers lacked the relevant skills to conduct the work independently, and could lead to the need for other partners to manage junior researchers from another country, in particular during project meetings and in relation to the reports they produced. The presumption that there would be a core group of eleven active senior partners who attended all meetings proved unrealistic. This had implications for communication between partners, as once funding was agreed the major communication framework related to project content was face-to-face meetings.

Face-to-face meetings were the high points of communication between partners and their research assistants. Partners and research assistants also corresponded by email, post and communicated by telephone with each other and the project coordinator in between meetings, but all issues and problems were brought to the meetings. The meetings were focal points, demonstrating and furthering effective project management and participant willingness to share disagreements, worries and concerns as well as positive views. Meetings were conducted with the aim of ensuring partner agreement and, even more importantly, the sharing of the same understandings leading to decisions on research instruments, analyses of data collected and the writing up. Discussion, negotiation and decision-making were structured through these meetings and, as the primary cross-national communication framework for the ongoing research process, functioned best for specific countries when senior partners were present as well as their research assistants.[3]

The phasing of the project incorporated strategies for facilitating communication. The background national reports in phase 1 helped partners to gain the same or similar knowledge of the three key areas across the nine countries before undertaking empirical research with Women's Studies past and current students. During phase 1, standardized reporting formats were designed for use in phase 2. The same research approaches were used to carry out primary and secondary analyses of national data. Time phases, work packages, specific partner responsibilities, and a series of meetings between partners and their research assistants facilitated the development of the study and the completion in each phase. Project management was well organized and detailed tasks and timings rigorously implemented.

Over the two years of the study, there were ten two-day meetings in seven countries of partners and their research assistants. The study began with project-based meetings, followed by a mid-term review and then a final review, while the remaining meetings were devoted to the relevant phase of the study.[4] In addition to focusing on the study, this series of ongoing partner meetings also involved seminar sessions with invited speakers, public meetings on the project with local participants and presentations on the study to other academics and conferences. Dissemination also was ongoing via the website as the study progressed. Of necessity meetings were practical and focused on achieving the tasks and outcomes for each phase. This reduced time for discussion of more fundamental issues arising from concepts and research methods.

## Concepts and intellectual mapping

Annette Jobert (1996) draws attention to the inchoate development of central concepts in cross-national research, such as education, training, employment and work. Because the definition and understanding of concepts are culturally specified in institutional practices and policies, the relationships between them are also conceptually localized. In our project this issue was experienced in an acute way over the use of the term 'course', in constructing the questionnaire. The term 'course' was particularly problematic as it was assumed to be a descriptor of the shared experience of Women's or Gender Studies providing a major similarity and connection between partner countries.

In English, 'course' has several meanings even when restricted to the educational context. It can be used interchangeably with module or refer to undergraduate or postgraduate degrees. The relevance of this to cross-national research was not recognized during the time the questionnaire was developed and finalized, a collective enterprise in which all partners and research assistants participated. An incorrect assumption, that all partners understood the term 'course' in the same way, either when used on its own or when linked to Women's Studies, guided the construction of the questionnaire. Only when questionnaires began to be returned did it become obvious that students in different national contexts did not always recognize themselves as Women's Studies students, for instance where gender content was incorporated into traditional social science and humanities disciplines. In Finland the term 'course' proved meaningless as degrees are organized by level. Elsewhere courses could be organized as modules or degrees and were not necessarily titled Women's or Gender Studies. The first insight into the problem was that the distinction in English between course and module was not fully conveyed to all partners.

As questionnaire returns increased, the problem with the literal translation of the word 'course' resurfaced. Some partners only realized after translation and circulation that the questions on courses did not reflect the educational system of their country, which made it difficult to obtain the required information from respondents. Other national researchers made changes at the questionnaire translation stage prior to circulation to fit their educational systems. It quickly became evident that excellent second-language skills do not eliminate language as a problem area. Further, not all partner countries had the full range of undergraduate and postgraduate degrees in Women's Studies. Practical problems arose: for example, the questionnaire offered columns for replies on types of courses such as modules, degrees etc., but when this structure did not conform to the national educational system, entries could be made in the wrong column.

Other conceptual problems began to surface, even though each partner translated or arranged translations of the questionnaire to be used in her country. English words, directly translated into another European language, could convey other meanings. For example, in Germany the word 'informal' (meaning work in the informal sector), was interpreted as work in the grey economy and students were unlikely to admit to this. Self-employment in the Netherlands could be interpreted as the degree of independence within public or private sector employment rather than self-employment as separate from salaried or waged labour.

There were a number of other issues raised by partners or their research assistants that reflected cultural differences between countries. Respondents were asked for views on experiences that could be interpreted as relatively straightforward or complex; that is, the impact of Women's Studies in a variety of situations. Respondents were also asked to remember past employment and earnings, which could be problematic in some cultural contexts, especially if students had had many short-term jobs. Asking questions about employment could be seen to be impolite or students could be unwilling to provide information on pay. Questions on quality of life were not always meaningful to respondents in all national settings. Students did not always know how to describe parental job titles and this was a greater problem in some countries than in others. In some national contexts both younger and older students could find it difficult to answer questions on life experiences, which was attributed to the way questions were asked, and students could view themselves as atypical, while in another national context age differences could be a factor increasing or decreasing the willingness or ability to answer questions.

As far as possible, past and current students were asked the same questions. As with other questions discussed in later meetings, any that might be interpreted differently by respondents were queried regarding their suitability for cross-national comparison. While the emphasis was on devising questions that would be understood in similar ways in all nine countries, questions that exposed cultural differences between countries could in fact result in rich data. One question known in advance to be problematic was to ask about ethnicity. There was considerable unease about asking this question. Even though partners and their research assistants forewarned that in some countries students would refuse to answer or would not understand the question, ethnicity as well as nationality in relation to students, their mothers and their fathers were included in the questionnaire. As anticipated, this question produced nationally varied answers in which of course non-reply also constituted data. The results and analysis of the questions on ethnicity are presented in Chapter 7 in this volume.

In discussing the questionnaire design, all partners were interested in adding questions that they thought would particularly illuminate the data for their country or that were routinely asked, for example when eliciting demographic information, in their country.[5] The expanding length of the questionnaire was recognized as problematic before its distribution, but no agreement could be reached on how to reduce it. Partners and their research assistants could not agree on a limited number of significant variables. As a result there were 313 variables in the past student questionnaire and 293 in the current student questionnaire. Before distribution a compressed layout reduced the number of pages, but the complexity of the layout with brief spaces for replies led to a reduction in replies. These issues were foreseen, but could not be overcome, given the need to make relatively quick group decisions with insufficient time to pilot questionnaires in the nine countries. A pilot would have helped to identify conceptual problems, and the issue of the questionnaire size and layout in obtaining completed questionnaires.

As experience with the questionnaire grew, issues for specific country respondents were noted, but furthering cross-cultural understanding of these differences could not be explored within the time frame and other limits of this project. Given these concerns, as the project progressed, the issue for partners and their research assistants began to focus on research methods.

## Quantitative and qualitative research methods

The value attributed to quantitative and qualitative methods seemed to be about more than differences in national research traditions and national cultures, but rather to be a restatement of the dispute within Women's Studies on research methods. The research origins of Women's Studies lie in qualitative methods (Bowles and Duelli Klein 1983; Roberts 1981; Stanley and Wise 1983). As a new subject area, the interview became the primary method for exploring women's experiences. Qualitative methods became accepted as the way to expose patriarchal social relations and the reality of women's lives (Harding 1986). Accompanied by a robust attack on the assumed objectivity in quantitative research, qualitative methods became valued over the quantitative. Women's Studies research training, including PhD research, has favoured qualitative methods, and quantitative research today remains somewhat discredited or at least not the favoured method of research in Women's Studies.

Twenty years later, Ann Oakley discusses the function of the quantitative and qualitative dichotomy as a gendered ideological representation. 'Within this gendering of methodology, experimental methods are seen as the "quantitative" and therefore the most masculine [ ... ] these processes of methodological development and gendering cannot be separated from the ways in which both science and social science developed; and the social relations in which they are embedded' (Oakley 2000: 3). In this dichotomy qualitative methods are the most feminine and the survey with its presentation of findings in numbers, whether descriptive or explanatory, represents the masculine. The EWSI project illustrates this ideological viewpoint.

As areas of difference were identified, the value of the survey data declined for some partners and research assistants. Over some months, feedback from researchers was followed by exchanges on the reliability and validity of the quantitative data – and views could be expressed with considerable passion. The proposed relationship between the survey method and interviews, with the survey as a means of producing limited data to be followed up and explored in depth in interviews, became less focused and ultimately was ruptured by the group decision to interview, in some countries, women who had not completed the questionnaire and adding new questions for interview that replicated those in the questionnaire. Some research assistants could be particularly adamant that the qualitative data were reliable and valid, representing the 'true' facts on Women's Studies, equal opportunities and employment in their country, while the quantitative data did not.

The basic issue with the quantitative data seemed to be their presentation in percentages, along with issues in obtaining questionnaire respondents. To reach a consensus among partners and research assistants, a summary page about the research methods was added to the quantitative data reports on the website. The page explains that while data are presented statistically, they are qualitative indicators because of the way the sample was constructed, i.e. non-random, and the results are specific to the sample rather than generalizable to the total population of past and present students. Not all were open to the view that as the quantitative and qualitative data were non-random samples, the same qualification on conclusions applied to both. Correspondence between interview and survey data findings did not always shift the relative value applied to each method.

Problems with comparison of statistical data usually derive from secondary analysis of data that are not fully comparable at the design and data collection stages. In this project the same questions were asked using the same sampling method. The heart of the dispute was the meanings that could be attributed to data acquired by two different methods. Whether the same reply to specific questions, obtained by quantitative or qualitative methods, signifies the same meaning to respondents is an issue within as well as between countries. However, similarity in meaning was likely to be assumed within countries, while partners and research assistants could be more at ease with assumed difference between countries.

The same issues also applied to qualitative data, but were largely unrecognized. The low degree of reliability, the possibility of repeating the same results, in qualitative research is due to the low degree of standardization of questions and also the low degree of standardization in the analysis of interview data (Denzin and Lincoln 1994, 2000). While the benefit of using the same analytical software for the analysis of the interview data was seen as desirable, among our partners and research assistants this was an underdeveloped research skill. Almost none of the researchers was trained in the use of any computer qualitative analysis package. ATLAS.ti was considered, but not all institutions had access to this software and the overall time-span of the project was too short to train researchers in its use.

Discussion on standardization by other means began by identifying key areas such as headings for the reports, the interview length and transcribing of interviews, but ultimately the lack of a common rigorous method of analysis was reflected in great diversity in the reports on the interviews. In comparison, the questionnaires were to be analysed using SPSS, and while not all partners had access to this programme, all were expected to obtain it so that they could access the data-set. Unlike ATLAS.ti, SPSS is more widely used throughout the European Union. Additionally, the analyses of national data were not to be conducted by partners, and partners had funds with which to purchase the version being used for later viewing of the data if their institution did not provide it. Unlike the interviews, the questionnaires were to be processed within one partner institution.

The research design required the collection of data by multiple methods, but approaching the same research questions through multiple methods, or triangulation by taking data from several sources, was not always accepted as increasing reliability and validity of the research findings. There is a growing literature on the relationship between quantitative and qualitative methods and their complementary use in research (Brannen 1992; Layder 1993; Todd 2004). By exploring feelings and complex relationships, qualitative research can provide greater depth of information, thereby furthering understanding obtained from quantitative data (Dale et al. 1988). The view that only qualitative data produce valid and reliable data could remain unshaken. Views on methods, as well as the nature of the topic, were reflected in the comparative reports, the final products of the research process. These showed some differences in their use of statistical and interview data.

A concern that readers might not understand that the descriptive statistics in comparative reports were based on a sample was not raised in relation to the similarly obtained interview data. Interpretation is a major issue in qualitative research as, 'good researchers do not claim that there is only one way of interpreting an event' (Janesick 2000: 393). Interpretation also raises questions about the appropriateness of the application of quantitative measures to qualitative data. 'The trinity of validity, generalisability and reliability, all terms from the quantitative paradigm' should be replaced 'with language that more accurately captures the complexity and texture of qualitative research' (ibid.). This view opens up a discussion of criteria for assessing the interpretive validity of qualitative research (Atheide and Johnson 1994).

### Comparability and non-harmonized data

Issues of comparability arise for cross-national research in the use of both harmonized and non-harmonized data (Glover 1996; Lijphart 1971; Ragin 1987; Collier 1991; Ember and Ember 2001). Harmonized data are critiqued for the loss of the specific meanings that are rooted in historical, economic, political and societal situations, while data rooted in non-harmonized specificities impede comparisons (Hantrais and Mangen 1996). From too general to too specific, these issues arise in the production and use of both primary and secondary data. While the same methods are available for national and cross-national studies, cross-cultural research methodologies are needed that address the central issues of equivalence of measurement and comparability of findings (Ember and Ember 2001; Harkness et al. 2003).

Standardization carried out to facilitate comparison between countries serves to raise in a more acute form the issue of diversity as distinctions fundamental to a particular country's occupational structure are lost or blurred (Glover 1989, 1996). The focus becomes fixed on historical and cultural discontinuities rather than convergence (Maurice 1979). There are dangers as well as benefits in a societal approach (Rubery 1992). Similarities between the unequal social position of women, when compared to that of men, may be lost sight of in a focus on differences between women in different national settings. Jill Rubery (1996) draws attention to the tendency of universal gender differences in Europe to arise out of the social construction of gender relations and attitudes, the organization of society into households and the division of labour between paid and unpaid work. The EWSI project provided examples of issues in comparability in both primary and secondary data research design, implementation and analysis.

Secondary analysis, a major method in cross-national studies, uses primary data gathered for other purposes to explore a different research issue (Hakim 1982). There are many benefits in the use of secondary analysis, including the testing of theoretical perspectives (Dale et al. 1988), combining categories to develop new variables and definitions, reducing costs and time that would be involved if collecting primary data, and access to historical data (Glover 1996). Attempting to use national data for cross-national comparisons, however, exposes a number of problems. Gremy (1989) describes these as technical, institutional and epistemological. Technical problems include the degree of familiarity of the researcher with the data and the level of documentation available. Institutional problems include gaining access to the data. Epistemological problems arise from primary data produced with a particular view of what constitutes knowledge and from a specific perspective. Other problems are understanding the structure of the data, the definitions used and the theoretical aspects of the research questions.

In the EWSI project we intended to compare data on women's occupations from 1945 to the present through secondary analysis of data in the nine countries. In some partner countries these data were available for only part of the period; for example, Spain after 1975. Over the time period classification systems changed within countries; women's employment data could be highly aggregated, employment categories could differ between countries. Even the most basic data on women's employment were not always available. While the project made limited use of secondary analysis, the advantages and disadvantages were obvious. Occupational classifications used in national employment data are based on a consensus that derives from specific cultural and historical contexts. One result of this consensus is limited information on women's employment, both in terms of time periods and employment sub-categories, which impedes cross-national comparisons. Non-harmonized and incomplete historical employment data on women reduced comparability between the nine countries.

## Comparability and harmonized data

Given the total lack of data-sets on Women's Studies courses in the nine countries, primary data were collected from past and current Women's Studies students on their experience of Women's Studies, prior and subsequent employment and equal opportunities. By using the same procedures, the aim was to produce a harmonized data-set for the nine countries. The harmonization process was also incorporated into the analysis of the primary data-set through the use of a standardized occupational classification scheme, ISCO-88 (ILO 1988). The inadequacy and non-comparability of the classification of women's employment in secondary data, the exclusion of the grey employment area, and the need for both vertical and horizontal employment data, led to a decision to use ISCO-88 to code employment of women, their mothers and fathers.

In ISCO-88, occupations are grouped on the basis of educational attainment rather than other distinctions. Occupational classifications are products of social, political and economic factors peculiar to each country. The distinction between private and public sector occupations and between employees and the self-employed are fundamental in some countries and not in others, emphasizing the importance of social identity as a guiding structure in the occupational classification (Hantrais and Mangen 1996). The conclusion that harmonized data will always be at the level of the lowest common denominator, providing less rather than more detail, distilling information rather than amplifying it (Glover 1996), proved accurate for the EWSI project.

The greatest problem in data processing was the coding of job titles using ISCO-88. The fit between descriptions and codes was not always obvious, different jobs carried different cultural meanings in partner countries and the ISCO-88 codes for women's jobs were both too general and incomplete. To eliminate variations in coding, with the exception of questionnaires received from the partner specializing in employment, coding was undertaken by the scientific coordinator prior to entry on SPSS. Liaison between the scientific coordinator and the employment specialist could not resolve the coding problems of a substantial minority of entries. Of the four-digit codes allocated to each job title by ISCO-88, only the first, the most general, could be used for comparative purposes. Given the structure of ISCCO-88, additional information would have been required to be able to use the remaining three digits with their increasing job specificity. This raised awareness that the decision to use ISCO-88 was taken without sufficient knowledge of this coding system and how it would affect the construction of the questionnaire. Once again, problems surfaced as a result of insufficient planning time and the lack of a pilot.

## Standardization

The primary strategy to introduce comparability was to standardize the collection, analysis and writing up of data produced by three different research methods: document research, quantitative survey and semi-structured interviews. Reporting formats identified issues of style, structure and content and provided a framework that ultimately contributed to synthesizing differences between countries in specific topic areas. The reporting formats provided a framework for the analysis and interpretation of national historical, political, institutional, social and cultural differences. For example, precise details were given for the national interview report format beginning with an introductory section providing details and numerical information about the interviewees.[6] Each national report was to provide information on the eight comparative report topic areas. The national reports were to have introductory paragraphs explaining these topic issues, their emergence in the data and the main findings of the interviews. Three quotations were to be drawn from the interviews to indicate the extremes; very positive and very negative, with an average response for each of the eight topics. The report was to end with a conclusion, best practice examples and policy recommendations regarding Women's Studies, education and women's employment under each of the eight topics. To encourage comparability between country-based reports on the interviews, the instructions were to summarize briefly the main contextual factors, the extremes of the experiences and to identify the norm. Direct quotations were to illustrate the points made in the summary and, where appropriate, data in table format and descriptive statistical data from the questionnaire survey were to be incorporated. As interviews were not translated as a whole, a coding system was developed to help partners identify those interviews cited in the reports so that further information could be requested from partners writing the comparative reports that would follow.

Standardization is also about shared understandings of research methods. Before sending in questionnaires to be entered into SPSS, partners were given instructions including how to check and number the questionnaires, to translate the very few open-ended questions, to 'clean up' or complete questionnaires if the respondent was to be interviewed, to examine for inconsistent replies, and to make a copy before posting. The difficulties for partners with no prior experience of the survey method and

SPSS in undertaking these tasks, however, could not be given sufficient time in the very packed two-day meetings. Explicit instructions were given on how to prepare for interviews, including prior reading of the interviewee's questionnaires, the agreed prompt questions, and headings and comparative report format guidelines.

Standardization was also pursued through increasing joint understanding of concepts critical to the successful conclusion of the study. Initially, for example, there was lack of clarity among partners about the meaning of the terms 'policy recommendation' and 'best practice'. The concepts of effectiveness and efficiency were suggested as ways of identifying ongoing or new ways of working that could be described as best practice and could provide the basis for a policy recommendation. There were a number of other suggestions, both conceptual and practical: for example, barriers to women's participation in education, employment and promotion could provide a way into identifying recommendations for research, monitoring and professional education. Gaining an agreed understanding of the concepts of 'policy recommendation' and 'best practice' developed over several meetings, culminating in national position papers based on interview data on the national problem areas partners wanted to address through best practice examples and policy recommendations.

The guidelines for best practice examples and policy recommendations called for simplicity and practicality with specific examples that distinguished between national and European Union levels. Policy recommendations were to be developed on Women's Studies training in Europe, on the use and effect of Women's Studies on employment and equal opportunities and to demonstrate best practice to support the development of the institutionalization of Women's Studies and the contribution of NGOs. Employment policy issues were seen as the need to generate high-quality employment for women in Europe; to overcome the wide variations in rates of women's employment in Europe; to expand areas of employment creation for women; to appreciate the relationship between Women's Studies and women's professionalization as a consequence of their training; to recognize the contribution of Women's Studies to innovation in employment, to job creation, to combating under-achievement and reducing unemployment. Education policy issues were seen to emerge from Women's Studies learning strategies that prevent and combat social exclusion; the adaptive response of formal education and training systems and their related policies and institutions to the challenges of lifelong learning for women; the development of pathways and bridges between Women's Studies learning and work; and the interaction between Women's Studies learning strategies and new trends in gender relations.

Partners were encouraged to think of policy as a means to enforce legitimacy and lobbying the European Union on issues such as the institutionalization of and student migration in Women's and Gender Studies. Partners distributed and spoke to best practice and policy recommendations arising from their data. The discussion that followed focused on the following areas: Women's Studies training in teacher training; institutionalization and full disciplinary status for Women's Studies; mainstreaming and lifelong learning; improving women's situation through permanent institutions such as equal opportunities bodies independent of political parties; introducing gender auditing and introductory courses in Women's Studies in schools; increasing networking of women and international co-operation around Women's Studies; introducing women commissioners for Women's Studies and employment and gender training for career advisers and employers; opening career centres for women; and funding further research projects in the areas of this study.

## Conclusions

Great expectations, limited resources and impossible time horizons, not infrequent experiences in research studies (Walker 1996), also applied to the EWSI project. Prior to submission, the major change to the proposal was made as a result of a request from one partner to reduce phase 1, the preliminary and planning phase of the project, from the first six months to three months. The three months 'released' through this process were added to the data collection phase of the project. On reflection there was agreement that limiting the planning phase of the project to three months proved to be an error; however, collecting the quantitative and qualitative data in six months might not have been possible.

Piloting the research questionnaire and interview questions and establishing a common base of research skills among partners and research assistants would have enriched the research process and possibly eliminated some issues. While these additional activities would add to the time needed to complete the study, building a research community in Europe requires directly confronting underlying issues that impede cross-national and cross-cultural research studies. Also, the lack of a sufficiently gender- and culturally-sensitive European employment classification scheme for use in this study reduced the effectiveness of both the national and cross-national comparisons of women's employment and employment progress. Improving classification schemes for women's employment would be of general benefit to European research.

Partners and their research assistants experienced a learning process and gaps in knowledge. For those who had not been involved previously in a European project, the learning curve was described as incredible. By the end of the first year, partners and research assistants were aware of the need for greater debate on terms and concepts, with 'course' used as the example of a term that caused problems in the process of data collection; the questionnaire needed discussion in more detail before its circulation to respondents; the questionnaire was too long and some questions were too complex, which resulted in incomplete answers; ISCO-88 was too detailed to allow replication in questionnaire format. These points indicated that the issue of translating what partners wanted to know and how they would find it out needed more time before data collection began.

The tight time schedule was thought to have affected the project. All agreed that the beginning of the project (the first three months) was particularly demanding as background data for country reports had to be collected and research instruments developed simultaneously. There were areas that should have been discussed, such as the different disciplinary backgrounds of partners and their research assistants. The research design was thought to need more discussion at the beginning of the project and, ideally, funded pre-proposal meetings. Problems with the questionnaire arose because of the lack of time during the first phase of the project. This raised awareness that the decision to use ISCO-88 was taken without sufficient knowledge of this coding system and how it would affect the construction of the questionnaire. Once again, problems surfaced as a result of insufficient planning time and the lack of a pilot.

Suggestions that might have short-circuited problems were for more meetings closer together earlier on, the need for piloting the questionnaire, the phasing of the various research instruments for full integration into the research process, more reflection on conceptual ideas and methodologies, more time for thinking through how the variables in the questionnaire would be operationalized and pre-coded, more discussion on qualitative data and comparative reports as the latter highlight both differences and similarities between participating countries. Working within a multi-disciplinary group required more sustained discussions about research methods. Turning these issues into positive insights on what partners learnt during the project and the actions that might follow meant thinking more about the dimensions of similarity and difference. National and cultural differences were underestimated initially and assumptions were made about agreements and understandings when events showed these to be unrealistic. It was regretted that the different time demands of consultancy work and research seem to be blurred in the European Union decision-making processes.

For all the differences and difficulties, partners and research assistants pursued the same methods of gathering and interpreting data. The repeated return to a discussion of best practice and policy recommendations enabled partners and research assistants to develop ways of thinking about the implementation of research that had not always been previous practice. This reflected national and disciplinary research traditions as well as the complexity of sifting data for good practice examples and reformulating findings as recommendations. It also reflected how to respond to differences within countries regarding the development and institutional arrangements for Women's Studies, equal opportunities and women's employment issues. Amid confusion and difference, the research demonstrated the value of Women's Studies and the contribution they can make to women, European societies more generally and furthering European Union socio-economic aims and objectives. Although there were issues, overall there was agreement that not only had the project achieved its aims, but also that there was continuing commitment to the dissemination of the research findings by partners individually and collectively.

## Notes

1 For further details see the introduction of this volume and the project website <www.hull.ac.uk/ewsi>

2 The initial plan for the questionnaire was to develop questions on personal and demographic data, including the impact on family life of taking one or more Women's Studies courses; previous employment and educational histories; motivations for pursuing Women's Studies and expectations, experiences, and evaluation of Women's Studies courses; prior and subsequent employment histories and how Women's Studies contributed to later employment; migration education experiences and their impact. This extensive list was added to when the study began with questions on the employment, nationality, ethnicity and date of birth of mothers and fathers and questions on equal opportunities. Once the questions were agreed these were translated into the appropriate language strictly following the question number of the English-language original. This facilitated SPSS data entry and analysis that followed. A standardized report form was developed to provide partners with statistical frequencies of replies to questions for past and for present students in each country.

The plan was to gather information through the questionnaire that could be followed up and further developed through face-to-face interviews with a sample of the questionnaire respondents. The criteria for the selection of twenty past and ten current students for interview were based on differences in employment experiences and expectations. The face-to-face interviews were to expand on the areas covered in the questionnaires providing detailed examples of the impact of Women's Studies on employment, equality, lifestyle and personal development. The interviews were conducted in the national language with a report in English on the interviews prepared by each partner.

3 The problem of senior partner participation in research projects is an

issue across such projects, and some project coordinators attempt to address this by requiring senior project partners to sign an agreement that they will be present at every project meeting and for the full duration of that meeting.

4 As an example of the range of agenda items to be discussed at meetings, the first meeting was devoted to ensuring there was shared understanding of the project and, as with all the later meetings, concluded with a provisional agenda for the next meeting. The meeting began with reports on the appointment of researchers, contractual obligations and deadlines, financial issues, the consortium agreement and the definition of success criteria for the European Union and each partner. The importance of smooth administration, on-time deliverables and dissemination were reviewed and agreed. The focus then switched to what had to be done by whom and when, how changes and disagreements would be handled and the strategy for information dissemination. This involved discussion of both phase 1 and phase 2 methods, and agreement was reached that the meetings would discuss issues as they arose. Prior to the first meeting a draft questionnaire and interview schedule had been prepared by the project coordinator and the scientific coordinator. The discussion centred on additional questions to be added, criteria for the distribution of questionnaires and deciding who should be interviewed, the proposed interface between the quantitative and qualitative methods, issues that partners foresaw in securing respondents and the timetable for final versions of the questionnaires, their translation, distribution, return and reports on the empirical data. The interview schedules were subject to a less rigorous timetable as these followed on after the survey data were completed.

5 A good example of this were questions about parents which are much more commonly asked in Germany, for instance, where they form part of one's *curriculum vitae* information, than in the UK where such questions contravene equal opportunities legislation.

6 The qualitative data reports from the project will be published in book format by the Ulrike Helmer Verlag, Frankfurt/Main, in the autumn of 2004.

# Notes on contributors

*Muriel Andriocci* was the French researcher for the EWSI project. After several years spent working as a freelance journalist in Paris, she obtained her BA, Masters and DEA degrees in sociology as a mature student at Toulouse-Le Mirail University. She is currently preparing her doctoral thesis on the relationship between academic Women's Studies and feminist consciousness-raising in France. She is an associate member of the Equipe Simone-SAGESSE feminist research centre and a board member of the National Association of Feminist Studies (ANEF).

*Gabriele Griffin* is Professor of Gender Studies at the University of Hull, UK. In 2001–03 she coordinated the EU-funded research project on 'Women's Employment, Women's Studies and Equal Opportunities in Europe' (EWSI) <www.hull.ac.uk/ewsi> on which much of this volume is based. She is currently co-ordinating another EU-funded research project on 'Integrative Research Methods in the Humanities and Social Sciences'. Recent publications include the co-edited volume (with Rosi Braidotti) *Thinking Differently: A Reader in European Women's Studies* (2002) and *Contemporary Black and Asian Women Playwrights in Britain* (2003).

*Jalna Hanmer* is Professor of Women's Studies at the University of Sunderland, UK and co-director of the International Centre for the Study of Violence and Abuse. She was a partner in the EU research project on Women's Employment and Women's Studies Training, and is currently in the EU Co-ordination Action on Human Rights Violations. Publication areas include violence against women; domestic violence and agency responses, including the criminal justice system, voluntary and statutory welfare agencies.

*Borbála Juhász* was the principal Hungarian researcher on the EWSI project. In 2003, she was appointed head of department of the equality section of the newly formed Ministry of Equal Opportunities in Hungary.

*Nicky Le Feuvre* obtained her PhD at the University of Birmingham before taking up a post as a senior lecturer in sociology and gender studies at Toulouse-Le Mirail University in 1991. She is director of the Equipe Simone-SAGESSE feminist research centre in Toulouse and has been involved in several European research projects on women's work and employment. She is a board member of the National Association of Feminist Studies (ANEF) and of the Interdisciplinary Network of Gender Studies Scholars (RING).

She is also co-editor of the Féminin & Masculin book series published by the Presses Universitaires du Mirail.

*Andrea Petö* is Associate Professor at University of Miskolc, Hungary, and a Visiting Professor at ELTE Ethnic and Minority Studies, Budapest. Recent publications include *Nõhistóriák. A politizáló magyar nõk története (1945–1951)* (1998) – and, as *Women in Hungarian Politics 1945–1951*, in English (2003); *Napasszonyok és Holdkisasszonyok. A mai magyar konzervatív nõi politizálás alaktana* [*Women of Sun and Girls of Moon. Morphology of Contemporary Hungarian Women Doing Politics*] (2003). She serves on the board of several journals in the field of women's history (*Gender and History*, *Clio*, *Visuoemene*, *Kultúra*, *Straipsniu rinktine*). At present she is working on gender and political conservatism with the support of a Bolyai Research Grant of the Hungarian Academy of Sciences (2002–05).

*Harriet Silius* is Professor of Women's Studies and Director of the Institute of Women's Studies, Åbo Akademi University, Finland. She is member of the board for the Nordic Research School in Interdisciplinary Gender Studies. Between 1999 and 2003 she was president of the Association for Feminist Education and Research in Europe (AOIFE). She is a member of several editorial boards of feminist journals. Professor Silius has published widely in the fields of sociology of professions, European welfare states, ethnicity, women's life stories and the institutionalization of Women's Studies. Recent publications include 'Women Jurists in Finland at the Turn of the Century: Breakthrough or Intermezzo?' in U. Schultz and G. Shaw (eds), *Women in the Legal Profession: A Challenge to Law and Lawyers* (2003) and 'Feminist Perspectives on the European Welfare State', in G. Griffin and R. Braidotti (eds), *Thinking Differently: A Reader in European Women's Studies* (2002).

*Isabel Carrera Suárez* is a senior lecturer and Pro-Vice Chancellor (Outreach) at the University of Oviedo, Spain, where she teaches Women's Studies and contemporary literatures in English. Her research and publications centre on the interaction of gender, postcolonialism and transcultural relations. She has contributed essays to international journals and books, and coordinated volumes on literatures in English and feminist studies. She has co-edited *Mujeres históricas, mujeres narradas* (2000); *Cambiando el conocimiento: universidad, sociedad y feminismo* (1999); *Mujer e investigación* (1995); *Como mujeres* (1994). She is also editor of the feminist research collection *Alternativas*. With colleagues from the Seminario de Estudios de la Mujer de la Universidad de Oviedo (SEMUO), she created the Women's Studies doctorate programme at the University of Oviedo, which has been running since 1995.

*Laura Viñuela Suárez* was the Spanish researcher for the EWSI project and is a PhD student at the University of Oviedo, Spain, where she has obtained a degree in Musicology and has attended the doctorate programme in Women's Studies. Her research interests range from popular music and other media to employment or disability, always with a gender perspective. At the moment she is attending a postgraduate course about women's employment at the University of Oviedo. She has developed a specialism on equal opportunities in Spain, and has lectured on this to many organizations.

*Jeannette van der Sanden* was the Dutch researcher for the EWSI project. She has an MA degree in social sciences, and specialized in Women's Studies. Her fields of interest are the women's movement, Women's Studies, and equal opportunities. She has worked as a researcher in the field of Women's Studies within the faculties of Medicine and Social Sciences at the University of Nijmegen. She has also worked as a staff member for positive action for female academic staff. At Utrecht University she worked as a researcher in the Department of Women's Studies in the Arts. Currently she is preparing her PhD on the institutionalization of Women's Studies in the Netherlands.

*Berteke Waaldijk* (1957) is a historian. She teaches in the Women's Studies department at Utrecht University, the Netherlands. She has published and edited books on the history of feminism in the Netherlands, on colonial culture, comparative studies of women and the history of social work. With Maria Grever she has written *Transforming the Public Sphere: The Dutch National Exhibition of Women's Labor in 1898* (2004).

# References

Aaron, J. and S. Walby (eds) (1991) *Out of the Margins: Women's Studies in the Nineties* (London: Taylor and Francis).

Acatiimi (2003) *AKAVAN työmarkkinatutkimus: Nuoret naisista puolet pätkätöissä* (Toukokuu: Acatiimi).

Acker, S. and D. Warren Piper (eds) (1984) *Is Higher Education Fair to Women?* (Guildford: SRHE and NFER-Nelson).

Agencies in Gonaives (2004) 'Haiti rebels declare independence and Americans leave', *Guardian*, 20 February 2004.

Alcoff, L. and E. Potter (eds) (1993) *Feminist Epistemologies* (London: Routledge).

Allen, D. (1987) 'Professionalism, Occupational Segregation by Gender and Control of Nursing' in E. Slavin (ed.), *The Politics of Professionalism, Opportunity, Employment, and Gender* (New York: Haworth Press), pp. 1–24.

Angeloff, T. (1999) 'Des miettes d'emploi: temps partiel et pauvreté', *Travail, genre et sociétés* (1): 43–70.

— (2000) *Le travail à temps partiel: un marché de dupes?* (Paris: Syros-La Découverte).

Atheide, J. and J. Johnson (1994) 'Criteria for Assessing Interpretive Validity in Qualitative Research', in N. K. Denzin and Y. S. L. Denzin (eds), *Handbook of Qualitative Research* (Thousand Oaks, CA: Sage).

Bahovec, E., N. Vodopivec and T. Salecl (2002) 'Slovenia', in G. Griffin (ed.), *Women's Employment, Women's Studies, and Equal Opportunities 1945–2001. Reports from Nine European Countries* (Hull: University of Hull Press).

Barazzetti, D. and M. Leone (2003) 'The Institutionalization of Women's Studies Training in Europe', Unpublished ms.

Barazzetti, D., C. Leccardi, M. Leone and S. Maggaraggia (2002) 'Italy', in G. Griffin (ed.), *Women's Employment, Women's Studies, and Equal Opportunities 1945–2001. Reports from Nine European Countries* (Hull: University of Hull Press).

— (2003) 'Qualitative Data Report: Italy', Unpublished ms.

Barrère-Maurisson, M.-A., M. Buffier-Morel and S. Rivier (2001) *Partage des temps et des tâches dans les ménages* (Paris: La Documentation française).

Bennetto, J. (2004) 'Anti-semitic assaults near record levels', *Independent*, 20 February 2004.

Benoit, C. (1994) 'Paradigm Conflict in the Sociology of the Professions', *Canadian Journal of Sociology*, 19(3): 303–29.

Bianchi, C., U. Gerhard, C. Leccardi, S. Magaraggia and M. Schmidbaur (2003) 'The Relationship between Women's Studies Training and Women's Employment Expectations' <www.hull.ac.uk/ewsi>

**References**

Bihr, A., and R. Pfefferkorn (1996) *Hommes/Femmes, l'introuvable égalité* (Paris: Editions de l'Atelier).

Black, I. (2004) 'Europe must stifle anti-semitism', *Guardian*, 20 February 2004.

Boland, E. (1987) *The Journey and Other Poems* (Manchester: Carcanet).

Bosch, M. (2004) 'The Spectacle of International Women's Suffrage', Unpublished conference paper, 'Das Jahrhundert des Feminismus', Frankfurt/ Main, 15 February 2004.

Bourdieu, P. (1984a) *Homo Academicus* (Paris: Editions de Minuit).

— (1984b) *Distinction. A Social Critique of the Judgement of Taste* (Cambridge, MA: Harvard University Press).

— (1989) *La Noblesse d'État. Grandes écoles et esprit de corps* (Paris: Editions de Minuit).

— (1990) 'La domination masculine', *Actes de la recherche en sciences sociales*, (84): 2–32.

Bourdieu, P. and L. Boltanski (1975) 'Le titre et le poste: rapports entre le système de production et le système de reproduction', *Actes de la recherche en sciences sociales*, 1(2): 95–107.

Bourdieu, P. and J. C. Passeron (1977) *Reproduction in Education, Society and Culture* (London: Sage).

Bowles, G. and R. Duelli Klein (eds) (1983) *Theories of Women's Studies* (London: Routledge and Kegan Paul).

Braidotti, R., E. Delhez, and C. Rammrath (1998) *The Institutionalisation of Gender Studies / Women's Studies in Europe* (Berne: Swiss Science Council).

Brannen, J. (ed.) (1992) *Mixing Methods: Qualitative and Quantitative Research* (Aldershot: Avebury).

Britton, D. (2000) 'The Epistemology of the Gendered Organization', *Gender and Society*, (14): 418–34.

Brousse, C. (2000) 'La répartition du travail domestique entre conjoints reste très largement spécialisé et inégale', *France, portrait social* (Paris: INSEE).

Buckley, M. (1989) *Women and Ideology in the Soviet Union* (London: Harvester Wheatsheaf).

Carrera Suárez, I. and L. Viñuela Suárez (2002) 'Spain', in G. Griffin (ed.), *Women's Employment, Women's Studies, and Equal Opportunities 1945–2001. Reports from Nine European Countries* (Hull: University of Hull Press).

— (2003a) 'Qualitative Data Report: Spain', Unpublished ms.

— (2003b) 'The Institutionalization of Equal Opportunities', Unpublished ms. <www.hull.ac.uk/ewsi>

Castle, S. (2004) 'Prodi promises to fight European anti-semitism', *Independent*, 20 February 2004.

Collier, D. (1991) 'The Comparative Method: Two Decades of Change', in D. A. Ruskow and K. Paul (eds), *Comparative Political Dynamics: Global Research Perspectives* (New York: HarperCollins).

Commaille, J. and C. Martin (1998) *Les enjeux politiques de la famille* (Paris: Bayard).

240

Commission of the European Communities (2002) *Final Commission Report on the Implementation of the Socrates Programme 1995–1999* (Brussels: European Commission).

Connell, R. W. (1987) *Gender and Power: Society, the Person and Sexual Politics* (Cambridge: Polity Press).

Crompton, R. (1987) 'Gender, Status and Professionalism', *Sociology*, 21(3): 413–28.

— (1999) *Restructuring Gender Relations and Employment: The Decline of the Male Breadwinner* (Oxford: Oxford University Press).

Crompton, R., and G. Birkelund (2000) 'Employment and Caring in British and Norwegian Banking: An Exploration Through Individual Careers', *Work, Employment and Society*, 14: 331–52.

Crompton, R. and F. Harris (1998) 'Gender Relations and Employment: The Impact of Occupation', *Work, Employment and Society*, 12: 297–315.

— (1999) 'Attitudes, Women's Employment and the Changing Domestic Division of Labour: A Cross-national Analysis', in R. Crompton (ed.), *Restructuring Gender Relations and Employment: The Decline of the Male Breadwinner* (Oxford: Oxford University Press).

Dale, A., and J. Glover (1989) 'Women at Work in Europe: The Potential Pitfalls of Using Published Statistics', *Employment Gazette*: 299–308.

Dale, A., S. Arber and M. Procter (1988) *Doing Secondary Analysis* (London: Unwin Hyman).

Daly, M. (2000) *The Gender Division of Welfare. The Impact of the British and German Welfare States* (Cambridge: Cambridge University Press).

Daly, M., and J. Lewis (2000) 'The Concept of Social Care and the Analysis of Contemporary Welfare States', *British Journal of Sociology*, 51: 281–98.

Davies, C. (1996) 'The Sociology of Professions and the Sociology of Gender', *Sociology*, 30(4): 661–8.

Denzin, N. K. and Y. S. Lincoln (eds) (1994) *Handbook of Qualitative Research* (Thousand Oaks, CA: Sage).

Denzin, N. K. and Y. S. Lincoln (eds) (2000) *Handbook of Qualitative Research* (revised edn) (Thousand Oaks, CA: Sage).

Dever, M. and E. Day (2001) 'Beyond the Campus: Some Initial Findings on Women's Studies, Careers and Employers', *Journal of International Women's Studies*, 2(2): 53–66.

Djuric, T. (1995) 'From National Economics to Nationalist Hysteria – Consequences for Women', in H. Lutz, A. Phoenix and N. Yuval-Davis (eds), *Crossfires: Nationalism, Racism and Gender in Europe* (London: Pluto Press).

Drglin, Z., E. D. Bahovec and R. Ščribar (2003) 'Employment Outcomes Following Women's Studies Training', Hull <www.hull.ac.uk/ewsi>

Dubois, E. C., G. P. Kelly, E. L. Kennedy et al. (1987) *Feminist Scholarship: Kindling in the Groves of Academe* (Urbana: University of Illinois Press).

Ellingsaeter, A. L. (1999) 'Dual Breadwinners Between State and Market', in R. Crompton (ed.), *Restructuring Gender Relations and Employment: The Decline of the Male Breadwinner* (Oxford: Oxford University Press).

References

Elliott, J., A. Dale and M. Egerton (2001) 'The Influence of Qualifications on Women's Work Histories, Employment Status and Earnings at Age 33', *European Sociological Review*, 17: 145–68.

Ember, C. and M. Ember (2001) *Cross-Cultural Research Methods* (Walnut Creek, CA: Alta Mira Press).

Esping-Andersen, G. (1990) *The Three Worlds of Welfare Capitalism* (Cambridge: Polity Press).

— (1999) *Social Foundations of Postindustrial Economies* (Oxford: Oxford University Press).

ETAN Expert Working Group on Women and Science (2002) *Science Policies in the European Union: Promoting Excellence through Mainstreaming Gender Equality* (Luxembourg: Office for Official Publications of the European Communities).

European Commission (1996a) *Bulletin on Women and Employment in the EC*, 8 (Brussels: European Commission).

— (1996b) *Bulletin on Women and Employment in the EC*, 9 (Brussels: European Commission).

— (2000) Directorate General for Education and Culture, *Survey into the Socioeconomic Background of Erasmus Students* (Brussels: European Commission).

Eurostat (1999) 'Mesures dynamiques de l'activité et du chômage, l'influence du facteur temps', *Statistiques en bref*, 18.

— (2000) 'Les bas salaires dans les pays de l'UE', *Statistics in Focus*, 3.

— (2001a) *Emploi et marché du travail dans les pays d'Europe centrale*, 01/2002, Populations Et Conditions Sociales (Luxembourg: Eurostat).

— (2001b) 'Employment Rates in Europe – 2000', *Statistics in Focus*, 8.

— (2001c) 'Taux d'emploi – Indicateurs généraux' (Luxembourg: Eurostat).

— (2002a) 'Disparités hommes–femmes parmi les chefs d'entreprises', *Statistiques en bref*, 3.

— (2002b) 'Enquête sur les forces de travail 2001' (Luxembourg: Eurostat).

— (2002c) 'La vie des femmes et des hommes en Europe. Un portrait statistique – Données 1980-2000' (Luxembourg: Eurostat).

— (2000d) 'L'influence des enfants sur le travail des femmes varie d'un Etat membre à l'autre – Les ménages où les deux partenaires travaillent constituent le modèle dominant', Press release, 21 May 2002.

— (2002e) 'Unemployment in the regions of the EU in 2001', *Statistics in Focus*, 7.

— (2003a) 'Les femmes dans l'UE', Press release, 27, 27 March 2003.

— (2003b) 'Origines sociales, niveau d'instruction et conséquences sur le marché du travail, le passage de l'école à la vie professionnelle chez les jeunes européens', *Statistiques en bref*, 6.

— (2003c) 'Students in tertiary education' (Luxembourg: Eurostat) <http://europa.eu.int/comm/eurostat>

Evetts, J. (2003) 'The Sociological Analysis of Professionalism: Occupational Change in the Modern World', *International Sociology*, 18 (2): 395–415.

Fagan, C. (2001) 'Time, Money and the Gender Order: Work Orientations and Working Time Preferences in Britain', *Gender, Work and Organisations*, 8: 239–66.

Feminist Anthology Collective (1981) *No Turning Back: Writings From the Women's Liberation Movement 1975–80* (London: Women's Press).

Ferrera, M. (1996) 'The Southern Model of the Welfare State in Social Europe', *Journal of European Public Policy*, 6: 17–37.

Fontana, A. and J. Frey (2000) 'The Interview: From Structured Questions to Negotiated Text', in N. K. Denzin and Y. S. Lincoln (eds), *Handbook of Qualitative Research* (Thousand Oaks, CA: Sage).

Fouquet, A., A. Gauvin and M.-T. Letablier (1999) 'Des contrats sociaux entre les sexes différents selon les pays de l'Union européenne', in B. M. d'Intagnano (ed.), *Egalité entre hommes et femmes : aspects économiques* (Paris: La Documentation française).

Fournier, V. (1999) 'The Appeal to "Professionalism" as a Disciplinary Mechanism', *Sociological Review*, 47: 280–307.

Frankenberg, R. (1993) *White Women, Race Matters: The Social Construction of Whiteness* (London: Routledge).

Freidson, E. (2001) *Professionalism* (Cambridge: Polity Press).

Freud, S. (1919) 'The Uncanny', in *Art and Literature*, Pelican Freud Library, vol. 14 (Harmondsworth: Penguin Books).

Friedan, B. (1963) *The Feminine Mystique* (New York: W.W. Norton).

Gaszi, J., A. Hars, B. Juhasz, A. Peto and S. Szabo (2002) 'Hungary', in G. Griffin (ed.), *Women's Employment, Women's Studies, and Equal Opportunities 1945–2001. Reports from Nine European Countries* (Hull: University of Hull Press).

Giacometti, M. (2002) 'Women in Italian Universities', *Industry and Higher Education*: 43–8.

Ginn, J. and S. Arber (1992) 'Towards Women's Independence: Pension Systems in Three Contrasting European Welfare States', *Journal of European Social Policy*, 2: 255–77.

Glover, J. (1989) 'The Classification of Occupations in Cross-National Research: Issues Relating to the Secondary Analysis of Large National Data Sets', *Cross-National Research Papers*: 80-2.

— (1993) 'Analyse secondaire et recherche comparative internationale: Problèmes et résultats', *Sociétés contemporaines*: 93–112.

— (1996) 'Epistemological and Methodological Considerations in Secondary Analysis', in L. Hantrais and S. Mangen (eds), *Cross-national Research Methods in the Social Sciences* (London: Frances Pinter).

Godelier, M. (1984) *L'idéel et le matériel* (Paris: Fayard).

Gremy, J.-P. (1989) 'Problèmes de l'analyse secondaire', in A. and E. Malinvaud Girard (eds), *Les enquêtes d'opinion et la recherche en sciences socials* (Paris: L'Harmattan).

Griffin, G. (2002a) 'Co-option or Transformation? Women's and Gender Studies Worldwide', in H. Flessner and Lydia Potts (eds), *Societies in Transition: Challenges for Women's and Gender Studies* (Opladen: Leske and Budrich).

Griffin, G. (2002b) 'Was haben wir erreicht? Eine kritische Auseinandersetzung mit dem "Schicksal" von Women's Studies im Vereinigten Koenigreich', *Feministische Studien*, 20(1): 70–86.

— (2003a) 'Qualitative Data Report: The UK', Unpublished ms.

— (2003b) *Employment and Women's Studies: The Impact of Women's Studies Training on Women's Employment in Europe. Final Report.* <www.hull.ac.uk/ewsi>

— (2003c) 'Thinking Differently: European Women's Studies', Plenary lecture delivered at the University of Konstanz as part of the international conference on 'Gender Studies zwischen Theorie und Praxis (Standortbestimmungen', University of Konstanz).

— (2003d) 'Humboldt, Mickey Mouse and Current European Research Programmes – or Where are the women in all this?', *Kvinder, Kon and Forskning*, 12 (2): 31–43.

— (ed.) (1994) *Changing Our Lives: Doing Women's Studies* (London: Pluto Press).

— (ed.) (2002) *Women's Employment, Women's Studies, and Equal Opportunities 1945–2001: Reports from Nine European Countries* (Hull: University of Hull Press).

Griffin, G. and R. Braidotti (eds) (2002a) *Thinking Differently. A Reader in European Women's Studies* (London: Zed Books).

Griffin, G. with R. Braidotti (2002b) 'Whiteness and European Situatedness', in G. Griffin and R. Braidotti (eds), *Thinking Differently: A Reader in European Women's Studies* (London: Zed Books).

Griffin, G. and J. Hanmer (2002) 'The UK', in G. Griffin (ed.), *Women's Employment, Women's Studies, and Equal Opportunities 1945–2001* (Hull: University of Hull Press).

— (2003) 'The Impact of Women's Studies Training on Women's Lifestyles and Everyday Life Practices', Unpublished ms. <www.hull.ac.uk/ewsi>

Griffin, G., M. Hester, S. Rai and S. Roseneil (eds) (1994) *Stirring It: Challenges for Feminism* (London: Taylor and Francis).

Guillaumin, C. (1992) *Sexe, race et pratique du pouvoir: l'idée de Nature* (Paris: Côté-Femmes).

Haicault, M. (1993) 'La doxa de sexe, une approche du symbolique dans les rapports sociaux de sexe', *Recherches féministes*, 6: 7–20.

Hakim, C. (1982) *Secondary Analysis in Social Research* (London: Allen and Unwin).

— (1994) 'A Century of Change in Occupational Segregation 1891–1991', *Journal of Historical Sociology*, 7(4): 435–545.

Hanmer, J. (1990) 'Faire des vagues', *Cahiers du GRIF*: 7–16.

Hanmer, J. and D. Wigglesworth (2003) *Summary Reports – Quantitative Data* <www.hull.ac.uk/ewsi>

Hantrais, L. and S. Mangen (eds) (1996) *Cross-national Research Methods in the Social Sciences* (London: Frances Pinter).

Harding, S. (1986) *The Science Question in Feminism* (Milton Keynes: Open University Press).

— (1987) *Feminism and Methodology* (Bloomington: Indiana University Press).

Harkness, J., F. Van de Vijver and J. Mohler (2003) *Cross-Cultural Survey Methods* (Hoboken, NJ: Wiley).

Hartsock, N. (1998) *The Feminist Standpoint Revisited* (Boulder, CO: Westview Press).

Hegewisch, A. (1995) 'A mi-chemin entre l'Amérique et l'Europe, les femmes et le chômage en Grande-Bretagne', *Cahiers du Mage*, 3–4: 11–24.

Heinen, J. and S. Portet (2002) 'Political and Social Citizenship: An Examination of the Case of Poland', in M. Molyneux and S. Razavi (eds), *Gender, Justice, Development and Rights* (Oxford: Oxford University Press).

Héritier, F. (1996) *Masculin/Féminin: la pensée de la difference* (Paris: Odile Jacob).

Hill, M. (ed.) (1997) *Whiteness: A Critical Reader* (New York: New York University Press).

hooks, b. (1994) *Teaching to Transgress* (London: Routledge).

Hull, G. T., P. B. Scott and B. Smith (eds) (1982) *But Some of Us are Brave: Black Women's Studies* (New York: City University Press of New York).

Humm, M. (1989) *The Dictionary of Feminist Theory* (London: Harvester Wheatsheaf).

Husu, L. (2001) *Sexism, Support and Survival in Academia: Academic Women and Hidden Discrimination in Finland* (Helsinki: Helsinki University Press).

ILO (1988) *ISCO-88 International Standard Classification of Occupations* (Geneva: International Labour Office).

Janesick, V. J. (2000) 'The Choreography of Qualitative Research Design: Minuets, Improvisations and Crystallization', in N. K. Denzin and Y. S. Lincoln (eds), *Handbook of Qualitative Research* (Thousand Oaks, CA: Sage).

Jaspard, M. and l'équipe Enveff (2001) 'Nommer et compter les violences envers les femmes', *Population et sociétés*: 1–4.

Jenson, J. (1986) 'Gender and Reproduction: Or Babies and the State', *Studies in Political Economy*, 20: 9–46.

Jenson, J. and M. Sineau (1998) *Qui doit garder le jeune enfant? Modes d'accueil et travail des mères dans l'Europe en crise* (Paris: Librairie Générale de Droit et de Jurisprudence).

Jobert, Annette (1996) 'Comparing Education, Training and Employment in Germany, the United Kingdom and Italy', in L. Hantrais and S. Mangen (eds), *Cross-national Research Methods in the Social Sciences* (London: Frances Pinter), pp. 76–83.

Juhász, B. (2003) 'Qualitative Data Report: Hungary', Unpublished ms.

Juhász, B., A. Peto, J. van der Sanden and B. Waaldijk (2003) 'The Relationship between Educational Migration and Women's Studies' Students' Employment', Unpublished ms. <www.hull.ac.uk/ewsi>

Junter-Loiseau, A. (1999) 'La notion de conciliation de la vie professionnelle et de la vie familiale. Révolution temporelle ou métaphore des discriminations?' *Cahiers du Genre*, 24: 73–98.

245

Kanter, R. M. (1977) *Men and Women of the Corporation* (New York: Basic Books).

Kay, J. (1997) 'Crown and Country', in M. Dooley (ed.), *Making for Planet Alice* (Newcastle upon Tyne: Bloodaxe Books).

Kergoat, D. (1982) *Les ouvrières* (Paris: Le Sycamore).

Kofman, E. (1993) 'Pour une théorie féministe de l'Etat: contradictions, complexité et confusion', in A. Gautier and J. Heinen (eds), *Le sexe des politiques socials* (Paris: Editions Côté-femmes).

Kolodny, A. (1998) *Failing the Future: A Dean Looks at Higher Education in the Twenty-First Century* (Durham NC: Duke University Press).

Korpi, W. (1980) 'Social Policy and Distributional Conflict in the Capitalist Democracies. A Preliminary Comparative Framework', *West European Politics*, 3: 296–316.

— (1985) 'Power Resources Approach Versus Action and Conflict: On Causal and Intentional Explanations in the Study of Power', *Sociological Theory*, 3: 31–45.

Kristeva, J. (1991) *Strangers to Ourselves* (New York: Harvester Wheatsheaf).

Layder, D. (1993) *New Strategies in Social Research* (Cambridge: Polity Press).

Le Feuvre, N. (1997) 'Women's Work and Employment in Europe', *Women in Europe: Convergence and Divergence from North to South* (Helsinki: Helsinki University Press).

— (2002) 'Women's Studies Qualifications and Professional Trajectories. Gender Studies in Europe', Studi di Genere in Europa. Conference Proceedings, European University Institute, Robert Schumann Centre for Advanced Studies and University of Florence, Department of Filologia moderna in association with Athena.

Le Feuvre, N. and M. Andriocci (2002a) 'France', in G. Griffin (ed.), *Women's Employment, Women's Studies, and Equal Opportunities 1945–2001. Reports from nine European Countries* (Hull: University of Hull Press).

— (2002b) 'Qualitative Data Report: France', Unpublished ms.

— (2003) 'Employment Opportunities for Women in Europe' Hull. <www.hull.ac.uk/ewsi>

Le Feuvre, N., J. Martin, C. Parichon and S. Portet (1999a) 'Employment, Family and Community Activities: A New Balance for Women and Men in France' (Dublin: Rapport à la Fondation européenne pour l'amélioration des conditions de vie et de travail).

Le Feuvre, N., M. Membrado and A. Rieu (1999b) *Les femmes et l'Université en Méditerranée* (Toulouse: Presses Universitaires du Mirail).

Leibfried, S. (1993) 'Towards a European Welfare State?' in C. Jones (ed.), *New Perspectives on the Welfare State in Europe* (London: Routledge).

Lewis, J. (1992) 'Gender and the Development of Welfare Regimes', *Journal of European Social Policy*, 2: 159–73.

Lijphart, A. (1971) 'Comparative Politics and Comparative Method', *American Political Science Review*, 65(3): 682–98.

Magee, B. (1966) *One in Twenty: A Study of Homosexuality in Men and Women* (London: Secker and Warburg).

Makkai, T. (1997) 'Social Policy and Gender in Eastern Europe', in D. Sainsbury (ed.), *Gendering Welfare States* (London: Sage).

Martin, C. (1997) 'La comparaison des systèmes de protection sociale en Europe. De la classification à l'analyse des trajectoires d'Etat providence', *Lien social et politiques – RIAC*, 37: 145–55.

Maruani, M. (1995) 'La traversée des turbulences: l'emploi féminin dans l'Europe des années quatre-vingt-dix', in M. de Manassein (ed.), *De l'égalité des sexes* (Paris: Centre national de documentation pédagogique).

— (1996) 'L'emploi féminin à l'ombre du chômage', *Actes de la recherche en sciences sociales*, 115: 48–57.

— (2002) *Les mécomptes du chômage* (Paris: Bayard).

Maurice, M. (1979) 'For a Study of the "Societal Effect": Universalism and Specificity in Organization Research', in C. J. and D. J. Hickson Lammers (eds), *Organizations Alike and Unlike: International and Inter-Institutional Studies in the Sociology of Organizations* (London: Routledge and Kegan Paul).

Mazari, S., U. Gerhard and U. Wischermann (2002) 'Germany', in G. Griffin (ed.), *Women's Employment, Women's Studies, and Equal Opportunities 1945–2001. Reports from Nine European Countries* (Hull: University of Hull Press).

Méda, D. (2001) *Le temps des femmes: pour un nouveau partage des roles* (Paris: Flammarion).

Meek, J. and J. Watts (2004) 'The life and death of a cockle picker', *Guardian*, 20 February 2004.

Morris, N. (2004) 'Minister "misled" MP over cocklers', *Independent*, 20 February 2004.

Muller, P. (2000) 'L'analyse cognitive des politiques publiques: vers une sociologie politique de l'action publique', *Revue française de science politique*, 50: 56–72.

Nauta, A. and J. A. M. Heesink (1992) 'Loopbaangedrag en loopbaanintentie van vrouwen. De invloed van psychologische, culturele en structurele factoren', *Gedrag en Organisatie*, 5(4): 215–35.

Oakley, A. (2000) *Experiments in Knowing: Gender and Method in the Social-Sciences* (Cambridge: Polity Press).

OECD (2002a) *Education at a Glance – OECD Indicators 2002* (Paris: UNESCO Institute for Statistics).

— (2002b) *Financing Education – Investments and Returns* (Paris: UNESCO Institute for Statistics).

— (2003) *Education at a Glance* (Paris: OECD).

O'Reilly, J. and C. Fagan (1998) *Part-Time Prospects: An International Comparison of Part-Time Work in Europe, North America and the Pacific Rim* (London: Routledge).

Owen, D. (1994a) *Black People in Great Britain: Social and Economic Circumstances. 1991 Census Statistical paper No. 6* (Warwick: Centre for Research in Ethnic Relations, University of Warwick).

— (1994b) *South Asian People in Great Britain: Social and Economic Circumstances. 1991 Census Statistical Paper No. 7* (Warwick: Centre for Research in Ethnic Relations, University of Warwick).

Oyen, E. (ed.) (1990) *Comparative Methodology: Theory and Practice in International Social Research* (London: Sage).

Papic, Z. (2002) 'Europe after 1989: Ethnic Wars, the Fascistization of Civil Society and Body Politics in Serbia', in G. Griffin and R. Braidotti (eds), *Thinking Differently: A Reader in European Women's Studies* (London: Zed Books).

Pateman, C. (1988) *The Sexual Contract* (Cambridge: Polity Press).

Pfau-Effinger, B. (1993) 'Modernisation, Culture and Part-time Employment: The Example of Finland and West Germany', *Work, Employment and Society*, 7: 383–410.

— (1996) 'Theorising Cross-national Differences in the Labour Force Participation of Women', Paper for the Seminar on Gender Relations, Employment and Occupational Segregation, University of Leicester.

— (1998) 'Gender Cultures and the Gender Arrangement: A Theoretical Framework for Cross-national Comparisons on Gender Innovation', *European Journal of Social Sciences*, 11: 1130–48.

— (1999) 'The Modernization of the Family and Motherhood in Western Europe', in R. Crompton (ed.), *Restructuring Gender Relations and Employment: The Decline of the Male Breadwinner* (Oxford: Oxford University Press).

Phoenix, A. (1995) 'Young People: Nationalism, Racism and Gender', in H. Lutz, A. Phoenix, and N. Yuval-Davis (eds), *Crossfires: Nationalism, Racism and Gender in Europe* (London: Pluto Press).

Piper, A. (1988) 'Cornered' (New York: John Weber Gallery).

— (1996) *Out of Order, Out of Sight* (Cambridge, MA: MIT Press).

Pirrie, A., V. Wilson, J. Powney and S. Hamilton (2002) *Gender Equality in SOCRATES: Final Report* (Edinburgh: Scottish Council for Research in Education).

Pollart, A. (2003) 'Women, Work and Equal Opportunities in Post-Communist Transition', *Work, Employment and Society*, 17: 331–57.

Press Association (2003) 'Tagging plan for asylum seekers', *Guardian*, 27 November 2003.

Price, L. (2002) 'Sexual Violence and Ethnic Cleansing: Attacking the Family', in G. Griffin and R. Braidotti (eds), *Thinking Differently: A Reader in European Women's Studies* (London: Zed Books).

Ragin, C. (1987) *The Comparative Method: Moving Beyond Qualitative and Quantitative Strategies* (Berkeley, CA: University of California Press).

— (1991) *Issues and Alternatives in Comparative Social Research* (Leiden: Brill).

Rainbird, H. (1996) 'Using the Vignette Method in Cross-Cultural Comparisons' in L. Hantrais and S. Mangen (eds), *Cross-national Research Methods in the Social Sciences* (London: Frances Pinter).

Rantalaiho, L. and H. Tuula (1997) *Gendered Practices of Working Life* (London: Macmillan).

Riska, E. (2003) 'The Career and Work of Pathologists: A Gender Perspective', *International Journal of Sociology and Social Policy*, 23(4–5): 59–79.

Roberts, H. (ed.) (1981) *Doing Feminist Research* (London: Routledge and Kegan Paul).

Rubery, J. (1992) 'Productive Systems, International Integration and the Single European Market', in A. Castro and J. Rubery (eds), *International Integration and Labour Market Organisation* (London: Academic Press).

— (1996) 'Mainstreaming Gender in Labour Market Policy Debates', in L. Hantrais and S. Mangen (eds), *Cross-national Research Methods in the Social Sciences* (London: Frances Pinter).

Rubery, J., M. Smith and C. Fagan (1999) *Women's Employment in Europe: Trends and Prospects* (London: Routledge).

Rubery, J., M. Smith and C. Fagan and D. Grimshaw (1996) *Women and the European Employment Rate: The Causes and Consequences of Variations in Female Activity and Employment Patterns in the European Union. Rapport à l'Unité pour l'égalité des chances* (Brussels: DGV, European Commission).

Ruivo, M., M. d. P. Gonzalez, and J. Varejao (1998) 'Why is Part-time Work so Low in Portugal and Spain?', in J. O'Reilly and C. Fagan (eds), *Part-Time Prospects* (London: Routledge).

Sainsbury, D. (1994) *Gendering Welfare States* (London: Sage).

— (1997) *Gender and Welfare State Regimes* (Oxford: Oxford University Press).

— (2001) 'Gender and the Making of Welfare States: Norway and Sweden', *Social Politics*, 8: 113–43.

Sassen, S. (1999) *Guests and Aliens* (New York: New Press).

Schmidbaur, M., S. Mazari, U. Gerhard and U. Wischermann (2003) 'Qualitative Data Report: Germany', Unpublished ms.

Schweitzer, S. (2002) *Les femmes ont toujours travaillé: une histoire du travail des femmes aux XIXème et XXème siècles* (Paris: Odile Jacob).

Scott, J. (1992) 'Experience', in J. Butler and J. W. Scott (eds), *Feminists Theorize the Political* (London: Routledge).

Silius, H. (1992) *Den kringgärdade kvinnligheten. Att vara kvinnlig jurist i Finland. [Contracted Femininity: The Case of Women Lawyers in Finland]* (Åbo, Finland: Åbo Akademi University Press).

— (1996) 'Finnish Gender Contracts', in K. C. Roy, C. A. Tisdell and H. C. Blomqvist (eds), *Economic Development and Women in the World Community* (Westport, CT: Praeger).

— (2002) 'Comparative Summary', in G. Griffin (ed.), *Women's Employment, Women's Studies, and Equal Opportunities 1945–2001. Reports from Nine European Countries* (Hull: University of Hull Press).

Silius, H. and S. Tuori (2003) 'The Professionalization of Women's Studies Graduates (Including the Academic Profession) in Europe' <www.hull.ac.uk/ewsi>

Silvera, R. (1998) 'Les femmes et la diversification des temps de travail : nouveaux enjeux, nouveaux risques', *Revue française des affaires sociales*, 3: 71–88.

Skelton, C. (1993) 'Women and Education', in D. Richardson and V. Robinson (eds), *Introducing Women's Studies* (Basingstoke: Macmillan).

Slapsak, S. (2002) 'Identities Under Threat on the Eastern Borders', in G. Griffin and R. Braidotti (eds), *Thinking Differently: A Reader in European Women's Studies* (London: Zed Books).

Stanley, L. and S. Wise (1983) *Breaking Out: Feminist Consciousness and Feminist Research* (London: Routledge and Kegan Paul).

Statistics Finland (1995) *Women and Men in Finland: Working Conditions* (Helsinki: Statistics Finland).

Threlfall, M. (ed.) (1996) *Mapping the Women's Movement* (London: Verso).

Titmuss, R. M. (1963) *Essays on the Welfare State* (London: Allen and Unwin).

— (1974) *Social Policy* (London: Allen and Unwin).

Todd, Z. (ed.) (2004) *Mixing Methods in Psychology: The Integration of Qualitative and Quantitative Methods in Theory and Practice* (New York: Psychology Press).

Tuori, S. (2003) 'Qualitative Data Report: Finland', Unpublished ms, Hull. <www.hull.ac.uk/ewsi>

Tuori, S. and H. Silius (2002) 'Finland', in G. Griffin (ed.), *Women's Employment, Women's Studies, and Equal Opportunities 1945–2001. Reports from Nine European Countries* (Hull: University of Hull Press).

Ungerson, C. (1990) *Gender and Caring: Work and Welfare in Britain and Scandinavia* (London: Harvester Wheatsheaf).

van der Sanden, J. with B. Waaldijk (2002) 'Netherlands', in G. Griffin (ed.), *Women's Employment, Women's Studies, and Equal Opportunities 1945–2001. Reports from Nine European Countries* (Hull: University of Hull Press).

Walker, R. (1996) 'Part Four: Evaluation', in L. Hantrais and S. Mangen (eds), *Cross-national Research Methods in the Social Sciences* (London: Frances Pinter).

Ware, V. (1992) *Beyond the Pale: White Women, Racism and History* (London: Verso).

White, M. (2004a) 'Cabinet split exposed over entry of EU jobseekers', *Guardian*, 12 February 2004.

— (2004b) 'Morecambe MP hits out at Home Office', *Guardian*, 20 February 2004.

Wintour, P. and D. Ward (2004) 'Cockle-picker warnings ignored, says Labour MP', *Guardian*, 12 February 2004.

Witz, A. (1992) *Professions and Patriarchy* (London: Routledge).

Woolf, V. (1982) *Three Guineas* [1934] (Harmondsworth: Penguin Books).

# Index